NOTES on the
PSALMS

WORKS BY
G. CAMPBELL MORGAN, D. D.

The Music of Life
The Corinthian Letters of Paul
The Triumphs of Faith
The Parables and Metaphors of Our Lord
The Voice of the Devil
The Bible Four Hundred Years after 1538
Mountains and Valleys in the Ministry of Jesus
Peter and the Church
The Great Physician
Preaching
The Answers of Jesus to Job
Great Chapters of the Bible
Hosea: the Heart and Holiness of God
Studies of the Four Gospels
    The Gospel According to Matthew
    The Gospel According to Mark
    The Gospel According to Luke
    The Gospel According to John
    The Set 4 Vols. Boxed
The Acts of the Apostles
The Teaching of Christ
The Crises of the Christ
Living Messages of the Books of the Bible
    Now Complete in Two Volumes.
    Vol. I, O.T.—Genesis to Malachi
    Vol. II, N.T.—Matthew to Revelation
The Ten Commandments
Discipleship

G. CAMPBELL MORGAN

NOTES on the
PSALMS

Fleming H. Revell Company
Old Tappan, New Jersey

To

DAVID MARTYN LLOYD-JONES

MY VALUED AND BELOVED COLLEAGUE DURING THE LAST
YEARS OF MY ACTIVE MINISTRY; A MAN LOYAL TO THE
WORD, AND A PREACHER OF EXCEPTIONAL ABILITY

THE PSALMS

In the Psalms, we look into the heart of all the saints, and, we seem to gaze into fair pleasure-gardens; into heaven itself, indeed; where bloom the sweet, refreshing, gladdening flowers of holy and happy thoughts about God and all His benefits. On the other hand, where will you find deeper, sadder, more piteous words of mourning than in the Psalms? In these again, we look into the heart of the saints, and we seem to be looking into death, yea, into hell itself. How gloomy, how dark it is there, because of the many sad visions of the wrath of God!

MARTIN LUTHER.

WHAT various and resplendent riches are contained in this treasury, it were difficult to find words to describe. . . . I am in the habit of calling this book, not inappropriately, "The Anatomy of all Parts of the Soul," for not an affection will any one find in himself, an image of which is not reflected in this mirror. Nay, all the griefs, sorrows, fears, misgivings, hopes, cares, anxieties; in short, all the disquieting emotions with which the minds of men art wont to be agitated, the Holy Spirit hath here pictured to the life.

CALVIN, Preface to *Commentary on the Psalms of David*.

CONTENTS

PSALMS—THE BOOK OF WORSHIP

Book.	Psalms.	Doxology.	Dominant Notes of Worship.	Divine Titles.			
				Jehovah.	Elohim.	Adonahy.	Jah.
I.	1 to 41	41–13	Jehovah—The Becoming One, The Helper. Adoring Worship.	275	68	14	—
II.	42 to 72	72–18, 19	Elohim — The Wonder-Working God. Wondering Worship.	32	234	19	1
III.	73 to 89	89–52	Elohim—Jehovah. The Mighty Helper. Ceaseless Worship.	44	80	15	—
IV.	90 to 106	106–48	Jehovah—The Governing King. Submissive Worship.	103	72	2	7
V.	107 to 150	150–1 to 6	Jehovah—The Redeemer. Perfected Worship.	236	40	12	32

PSALMS

INTRODUCTORY

The word "Psalms" is the Anglicized form of a Greek word, which really means a poem set to music. The Hebrew title of the book was simply Praises, or Book of Praises. It is pre-eminently the worship-book of the Hebrew people, and consists of a collection of songs which express the attitude of the soul in the presence of God, when contemplating past history, existing conditions, or prophetic hopes. The whole collection consists, in the Hebrew Bible, of five books. In the English and American Revisions this sub-division is shown.

We have no definite proof who the editor was. His method becomes evident by an examination of the grouping of the psalms. It is perfectly clear that neither authorship nor chronology was in his view. Eusebius declares that "The psalms are disposed according to a law of inward affinity"; and Dr. Anderson says, "It must be remembered that every attempt to classify and arrange the psalms apart from the division of the whole Psalter into the five books as found in our Hebrew Bible, the Septuagint, Syriac, and Vulgate Versions—every such attempt is confessedly imperfect, and more or less arbitrary."

The key to the method of the editor is to be found in the doxologies with which the books close. Each of the five has such a doxology, and an examination of these will reveal a certain conception of God, and an attitude of the soul in worship resulting from such conception. The doxology for each will be found as follows:

9

Book I.   Psalm 41–13.   Worship of Jehovah as the Be-
                                coming One, Who is the Helper.

Book II.   Psalm 72–18, 19.   Worship of Jehovah as the Won-
                                der-working God.

Book III.   Psalm 89–52.   Worship of Jehovah ceaseless.

Book IV.   Psalm 106–48.   Worship of Jehovah rendered.

Book V.   Psalm 150–1 to 6. Worship of Jehovah consum-
                                mated.

The individual psalms are natural expressions by many
authors, at various times, under differing circumstances, of the
consciousness of God. The editing gathers these individual
songs around the notes of truth dominant in each.

These notes are indicated in each book by the particular
title of Jehovah which predominates. The subject of the
Divine titles is too great a one to be discussed at length now;
but as an introduction to the study of the Psalter, recognition
of difference is necessary. The proportion in which the four
titles are used in the book of Psalms, as indicated in the dia-
gram, is a somewhat rough one. Under Elohim are included
El and Eloah, because while there is a minor difference of
suggestion between the singular and the plural, the underlying
thought is the same. So also with reference to Adonahy and
Adon.

JEHOVAH. In the ancient Hebrew Scriptures this particular
title was always written in the form of a tetragrammaton—
YHVH—and there are differences of opinion as to what the
actual form of the word should be. Without entering into any
discussion of the varied interpretations, I adopt that of Mr.
Joseph Rotherham in the EMPHASIZED BIBLE, both as to spell-
ing and significance. He claims that the word thus abbreviated
is Yahweh, and interprets it as meaning "the Becoming One."
In his Bible, he says, "Yahweh is almost always regarded as

the third person singular, masculine, imperfect tense, from the root Hawah, an old form of the root Hayah. The one meaning of Hawah is 'become.' So that the force of Yahweh, thus derived as a verb, would be, 'He will become,' or, as expressive of use and wont as a noun, it is, 'He who becometh,' 'the Becoming One.' "

In a letter written to me in the course of correspondence on the subject, referring to this meaning, Mr. Rotherham said:—

" 'He becometh,' that is, 'He who becometh,' 'the Becoming One'; becoming to His people whatever in His rich favour He pleases, in order to meet their need, and at last becoming Man."

The truth, therefore, suggested by the use of this word is always that, first of the essential Being of God which enables Him to become; and by deduction, that God in infinite grace does become whatever man needs.

ELOHIM. This is a plural noun, but it is plural in a sense peculiar to the Hebrew language. Canon Girdlestone says:—

"It is well known that the Hebrews often expressed a word in the plural, so as to give it a special or technical meaning, as in the case of the words, blood, water, wisdom, salvation, righteousness, life. . . . It is implied that the word in the singular number is not large enough to set forth all that is intended; and so, in the case of the Divine Name, the plural form expresses the truth that the finite word conveys an inadequate idea of the Being Whom it represents. Other names of God will be found to be plural also, and it is worthy of notice that in the well-known passage in Ecclesiastes (xii. 1) the Hebrew runs thus, 'Remember now thy Creators in the days of thy youth.' "

The root idea is that of strength or might, and the thought of God suggested by it is that of His strength as revealed in creation, and in all the operations of His power.

ADONAHY. This is again plural in form. Its simple signification is "Master" or "Lord"; and the thought it suggests is that of sovereign supremacy.

JAH. This is the shorter form of the name Jehovah, and is only found in Scripture; twice in Exodus, a few times in Isaiah, and in thirty-five passages in the book of Psalms.

These names reveal the doctrine of God, which creates man's worship. Recognizing that Jehovah and Jah have the same essential significance, there are three lines of thought suggested. First, the essential Being of God, and the fact that He becomes in grace what man needs. Second, the essential Might of God, and the fact that it operates in power. Third, the essential Lordship of God, and His consequent sovereignty over man.

The analyses are intended to help in the study of the collection, as to the conceptions impelling to worship.

BOOK I.
PSALMS 1–41

BOOK I.—PSALMS 1-41

DOXOLOGY

"Blessed be the Lord, the God of Israel,
From everlasting and to everlasting. Amen, and Amen." **Ps. 41-13.**

A. THE TITLE.	B. THE RELATION.	C. THE QUANTITY.	D. THE QUALITY.
"Jehovah." The mysterious name, suggestive of essential Being, becoming whatever is needed by men, and therefore uniformly used as indicating God's relation to His people as Helper.	"The God of Israel." "God." Elohim. The idea of Supremacy. "Of Israel." The chosen People.	"From everlasting to everlasting." "The word 'everlasting' means the concealed or vanishing point; and suggests the mysterious past, and the unknown future. In its use here it reminds the heart of the eternity of God."	"Blessed." The root idea is that of prostration in the attitude of adoration. "Amen, and Amen." The consent of all to such adoration.

The Divine Name.

The prevailing Name in this book is Jehovah. It occurs in every psalm at least twice, and in one (xxix), as many as 18 times.

"God" is found 18 times in the singular, 50 times in the plural; in all 68 times. From 13 psalms it is absent altogether. The general title "Lord" (Adonahy) only occurs 14 times in all, and these occasions are all in 8 psalms.

The Dominant Thought.

The dominant thought in this book is that of God as Jehovah, the Helper of His people. The psalms are songs of varying emotion, and differing condition, but all express themselves in harmony with this note.

ANALYSIS

A. AUTHORITY ESTABLISHED. 1–8		B. AUTHORITY DEFENDED. 9–15		C. AUTHORITY ADMINISTERED. 16–41	
I. The Foundations.	1–2	I. The Need.	9, 10	I. The Person.	16 to 24
i. Obedience and Disobedience.	1	i. The Throne and the Enemy.	9	(See Titles.)	
ii. The enthroned King.	2	ii. Appeal for Action.	10		
II. The Experiences.	3–7	II. The Activity.	11 to 15	II. The Process.	25 to 39
(See Titles.)		(See Titles.)		i. Songs of Assurance.	25 to 29
				(See Titles.)	
				ii. Songs of Appropriation.	30
				(See Titles.)	34
				iii. Songs of Aspiration.	35 to 39
				(See Titles.)	
III. The ultimate Purpose.	8			III. The Person.	40, 41

PSALM 1

Jehovah's Law, A Contrast; Obedience and Disobedience

BLESSED is the man that walketh not in the counsel of the wicked,
Nor standeth in the way of sinners,
Nor sitteth in the seat of scoffers:
2 But his delight is in the law of Jehovah;
And on his law doth he meditate day and night.
3 And he shall be like a tree planted by the streams of water,
That bringeth forth its fruit in its season,
Whose leaf also doth not wither;
And whatsoever he doeth shall prosper.
4 The wicked are not so,
But are like the chaff which the wind driveth away.
5 Therefore the wicked shall not stand in the judgment,
Nor sinners in the congregation of the righteous.
6 For Jehovah knoweth the way of the righteous;
But the way of the wicked shall perish.

The master thought of this psalm is that of the law of Jehovah. The obedient and disobedient are placed in sharp contrast. This contrast is vividly seen by bringing together the first and last words of the psalm—"blessed," "perish." The former word describes the issue of obedience; the latter, the result of disobedience. The conditions of blessedness are stated negatively and positively. Negatively there must be complete separation from fellowship with such as are disobedient. The graduation in description must not be omitted; "walketh," "standeth," "sitteth," "counsel," "way," "seat"; "wicked," "sinners," "scornful." The positive condition is twofold; delight, and meditation in the law. This, moreover, must be continuous, "day and night." The experience of blessedness is described under the figure of a tree planted, bearing fruit, with evergreen leaf. Moreover, such a man prospers in all he does.

Then comes the contrast. Let the statement, "The wicked are not so" be considered in the light of all that has been said; that is, in the former part of the psalm cancel the negations where they stand, and insert them where they are not. The condition of the wicked is then summarized, and the contrast is perfected. Instead of the tree planted, they are chaff driven away. They will be unable to stand the test of judgment, and therefore are excluded from the assembly of the righteous. The psalm ends with a summary. "The way of the righteous" is known to Jehovah. "The way of the wicked" perishes, that is, runs out, and is lost in the wood.

PSALM 2

Jehovah's King. Folly of Rebellion. Wisdom of Submission

WHY do the nations rage,
And the peoples meditate a vain thing?
2 The kings of the earth set themselves,
And the rulers take counsel together,
Against Jehovah, and against his anointed, *saying,*
3 Let us break their bonds asunder,
And cast away their cords from us.
4 He that sitteth in the heavens will laugh:
The Lord will have them in derision.
5 Then will he speak unto them in his wrath,
And vex them in his sore displeasure:
6 Yet I have set my king
Upon my holy hill of Zion.
7 I will tell of the decree:

Jehovah said unto me, Thou art my son;
This day have I begotten thee.
8 Ask of me, and I will give *thee* the nations for thine inheritance,
And the uttermost parts of the earth for thy possession.
9 Thou shalt break them with a rod of iron;
Thou shalt dash them in pieces like a potter's vessel.
10 Now therefore be wise, O ye kings:
Be instructed, ye judges of the earth.
11 Serve Jehovah with fear,
And rejoice with trembling.
12 Kiss the son, lest he be angry, and ye perish in the way,
For his wrath will soon be kindled.
Blessed are all they that take refuge in him.

This is the psalm of Jehovah's King. It is impossible to fix the event for which it was written and to which it first referred.

The wider application is perfectly patent. To whatsoever king the words first applied, the singer was looking to the ideal King, and his song has found fulfilment in Christ.

It is very interesting to notice how this psalm is interwoven with the thinking of the New Testament. To study it carefully, first of all we must discover the speakers in each case. The psalmist opens with a description of the nations in opposition to Jehovah and His King. This is given in the form of a question as to why they are in such attitude. He then proceeds to declare the contempt of the Lord for them, and in verse 6 Jehovah is the Speaker, announcing that notwithstanding all their opposition, He has appointed His King.

The next section (vers. 7-9) gives us the words of the anointed King, Who declares the decree of His Kingship. The Son of Jehovah is to receive dominion from His Father, and exercise it for the subjugation of all these opposing forces. The order of procedure is indicated; "inheritance," "possession," "administration." The psalm ends with an appeal to the kings and judges to manifest their wisdom by submitting themselves to Jehovah's King.

PSALM 3

Jehovah's Salvation. Confidence in Peril

JEHOVAH, how are mine adversaries increased!
Many there are that rise up against me.

2 Many there are that say of my soul,
There is no help for him in God.

3 But thou, O Jehovah, art a shield about me;
My glory, and the lifter up of my head.

4 I cry unto Jehovah with my voice,

And he answereth me out of his holy hill.

5 I laid me down and slept;
I awaked; for Jehovah sustaineth me.

6 I will not be afraid of ten thousands of the people
That have set themselves against me round about.

7 Arise, O Jehovah; save me, O my God:
For thou hast smitten all mine enemies upon the cheek bone;

| Thou hast broken the teeth of the wicked. | 8 Salvation belongeth unto Jehovah:
Thy blessing be upon thy people. |

This is a morning psalm. It is the song of a soul whose circumstances are those of grave peril as a new day dawns. The consciousness of difficulty is first uttered. Adversaries are increased, and the bitterest part of the pain is that these mock him, declaring "There is no help for him in God."

Immediately succeeding are the words which tell of the sufferer's confidence, and its reason. Jehovah is at once "Shield" and "Glory," and "Lifter up." Between this man and Jehovah there is established communion—"I cry," and "He answereth."

Then follows the language of courage. He has "slept" and "awaked," because Jehovah sustained him. In this assurance he will not be afraid of the increased adversaries. Then out of these circumstances of peril and conviction of safety, the prayer arises for salvation, and is accompanied by the assertion that Jehovah has already heard and answered. A consciousness of the constancy of the Divine love has always been the strength of a trusting soul amid circumstances of the greatest peril. If that is lost, all is lost. If that be maintained no great waters can overwhelm.

PSALM 4

Jehovah's Countenance the Cause of Confidence

ANSWER me when I call,
O God of my righteousness;
Thou hast set me at large *when
I was* in distress:
Have mercy upon me, and hear
my prayer.
2 O ye sons of men, how long shall
my glory be turned into dishonor?

How long will ye love vanity, and
seek after falsehood?
3 But know that Jehovah hath set
apart for himself him that is
godly:
Jehovah will hear when I call
unto him.
4 Stand in awe, and sin not:

Commune with your own heart upon your bed, and be still.
5 Offer the sacrifices of righteousness,
And put your trust in Jehovah.
6 Many there are that say, Who will show us *any* good?
Jehovah, lift thou up the light of thy countenance upon us.

7 Thou hast put gladness in my heart,
More than *they have* when their grain and their new wine are increased.
8 In peace will I both lay me down and sleep;
For thou, Jehovah, alone makest me dwell in safety.

This is a song of the evening. The general circumstances out of which it rises are the same as those of the previous psalm. Now, however, the day into which the singer marched with confidence, is over. The evidences of strain are manifest, and yet the dominant thought is that of victory won, and confidence increased.

The opening words constitute a petition in the midst of which the singer declares that God has delivered him. He appeals to the "sons of men," to those who, according to his morning psalm declared, "There is no help for him in God." He now asks them how long they will turn His glory into dishonour, "love vanity," and "seek after falsehood." The experiences of another day enable him to declare that Jehovah is great. He warns them to "stand in awe," to think of it, and "be still."

The testimony merges into an appeal to those who do not know Jehovah. They are pessimists, dissatisfied in the midst of life, and asking, "Who will show us any good?" Out of his experience of Jehovah's goodness he affirms that he has found gladness more than the men who have been in circumstances of material prosperity. The song ends with words that breathe his deep content, "In peace will I both lay me down and sleep"; and the reason is that though he is alone, or in solitude, Jehovah makes him dwell safely.

PSALM 5

Jehovah's Leading in Time of Persecution

GIVE ear to my words, O Jehovah,
Consider my meditation.

2 Hearken unto the voice of my
cry, my King, and my God;
For unto thee do I pray.

3 O Jehovah, in the morning shalt
thou hear my voice;
In the morning will I order *my
prayer* unto thee, and will
keep watch.

4 For thou art not a God that
hath pleasure in wickedness:
Evil shall not sojourn with thee.

5 The arrogant shall not stand in
thy sight:
Thou hatest all workers of iniquity.
Thou wilt destroy them that
speak lies:
Jehovah abhorreth the bloodthirsty and deceitful man.

7 But as for me, in the abundance
of thy loving kindness will I
come into thy house:
In thy fear will I worship toward thy holy temple.

8 Lead me, O Jehovah, in thy
righteousness because of mine
enemies.
Make thy way straight before
my face.

9 For there is no faithfulness in
their mouth;
Their inward part is very wickedness;
Their throat is an open sepul-
chre;
They flatter with their tongue.

10 Hold them guilty, O God;
Let them fall by their own
counsels;
Thrust them out in the multitude of their transgressions;
For they have rebelled against
thee.

11 But let all those that take
refuge in thee rejoice,
Let them ever shout for joy, because thou defendest them:
Let them also that love thy
name be joyful in thee.

12 For thou wilt bless the righteous;
O Jehovah, thou wilt compass
him with favor as with a
shield.

This is another song of the morning. It opens with language which reveals the reason of the soul's assurance as it faces another day. First are petitions asking the attention of Jehovah. These are followed by words which reveal at once the singer's conception of personal responsibility, and the reason of his confidence in God.

As to the former, the day is to be begun in prayer, "O Jehovah, in the morning shalt Thou hear my voice." It is,

moreover, to be arranged as in the sight of God, "In the morning will I order unto Thee, and will keep watch." The attitude
of God toward wickedness and evil men is then declared. This
attitude at once makes the singer sure of his safety as against
the opposition of evil men, and causes his care concerning his
own condition before God. Turning his eyes towards the
enemies that wait for him whom he describes, he seeks the
Divine guidance, desiring most of all to see plainly before his
face the way of Jehovah. As he goes forth to meet these enemies he does so with a prayer that God will defeat their
counsels, and vindicate those who put their trust in Him.
There is no doubt or uncertainty in his heart. The things he
asked for he is assured he will receive, and with an affirmation
of this confidence the song ends.

PSALM 6

Jehovah's Deliverance in Time of Chastisement

O JEHOVAH, rebuke me not
in thine anger,
Neither chasten me in thy hot
displeasure.
2 Have mercy upon me, O Jehovah; for I am withered away:
O Jehovah, heal me; for my
bones are troubled.
3 My soul also is sore troubled:
And thou, O Jehovah, how long?
4 Return, O Jehovah, deliver my
soul:
Save me for thy loving-kindness'
sake.
5 For in death there is no remembrance of thee:
In Sheol who will give thee
thanks?
6 I am weary with my groaning;

Every night make I my bed to
swim;
I water my couch with my
tears.
7 Mine eye wasteth away because
of grief;
It waxeth old because of all
mine adversaries.
8 Depart from me, all ye workers
of iniquity;
For Jehovah hath heard the
voice of my weeping.
9 Jehovah hath heard my supplication;
Jehovah will receive my prayer.
10 All mine enemies shall be put to
shame and sore troubled:
They shall turn back, they shall
be put to shame suddenly.

This is known as the first of the seven great penitential psalms. It is somewhat weak in its note of true penitence, and is not to be compared with some which follow in this respect. It is rather a cry for deliverance from the pain and the sorrow and chastisement, than from the sin which causes it.

The first seven verses are full of the misery of the man. He is perfectly conscious of the meaning of his suffering. He knows that it is chastisement, and under the pressure of it he sobs for deliverance. The light breaks upon the darkness in his confident consciousness of Jehovah's attention and willingness to help him.

If this be considered a psalm of penitence it is remarkable rather as a revelation of the tender compassion of Jehovah, than of the true note of repentance. There is not a single sentence which reveals any profound consciousness of the sinfulness of sin. The saving grace of it, so far as the sinner is concerned, is that it recognizes Jehovah's rebuke and chastening. The desire preeminently manifest is that of escape from the suffering and the sorrow. Notwithstanding the shallowness of the sense of sin, the fact of the recognition of the hand of Jehovah seems to be enough and in answering pity and power the deliverance and the comfort sought are granted.

PSALM 7

Jehovah's Deliverance Confidently Hoped In

O JEHOVAH my God, in thee do I take refuge:
Save me from all them that pursue me, and deliver me,

2 Lest they tear my soul like a lion,
Rending it in pieces, while there is none to deliver.

3 O Jehovah my God, if I have done this;
If there be iniquity in my hands;

4 If I have rewarded evil unto him that was at peace with me
(Yea, I have delivered him that without cause was mine adversary);

5 Let the enemy pursue my soul, and overtake it;
Yea, let him tread my life down to the earth,
And lay my glory in the dust.

6 Arise, O Jehovah, in thine anger;
Lift up thyself against the rage
of mine adversaries,
And awake for me; thou hast
commanded judgment.

7 And let the congregation of the
peoples compass thee about;
And over them return thou on
high.

8 Jehovah ministereth judgment
to the peoples:
Judge me, O Jehovah, according
to my righteousness, and to
mine integrity that is in me.

9 Oh let the wickedness of the
wicked come to an end, but
establish thou the righteous:
For the righteous God trieth
the minds and hearts.

10 My shield is with God,
Who saveth the upright in
heart.

11 God is a righteous judge,
Yea, a God that hath indignation every day.

12 If a man turn not, he will whet
his sword;
He hath bent his bow, and made
it ready;

13 He hath also prepared for him
the instruments of death;
He maketh his arrows fiery
shafts.

14 Behold, he travaileth with iniquity;
Yea, he hath conceived mischief,
and brought forth falsehood.

15 He hath made a pit, and digged
it,
And is fallen into the ditch
which he made.

16 His mischief shall return upon
his own head,
And his violence shall come
down upon his own pate.

17 I will give thanks unto Jehovah
according to his righteousness,
And will sing praise to the name
of Jehovah Most High.

This is a song of confidence and appeal in circumstances of the most trying description. He is persecuted by enemies, some one among them being violent and cruel. The basis of their attack would seem to be some charge they make against him of wrong-doing. He vehemently denies the charge, and cries to Jehovah for vindication, which he firmly believes the God Who tries the hearts of men will surely grant.

In the first part of the psalm the story of personal need is told. The ruthlessness of the foe is the reason for his appeal. The declaration of personal innocence follows. If the charges were true, then would the heaviest judgments be just. They are untrue, as God is witness. Then let Jehovah appear on be-half of the innocent, against the guilty. Then follows the general affirmation of the equity of God upon which the singer builds his confidence. God is righteous. The way of wicked-ness cannot prosper. It creates its own destruction. The pit digged is the grave of the man who digs it. The mischief and violence meditated return as retribution upon the evil-doer.

The psalm is a song of confidence in the reign of God in equity over all men, and the consequent certainty that inno-cence will be vindicated in this particular case. Thanksgiving is according to Jehovah's righteousness.

PSALM 8

Jehovah's Excellence Manifest in Nature and Man

O JEHOVAH, our Lord,
How excellent is thy name in all the earth,
Who hast set thy glory upon the heavens!

2 Out of the mouth of babes and sucklings hast thou established strength,
Because of thine adversaries,
That thou mightest still the enemy and the avenger.

3 When I consider thy heavens, the work of thy fingers,
The moon and the stars, which thou hast ordained;

4 What is man, that thou art mindful of him?
And the son of man, that thou visitest him?

5 For thou hast made him but little lower than God,
And crownest him with glory and honor.

6 Thou makest him to have do-minion over the works of thy hands;
Thou hast put all things under his feet:

7 All sheep and oxen,
Yea, and the beasts of the field,

8 The birds of the heavens, and the fish of the sea,
Whatsoever passeth through the paths of the seas.

9 O Jehovah, our Lord,
How excellent is thy name in all the earth!

This is a great song of worship. It opens and closes with the same words. These words enclose the psalm, and create its burden. The matters lying between are the proofs of the open-ing and closing statements. They are two. The manifestation of Jehovah's excellencies in nature and man. These are first briefly stated (vers. 1b, 2) and then more particularly described (vers. 3–8).

The principal manifestation is in man, and this is revealed in both sections. The outlook on nature is toward the encompassing heaven, all the glory of which is expressed in one inclusive thought—Jehovah has set His glory there. From this he turns to the little children of the human race, and in them he finds a perfection of praise absent from the glorious heaven. It is such as "to still the enemy and the avenger."

These two facts are then more particularly considered. The first impression suggests the littleness of man. In the presence of the glorious heaven man seems beneath consideration. Yet it is not so. Man is greater than all. He is but little lower than God. His place is that of dominion. The contemplation of the heaven leads to the consideration of man. This creates first a wonder at Jehovah's consideration of him. This consideration issues in investigation, and man is found nearer to God than the heavens. The issue is worship. It is the true order of creation. Through man's sin it has been lost. Through Jesus it is being restored.

PSALM 9

Jehovah's Righteous Rule Rejoiced In

I WILL give thanks unto Jehovah with my whole heart;
I will show forth all thy marvellous works.

2 I will be glad and exult in thee;
I will sing praise to thy name, O thou Most High.

3 When mine enemies turn back,
They stumble and perish at thy presence.

4 For thou hast maintained my right and my cause;
Thou sittest in the throne judging righteously.

5 Thou hast rebuked the nations, thou hast destroyed the wicked;
Thou hast blotted out their name for ever and ever.

6 The enemy are come to an end, they are desolate for ever;
And the cities which thou hast overthrown,
The very remembrance of them is perished.

7 But Jehovah sitteth *as king* for ever:

He hath prepared his throne for judgment;

8 And he will judge the world in righteousness,
He will minister judgment to the peoples in uprightness.

9 Jehovah also will be a high tower for the oppressed,
A high tower in times of trouble;

10 And they that know thy name will put their trust in thee;
For thou, Jehovah, hast not forsaken them that seek thee.

11 Sing praises to Jehovah, who dwelleth in Zion:
Declare among the people his doings.

12 For he that maketh inquisition for blood remembereth them;
He forgetteth not the cry of the poor.

13 Have mercy upon me, O Jehovah;
Behold my affliction *which I suffer* of them that hate me,
Thou that liftest me up from the gates of death;

14 That I may show forth all thy praise.

In the gates of the daughter of Zion
I will rejoice in thy salvation.

15 The nations are sunk down in the pit that they made:
In the net which they hid is their own foot taken.

16 Jehovah hath made himself known, he hath executed judgment:
The wicked is snared in the work of his own hands.

17 The wicked shall be turned back unto Sheol,
Even all the nations that forget God.

18 For the needy shall not always be forgotten,
Nor the expectation of the poor perish for ever.

19 Arise, O Jehovah; let not man prevail:
Let the nations be judged in thy sight.

20 Put them in fear, O Jehovah:
Let the nations know themselves to be but men.

The burden of this psalm is that of thanksgiving for Jehovah's righteous rule by which He has overcome the enemies of the chosen people. It is almost exclusively a song of thanksgiving. There are a few brief petitions, but they are intimately related to the measures of praise. These songs of praise move from the personal to the general. First, deliverances wrought for the singer are celebrated (vers. 1–4); then the government of the enthroned Jehovah among the nations, a government based upon righteousness, is sung (vers. 5–8); and next the tenderness of Jehovah toward the oppressed, and His unfailing succour of the needy, is declared (vers. 9, 10). The song of the singer then becomes a cry to others to join in the chorus (vers. 11, 12). Then follows a cry for mercy which immediately merges into praise, and the thanksgiving moves out in the same order from personal (vers. 13, 14) to general (vers. 15, 16).

The whole ends with a declaration of the certainty of the Divine government, and a final prayer for its clear manifestation. The psalm is a great pattern of praise on a far too much neglected level in our day. We praise God much for His mercy. This is right, but it is a good thing to recognize His righteous rule, and to praise Him for that.

PSALM 10

Jehovah's Judgment Besought

WHY standest thou afar off, O Jehovah?
Why hidest thou thyself in times of trouble?

2 In the pride of the wicked the poor is hotly pursued;
Let them be taken in the devices that they have conceived.

3 For the wicked boasteth of his heart's desire,
And the covetous renounceth, yea, contemneth Jehovah.

4 The wicked, in the pride of his countenance, saith, He will not require it.
All his thoughts are, There is no God.

5 His ways are firm at all times;
Thy judgments are far above out of his sight:
As for all his adversaries, he puffeth at them.

6 He saith in his heart, I shall not be moved;

To all generations I shall not be in adversity.

7 His mouth is full of cursing and deceit and oppression:
Under his tongue is mischief and iniquity.

8 He sitteth in the lurking-places of the villages;
In the secret places doth he murder the innocent;
His eyes are privily set against the helpless.

9 He lurketh in secret as a lion in his covert;
He lieth in wait to catch the poor:
He doth catch the poor, when he draweth him in his net.

10 He croucheth, he boweth down,
And the helpless fall by his strong ones.

11 He saith in his heart: God hath forgotten,
He hideth his face, he will never see it.

12 Arise, O Jehovah; O God, lift
   up thy hand:
   Forget not the poor.
13 Wherefore doth the wicked con-
   temn God,
   And say in his heart, Thou wilt
   not require *it*?
14 Thou hast seen *it*; for thou be-
   holdest mischief and spite, to
   requite it with thy hand:
   The helpless committeth *himself*
   unto thee;
   Thou hast been the helper of
   the fatherless.
15 Break thou the arm of the
   wicked;

And as for the evil man, seek
   out his wickedness till thou
   find none.
16 Jehovah is King for ever and
   ever:
   The nations are perished out of
   his land.
17 Jehovah, thou hast head the desire of the meek:
   Thou wilt prepare their heart,
   thou wilt cause thine ear to
   hear;
18 To judge the fatherless and the
   oppressed,
   That man who is of the earth
   may be terrible no more.

In the Septuagint and other versions, probably the ancient Hebrew, psalms ix and x appear as one. There is a clear connection between them, but it is that of contrast. In the former the singer has rejoiced in the exercise of Jehovah's rule in the whole earth. In this he mourns what seems to be the abandonment of His own people.

There is first the protesting cry of the heart against what seems to be Divine indifference to the injustice being wrought by the wicked against the poor (vers. 1, 2). This injustice is then described in detail. It is a graphic description of the brutality of earthly rule when it has forgotten God, or says in its ignorance that God has forgotten it. The picture would fit many times of misrule on the pages of human history. There is a heart cry to Jehovah; to God to interfere. If the psalm opens in complaint, it closes in confidence. The wicked man is wrong about God. He does see and know. The cry of the oppressed He hears. Deliverance must come, for Jehovah is King. Not once nor twice, but often the man of faith has been driven to cry out in complaint in presence of the oppression of man by man. Happy is the man whose faith causes him to utter his complaint directly to Jehovah. The issue of such action is ever a renewed consciousness of the certainty of the Divine government, and the necessary rightness of the ultimate issue.

PSALM 11

Jehovah's Throne the Foundation

IN Jehovah do I take refuge:
How say ye to my soul,
Flee *as* a bird to your mountain;
2 For, lo, the wicked bend the bow,
They make ready their arrow
upon the string,
That they may shoot in darkness
at the upright in heart;
3 If the foundations be destroyed,
What can the righteous do?
4 Jehovah is in his holy temple;
Jehovah, his throne is in heaven;

His eyes behold, his eye-lids try,
the children of men.
5 Jehovah trieth the righteous;
But the wicked and him that
loveth violence his soul hateth.
6 Upon the wicked he will rain
snares;
Fire and brimstone and burning
wind shall be the portion of
their cup.
7 For Jehovah is righteous; he
loveth righteousness:
The upright shall behold his face.

This psalm is the answer of faith to the advice of fear. Both are alike conscious of immediate peril. Fear sees only the things that are near. Faith takes in the larger distances. If the things fear sees are indeed all, its advice is excellent. When the things which faith sees are realized, its determination is vindicated. The advice of fear is found in the words beginning, "Flee as a bird," and ending, "What can the righteous do?" The name and thought of God are absent. The peril is seen vividly and accurately. It is wicked in its nature; imminent, the bow is bent; subtle, they "shoot in darkness." The very foundations are destroyed. There is nothing for it now but to flee!

The rest of the psalm is the answer of faith. The first vision of faith is that of Jehovah enthroned. That is the supreme foundation. Then He also sees the peril. Do the wicked watch the righteous? Jehovah watches the wicked! Are the righteous tried in the process? Jehovah presides over the trial!

Are the wicked going to shoot? So is Jehovah—snares and brimstone!

Perhaps among all the psalms none reveals more perfectly the strenuous hold of faith. It is the man who measures things by the circumstances of the hour who is filled with fear, and counsels and practises flight! The man who sees Jehovah enthroned and governing has no panic.

PSALM 12

Jehovah's Rule in the Midst of Ungodliness

HELP, Jehovah; for the godly man ceaseth;
For the faithful fail from among the children of men.
2 They speak falsehood every one with his neighbor:
With flattering lip, and with a double heart, do they speak.
3 Jehovah will cut off all flattering lips,
The tongue that speaketh great things;
4 Who have said, With our tongue will we prevail;
Our lips are our own: who is lord over us?

5 Because of the oppression of the poor, because of the sighing of the needy,
Now will I arise, saith Jehovah;
I will set him in the safety he panteth for.
6 The words of Jehovah are pure words;
As silver tried in a furnace on the earth,
Purified seven times.
7 Thou wilt keep them, O Jehovah,
Thou wilt preserve them from this generation for ever.
8 The wicked walk on every side,
When vileness is exalted among the sons of men.

Out of a consciousness of the terrible evil of his times the worshipper cries to Jehovah for help. The failure of godly men and faithful souls is always the gravest peril which can threaten a nation or an age. There is no trouble which more heavily afflicts the heart of the trusting. The note here is more characterized by faith than that of psalm x. Here is a cry for help, but no suggestion that God is indifferent. Indeed there is an immediate affirmation of confidence in the interest and interference of God.

It is very beautiful to notice how in answer to the cry and the affirmation of confidence, Jehovah speaks, so that the singer hears Him, and is able to announce His declaration in response ere the song ceases. This answer of Jehovah is most precious. It promises the preservation of the trusting. The psalmist breaks out into praise of the purity of His words, and declares that Jehovah will "keep them," and "preserve them." The "them" here refers to the words. There is no promise made of widespread revival or renewal. It is the salvation of a remnant and the preservation of His own words which Jehovah promises.

Thus the psalm ends with a description of the same condition which it at first describes. It is the cry of a godly soul amid prevailing ungodliness for help; and it is answered.

PSALM 13

Jehovah's Succour Sought by the Afflicted

HOW long, O Jehovah? wilt thou forget me for ever? How long wilt thou hide thy face from me?
2 How long shall I take counsel in my soul, Having sorrow in my heart all the day? How long shall mine enemy be exalted over me?
3 Consider *and* answer me, O Jehovah my God:
Lighten mine eyes, lest I sleep the *sleep* of death;
4 Lest mine enemy say, I have prevailed against him; *Lest* mine adversaries rejoice when I am moved.
5 But I have trusted in thy lovingkindness; My heart shall rejoice in thy salvation.
6 I will sing unto Jehovah, Because he hath dealt bountifully with me.

This little psalm is very full of beauty as it traces the way by which many a tried and tempest-tossed soul has found consolation and strength. There is first of all the cry of despair. Foes are oppressing the man of faith. There seems to be no succour even from Jehovah. Yet carefully note that his faith in Jehovah Who is his God, abides. He is able to help. To Him then he cries.

This is a lesson of profound value. If the heart be overburdened and Jehovah seems to hide His face, let the story of woe be told to Him. It is a holy exercise. Men may not understand it. They may even charge us with failing faith, when as a matter of fact in the sweeping of the storm as all other anchorage crumbles and passes, faith is fastening itself more surely upon the Rock.

How does the psalm end? With a song of triumph. Yet it is a song of faith, for deliverance is not yet realized. How then does the song emerge from the wail? Carefully examine the words:—

> "But I *have* trusted in Thy mercy;
> My heart shall rejoice in Thy salvation."

That backward look has served to remind the troubled heart of deliverances wrought, and a new confidence is born of the memory which utters itself in a song. It is good to "forget the things behind" if the memory of them would hinder present consecration. It is also good to remember all the way Jehovah has led us when the day is dark with fear.

PSALM 14

Jehovah's Knowledge of the Godless

THE fool hath said in his heart,
  There is no God.
They are corrupt, they have done
  abominable works;
There is none that doeth good.
2 Jehovah looked down from heaven
  upon the children of men,
To see if there were any that did
  understand,
That did seek after God.

They are all gone aside; they are
  together become filthy;
There is none that doeth good,
  no, not one.
4 Have all the workers of iniquity
  no knowledge,
Who eat up my people *as* they
  eat bread,
And call not upon Jehovah?
5 There were they in great fear;

For God is in the generation of the righteous.
6 Ye put to shame the counsel of the poor,
Because Jehovah is his refuge.

7 Oh that the salvation of Israel were come out of Zion!
When Jehovah bringeth back the captivity of his people,
Then shall Jacob rejoice, *and* Israel shall be glad.

Here the psalmist utters his own consciousness of the meaning of godlessness. In its essence it is folly. The word "fool" here stands for moral perversity rather than intellectual blindness. This is repeated in the declaration, "They are corrupt," and in the statement that their works are abominable. To his own testimony he adds the statement of the Divine outlook upon humanity. It is the same. Men do not recognize Him, and their doings are therefore evil.

The psalmist then looks at certain occasions without naming them. "There" refers to some occasion of deliverance wrought by God for His people. The thought is that when God was recognized by His people their enemies were filled with fear. Then there is a contrasting picture of the oppressed people of God put to shame, "because Jehovah is his refuge"; the thought being that the refuge was neglected, and the chosen therefore rejected (see Ps. liii. 5). The thought of the whole psalm is that the safety of godliness, and the peril of ungodliness. Jehovah cannot be deceived. He knows, and this, events always prove. The psalm ends with a sigh for the coming of the day of deliverance.

PSALM 15

Jehovah's Friend Described

JEHOVAH, who shall sojourn in thy tabernacle?
Who shall dwell in thy holy hill?
2 He that walketh uprightly, and worketh righteousness,
And speaketh truth in his heart;

3 He that slandereth not with his tongue,
Nor doeth evil to his friend,
Nor taketh up a reproach against his neighbor;

4 In whose eyes a reprobate is despised,
But who honoreth them that fear Jehovah;
He that sweareth to his own hurt, and changeth not;

5 He that putteth not out his money to interest,
Nor taketh reward against the innocent.
He that doeth these things shall never be moved.

This psalm declares the terms of friendship between man and Jehovah. The opening questions describe the privileges of friendship. To sojourn does not necessarily mean to stay for a brief time. Length of stay is not suggested by the word, but rather the position of one who receives hospitality, a guest. To dwell is to reside permanently. The picture is that of a resident of the City of God, who has free and welcome access to His presence. To whom are such high privileges granted? The answer is first stated in general terms, and then illustrations are given.

In general terms the friend of God is one whose general deportment is perfect, whose activity is right, whose inner thoughts are pure. The test of all this is in a man's attitude to his fellowman, which is described. The man fulfilling these conditions is never moved from his residence in the holy hill, nor excluded from the hospitality of Jehovah's tent. The outcome of true friendship with Jehovah is friendship for man. Therefore, the condition for continued friendship with Jehovah is loyal friendship to man.

PSALM 16

Jehovah the Portion of the Trusting

PRESERVE me, O God; for in thee do I take refuge.
2 *O my soul*, thou hast said unto Jehovah, Thou art my Lord:
I have no good beyond thee.
3 As for the saints that are in the earth,

They are the excellent in whom is all my delight.
4 Their sorrows shall be multiplied that give gifts for another *god*:
Their drink-offerings of blood will I not offer,

Nor take their names upon my
lips.
5 Jehovah is the portion of mine
inheritance and of my cup:
Thou maintainest my lot.
6 The lines are fallen unto me in
pleasant places;
Yea, I have a goodly heritage.
7 I will bless Jehovah, who hath
given me counsel;
Yea, my heart instructeth me
in the night seasons.
8 I have set Jehovah always before me:
Because he is at my right hand,
I shall not be moved.

9 Therefore my heart is glad, and
my glory rejoiceth:
My flesh also shall dwell in
safety.
10 For thou wilt not leave my soul
to Sheol;
Neither wilt thou suffer thy
holy one to see corruption.
11 Thou wilt show me the path of
life:
In thy presence is fulness of
joy;
In thy right hand there are
pleasures for evermore.

This is a song of satisfaction. The singer is not one who is
unfamiliar with peril. The opening sentence is a sigh revealing the consciousness thereof, and towards the close, the
shadows of Sheol and the terror of corruption are recognized.
Yet these things only find a place here that they may be cancelled by the facts which create a sense of triumph over all
peril. Jehovah is the one and all sufficient good, and the
saints are the friends of the singer because they are also the
friends of Jehovah. With those who exchange Jehovah for
another god, the psalmist will have no fellowship. The fact
that Jehovah is the supreme Good is developed in descriptive
measures. He is a present Good, and the Hope of all the
future; a present Possession, creating pleasant places, and
perpetual power. As to the future, the last enemies are not to
overcome the trusting, and beyond victory over them is the
presence of the King, and the place of His right hand, with
fullness of joy, and pleasures for evermore.

The hope of this singer found its perfect fulfilment only in
the Man of perfect trust, and through Him in all who share
His life, through the mystery of that death, from which He
came triumphantly to enter into the eternal joys.

PSALM 17

Jehovah Appealed to, to Exercise Judgment

HEAR the right, O Jehovah,
    attend unto my cry;
Give ear unto my prayer, that
    goeth not out of feigned lips.
2 Let my sentence come forth
    from thy presence;
Let thine eyes look upon equity.
3 Thou hast proved my heart;
    thou hast visited me in the
    night;
Thou hast tried me, and findest
    nothing;
I am purposed that my mouth
    shall not transgress.
4 As for the works of men, by the
    word of thy lips
I have kept me from the ways
    of the violent.
5 My steps have held fast to thy
    paths,
My feet have not slipped.
6 I have called upon thee, for
    thou wilt answer me, O God:
Incline thine ear unto me, *and*
    hear my speech.
7 Show thy marvellous loving-
    kindness,
O thou that savest by thy right
    hand them that take refuge
    in thee
From those that rise up *against
    them.*
8 Keep me as the apple of the
    eye;
Hide me under the shadow of
    thy wings,

9 From the wicked that oppress
    me,
My deadly enemies that com-
    pass me about.
10 They are inclosed in their own
    fat:
With their mouth they speak
    proudly.
11 They have now compassed us
    in our steps;
They set their eyes to cast *us*
    down to the earth.
12 He is like a lion that is greedy
    of his prey,
And as it were a young lion
    lurking in secret places.
13 Arise, O Jehovah,
Confront him, cast him down:
Deliver my soul from the
    wicked by thy sword;
14 From men by thy hand, O Je-
    hovah,
From men of the world, whose
    portion is in *this* life,
And whose belly thou fillest
    with thy treasure:
They are satisfied with children,
And leave the rest of their sub-
    stances to their babes.
15 As for me, I shall behold thy
    face in righteousness;
I shall be satisfied, when I
    awake, with *beholding* thy
    form.

This psalm is generally conceded to be closely linked with
the preceding one. There is an evident similarity of outlook.
In each case the singer declares his abstention from complicity

with ungodly men. In both psalms God is appealed to, and the final hope of the soul is that of fuller communion with Him. Yet, of course, the chief impression of comparison is that of contrast. In the former, peril is referred to incidentally. Here, it is described, and is the occasion of the outpouring of the soul. The two exercises of priesthood are exemplified in these psalms. In the first the sacrifices of praise are offered. In this the petitions of need are presented.

First, the ground of appeal is that of the singer's uprightness of heart, and speech, and action. It then moves into another and higher realm, that of the singer's confidence in God. He is known to be the One Who saves the trusting. The consciousness of His tenderness is manifest in the expressions used:—

> "Keep me as the apple of the eye,
> Hide me under the shadow of Thy wings."

After a description of the immediate peril the singer again appeals for help, and the song ends with the expression of assured blessing, and the declaration of the one and only full satisfaction.

PSALM 18

Jehovah Worshipped

I LOVE thee, O Jehovah, my strength.

2 Jehovah is my rock, and my fortress, and my deliverer;
My God, my rock, in whom I will take refuge;
My shield, and the horn of my salvation, my high tower.

3 I will call upon Jehovah, who is worthy to be praised:
So shall I be saved from mine enemies.

4 The cords of death compassed me,
And the floods of ungodliness made me afraid,

5 The cords of Sheol were round about me;
The snares of death came upon me.

6 In my distress I called upon Jehovah,
And cried unto my God:
He heard my voice out of his temple,
And my cry before him came into his ears.

7 Then the earth shook and trembled;
The foundations also of the mountains quaked
And were shaken, because he was wroth.

8 There went up a smoke out of his nostrils,
And fire out of his mouth devoured:
Coals were kindled by it.

9 He bowed the heavens also, and came down;
And thick darkness was under his feet.

10 And he rode upon a cherub, and did fly:
Yea, he soared upon the wings of the wind.

11 He made darkness his hiding-place, his pavilion round about him,
Darkness of waters, thick clouds of the skies.

12 At the brightness before him his thick clouds passed,
Hailstones and coals of fire.

13 Jehovah also thundered in the heavens,
And the Most High uttered his voice,
Hailstones and coals of fire.

14 And he sent out his arrows, and scattered them;
Yea, lightnings manifold, and discomfited them.

15 Then the channels of waters appeared,
And the foundations of the world were laid bare,
At thy rebuke, O Jehovah,
At the blast of the breath of thy nostrils.

16 He set from on high, he took me;

He drew me out of many waters.

17 He delivered me from my strong enemy,
And from them that hated me; for they were too mighty for me.

18 They came upon me in the day of my calamity;
But Jehovah was my stay.

19 He brought me forth also into a large place;
He delivered me, because he delighted in me.

20 Jehovah hath rewarded me according to my righteousness;
According to the cleanness of my hands hath he recompensed me.

21 For I have kept the ways of Jehovah,
And have not wickedly departed from my God.

22 For all his ordinances were before me,
And I put not away his statutes from me.

23 I was also perfect with him,
And I kept myself from mine iniquity.

24 Therefore hath Jehovah recompensed me according to my righteousness,
According to the cleanness of my hands in his eyesight.

25 With the merciful thou wilt show thyself merciful;
With the perfect man thou wilt show thyself perfect;

26 With the pure thou wilt show thyself pure;
And with the perverse thou wilt show thyself froward.

27 For thou wilt save the afflicted people;

But the haughty eyes thou wilt
bring down.
28 For thou wilt light my lamp:
Jehovah my God will lighten
my darkness.
29 For by thee I run upon a troop;
And by my God do I leap over
a wall.
30 As for God, his way is perfect:
The word of Jehovah is tried;
He is a shield unto all them that
take refuge in him.
31 For who is God, save Jehovah?
And who is a rock, besides our
God,
32 The God that girdeth me with
strength,
And maketh my way perfect?
33 He maketh my feet like hinds'
feet:
And setteth me upon my high
places.
34 He teacheth my hands to war;
So that mine arms do bend a
bow of brass.
35 Thou hast also given me the
shield of thy salvation;
And thy right hand hath holden
me up,
And thy gentleness hath made
me great.
36 Thou hast enlarged my steps
under me,
And my feet have not slipped.
37 I will pursue mine enemies, and
overtake them;
Neither will I turn again till
they are consumed.
38 I will smite them through, so
that they shall not be able to
rise:
They shall fall under my feet.
39 For thou hast girded me with
strength unto the battle:

Thou hast subdued under me
those that rose up against me
40 Thou hast also made mine enemies turn their backs unto
me,
That I might cut off them that
hate me.
41 They cried, but there was none
to save;
Even unto Jehovah, but he answered them not.
42 Then did I beat them small as
the dust before the wind;
I did cast them out as the mire
of the streets.
43 Thou hast delivered me from
the strivings of the people;
Thou hast made me the head of
the nations:
A people whom I have not
known shall serve me.
44 As soon as they hear of me they
shall obey me;
The foreigners shall submit
themselves unto me.
45 The foreigners shall fade away,
And shall come trembling out
of their close places.
46 Jehovah liveth; and blessed be
my rock;
And exalted be the God of my
salvation,
47 Even the God that executeth
vengeance for me,
And subdueth peoples under
me.
48 He rescueth me from mine enemies;
Yea, thou liftest me up above
them that rise up against me;
Thou deliverest me from the
violent man.
49 Therefore I will give thanks
unto thee, O Jehovah, among
the nations,

And will sing praises unto thy name.
50 Great deliverance giveth he to his king,
And showeth loving kindness to his anointed,
To David and to his seed, for evermore.

This is one of the most majestic and beautiful of the worship psalms. It is at once a perfect pattern of praise, and therefore a great revelation of the method and might and mercy of God. So clear and simple is it in its movement and language that nothing need be said of it save perhaps to suggest an analysis to aid in its study.

PROLOGUE OF PRAISE (vers. 1–3). Here the psalmist pours out the gladness and gratitude of his heart which thrills with the highest spirit of adoration.

THE PERIL AND DELIVERANCE (vers. 4–19). The terrible nature of the peril is first made clear, and then the story of the might and majesty of Jehovah's process is told, and the fact of deliverance declared.

THE PRINCIPLE (vers. 20–29). The reason of the Divine deliverance is declared, and the truth of perpetual importance, that God is to man what man is to God, is affirmed.

THE RESULTANT CONFIDENCE (vers. 30–45). Again the song breaks forth in almost tumultuous joy. Absolute confidence in God, and assurance of continued triumph are based upon experiences already gained of His goodness.

EPILOGUE OF PRAISE (vers. 46–50). The anthem ends with further sentences which group the benefits conferred upon the king by his God, and attest his determination to praise Him among the nations.

PSALM 19

Jehovah Revealed in Nature and Law

THE heavens declare the glory of God;
And the firmament showeth his handiwork.

2 Day unto day uttereth speech, And night unto night showeth knowledge.
3 There is no speech nor language;

Their voice is not heard.

4 Their line is gone out through all the earth,
And their words to the end of the world.
In them hath he set a tabernacle for the sun,

5 Which is as a bridegroom coming out of his chamber,
And rejoiceth as a strong man to run his course.

6 His going forth is from the end of the heavens,
And his circuit unto the ends of it;
And there is nothing hid from the heat thereof.

7 The law of Jehovah is perfect, restoring the soul:
The testimony of Jehovah is sure, making wise the simple.

8 The precepts of Jehovah are right, rejoicing the heart:
The commandment of Jehovah is pure, enlightening the eyes.

9 The fear of Jehovah is clean, enduring for ever:

The ordinances of Jehovah are true, *and* righteous altogether.

10 More to be desired are they than gold, yea, than much fine gold;
Sweeter also than honey and the droppings of the honeycomb.

11 Moreover by them is thy servant warned:
In keeping them there is great reward.

12 Who can discern *his* errors? Clear thou me from hidden *faults*.

13 Keep back thy servant also from presumptuous *sins*;
Let them not have dominion over me:
Then shall I be upright,
And I shall be clear from great transgression.

14 Let the words of my mouth and the meditation of my heart
Be acceptable in thy sight,
O Jehovah, my rock, and my redeemer.

The burden of this psalm is that of the twofold revelation of Jehovah. He is revealed in nature and in law. Yet in nature Jehovah is revealed as God, and not by those especial qualities suggested by the great name Jehovah. Moreover, in the law God is revealed as Jehovah, rather than by the facts of His wonder-working power. This differentiation is justified by the names as used.

In the first six verses, which deal with the nature revelation, the name God appears once, and Jehovah not at all. In the last eight verses, which speak of the law revelation, the name Jehovah appears seven times, and God not at all. It is one Sovereign Ruler Who is revealed, and He is referred to by name eight times in all. Nature speaks to nature. Day has its message to itself, and night to itself. Without articulation the message is constantly delivered in the circuit of the sun. To man, higher than all nature (see Ps. viii), an articulate message is given. A word is spoken. It is the great law of Jehovah —"perfect," "sure," "right," "pure," "clean," "true," "righteous." Mark well the sevenfold description, and how perfectly all the needs of man are met. Great and wondrous, God is known in nature by nature through the speech of a great silence; and revealed to man in messages which answer all his questionings, and govern all his ways.

PSALM 20

Jehovah Appealed to for Help on Behalf of the King

JEHOVAH answer thee in the day of trouble;
The name of the God of Jacob set thee upon high;
2 Send thee help from the sanctuary,
And strengthen thee out of Zion;
3 Remember all thy offerings,
And accept thy burnt-sacrifice;
4 Grant thee thy heart's desire,
And fulfil all thy counsel.
5 We will triumph in thy salvation,
And in the name of our God we will set up our banners:
Jehovah fulfil all thy petitions.

6 Now know I that Jehovah saveth his anointed:
He will answer him from his holy heaven
With the saving strength of his right hand.
7 Some *trust* in chariots, and some in horses;
But we will make mention of the name of Jehovah our God.
8 They are bowed down and fallen;
But we are risen, and stand upright.
9 Save, Jehovah:
Let the King answer us when we call.

This and the next psalms are certainly closely connected. The first is the prayer of the people on behalf of the king as he goes forth to battle. The first five verses were sung in chorus, and express the consciousness of the supreme need in this day of trouble. The foes are gathered, the battle must be fought. Help must come from the sanctuary, and strength from Zion. In the name of God the banners must be set up.

The next verse is a solo. The voice of the king is heard announcing his confidence in Jehovah. Immediately the chorus takes up the music, and contrasts the confidence of the foe in chariots and horses, with that of those who follow the king, in the name of Jehovah Who is their God. Following the contrast of confidence is that of issue: "They are bowed down and fallen," "We are risen, and stand upright."

The whole ends with a prayer in such form as recognizes the kingship of Jehovah. To-day the weapons of our warfare are no longer carnal, but we have a conflict to wage, and the secrets of strength for us are revealed as clearly here, as for those of olden times.

PSALM 21

Jehovah Praised as the Strength of the King

THE king shall joy in thy strength, O Jehovah;
And in thy salvation how greatly shall he rejoice!

2 Thou hast given him his heart's desire,
And hast not withholden the request of his lips.

3 For thou meetest him with the blessings of goodness:
Thou settest a crown of fine gold on his head.

4 He asked life of thee, thou gavest it him,
Even length of days for ever and ever.

5 His glory is great in thy salvation:
Honor and majesty dost thou lay upon him.

6 For thou makest him most blessed for ever:
Thou makest him glad with joy in thy presence.

7 For the king trusteth in Jehovah;
And through the lovingkindness of the Most High he shall not be moved.

8 Thy hand will find out all thine enemies;
Thy right hand will find out those that hate thee.

9 Thou wilt make them as a fiery furnace in the time of thine anger:
Jehovah will swallow them up in his wrath,
And the fire shall devour them.

10 Their fruit wilt thou destroy from the earth,
And their seed from among the children of men.

11 For they intended evil against thee;
They conceived a device which they are not able to perform.

12 For thou wilt make them turn
    their back;
Thou wilt make ready with thy
    bowstrings against their face.

13 Be thou exalted, O Jehovah, in
    thy strength;
So will we sing and praise thy
    power.

The battle is over; the victory is won, and the assembled people sing the song of the victory. This song while it celebrates one victory, runs beyond it, and praises Jehovah for all He has done for the King. They had prayed, "Grant thee thy heart's desire" (xx. 4). The prayer is answered, and now they sing, "Thou hast given him his heart's desire" (xxi. 2). They had sung of victory because their trust was in the name of Jehovah (xx. 7, 8). Victory has been won, and now they celebrate it (xxi. 7–12).

The contrast is very vivid between the king trusting in Jehovah, and therefore sustained, supplied, and led in triumph; and the enemies who intended evil against Jehovah, and who are swallowed up, and destroyed, and utterly overcome. From the experience of the king the whole nation learns its lesson. The opening declaration, "The king shall joy in Thy strength," issues in the final prayer:—

"Be Thou exalted, O Jehovah, in Thy strength;
So will we sing and praise Thy power."

Again let us remember our conflict is spiritual, and still the ancient hymn is ours, for our King also triumphed through the strength of Jehovah, and to our final victories we follow in His train.

PSALM 22

Jehovah the Succourer of the Afflicted One

MY God, my God, why hast
    thou forsaken me?
Why art thou so far from helping me, *and from* the words
    of my groaning?

2 O my God, I cry in the daytime, but thou answerest not;
And in the night season, and
    am not silent.

3 But thou art holy,

O thou that inhabitest the praises of Israel.

4 Our fathers trusted in thee: They trusted, and thou didst deliver them.

5 They cried unto thee, and were delivered: They trusted in thee, and were not put to shame.

6 But I am a worm, and no man; A reproach of men, and despised of the people.

7 All they that see me laugh me to scorn: They shoot out the lip, they shake the head, *saying,*

8 Commit *thyself* unto Jehovah; let him deliver him: Let him rescue him, seeing he delighteth in him.

9 But thou art he that took me out of the womb; Thou didst make me trust *when I was* upon my mother's breasts.

10 I was cast upon thee from the womb; Thou art my God since my mother bare me.

11 Be not far from me; for trouble is near; For there is none to help.

12 Many bulls have compassed me; Strong bulls of Bashan have beset me round.

13 They gape upon me with their mouth, *As* a ravening and a roaring lion.

14 I am poured out like water, And all my bones are out of joint: My heart is like wax; It is melted within me.

15 My strength is dried up like a potsherd; And my tongue cleaveth to my jaws; And thou hast brought me into the dust of death.

16 For dogs have compassed me: A company of evil-doers have inclosed me; They pierced my hands and my feet.

17 I may count all my bones. They look and stare upon me;

18 They part my garments among them, And upon my vesture do they cast lots.

19 But be not thou far off, O Jehovah: O thou my succor, haste thee to help me.

20 Deliver my soul from the sword, My darling from the power of the dog.

21 Save me from the lion's mouth; Yea, from the horns of the wild-oxen thou hast answered me.

22 I will declare thy name unto my brethren: In the midst of the assembly will I praise thee.

23 Ye that fear Jehovah, praise him; All ye the seed of Jacob, glorify him; And stand in awe of him, all ye the seed of Israel.

24 For he hath not despised nor abhorred the affliction of the afflicted; Neither hath he hid his face from him; But when he cried unto him, he heard.

25 Of thee cometh my praise in the
   great assembly:
   I will pay my vows before them
   that fear him.
26 The meek shall eat and be satisfied;
   They shall praise Jehovah that
   seek after him:
   Let your heart live for ever.
27 All the ends of the earth shall
   remember and turn unto Jehovah;
   And all the kindreds of the
   nations shall worship before
   thee.
28 For the kingdom is Jehovah's;

And he is the ruler over the
nations.
29 All the fat ones of the earth
   shall eat and worship:
   All they that go down to the
   dust shall bow before him,
   Even he that cannot keep his
   soul alive.
30 A seed shall serve him;
   It shall be told of the Lord unto
   the *next* generation.
31 They shall come and shall declare his righteousness
   Unto a people that shall be
   born, that he hath done it.

Whatever may have been the local conditions creating this
psalm, it has become so perfectly and properly associated with
the One Son of God, that it is almost impossible to read it in
any other way. This and the two following psalms constitute
a triptych of tablets upon which are written the story of the
Christ in His work as Saviour, Shepherd, and Sovereign.

As to this first, seeing that in the supreme mystery of the
Passion Jesus quoted the first words, we are justified in reading it in the light of that Cross. It has two great movements.
The first admits us, so far as that can be, to the lonely suffering of the Victim on the altar of sacrifice (vers. 1–21). The
second brings us into the presence of that joy of the Victor, as
through the travail He saw the triumph (vers. 22–31).

In reverently reading the first, we must understand that all
the desolation was the experience of One Who had entered the
sinner's place. In rejoicingly reading the second, we must
recognize that the height of joy is that of ability to proclaim
an evangel to those in need. And this is enough to write. For
the rest let the Spirit, Who is the one Interpreter of the Christ
of God, speak to our hearts, and let us in amazement worship
and obey.

PSALM 23

Jehovah the Shepherd of His Own

JEHOVAH is my shepherd; I shall not want.

2 He maketh me to lie down in green pastures;
He leadeth me beside still waters.

3 He restoreth my soul:
He guideth me in the paths of righteousness for his name's sake.

4 Yea, though I walk through the valley of the shadow of death,
I will fear no evil; for thou art with me;

Thy rod and thy staff, they comfort me.

5 Thou preparest a table before me in the presence of mine enemies:
Thou has anointed my head with oil;
My cup runneth over.

6 Surely goodness and lovingkindness shall follow me all the days of my life;
And I shall dwell in the house of Jehovah for ever.

In the Messianic application this psalm properly follows that in which the work of the Christ as Saviour is portrayed. It is to those whom He has won through His passion that He becomes known as the Shepherd. Of course this psalm as written is even more wonderful for the fact that its author did not live in the light of Jehovah which has come to us through the Incarnation. It shows us how very clearly faith saw through the mists of those preparatory days to some of the most precious things about God. We still read the wonderful words, and understand them of Jehovah, but the revelation of Him in Jesus is our interpretation, and the psalm becomes richer for that fact. It is an unruffled song of rest. All the circumstances of the pilgrimage, want, weariness, journeyings, wanderings, perplexities, the shadowed mysteries of the valleys, the thronging enemies, and the infinite beyond, are present; and the singer knows them. They are, however, only mentioned to sing of their negation by the graciousness of the Shepherd. Want is cancelled. For weariness He has green pastures of rest. On journeys He leads by pleasant ways. From wanderings He restores. Through perplexities He guides, and that by right ways. In the valleys of death's shadow His presence cancels fear. In the presence of enemies He makes a feast, and is a Host royal in bounty. And finally the path runs on, not into a tangled wilderness, but to the King's own palace.

PSALM 24

Jehovah Conquering Through the King

THE earth is Jehovah's, and the fulness thereof;
The world, and they that dwell therein.

2 For he hath founded it upon the seas,
And established it upon the floods.

3 Who shall ascend into the hill of Jehovah?
And who shall stand in his holy place?

4 He that hath clean hands, and a pure heart;
Who hath not lifted up his soul unto falsehood,
And hath not sworn deceitfully.

5 He shall receive a blessing from Jehovah,
And righteousness from the God of his salvation.

6 This is the generation of them that seek after him,
That seek thy face, *even* Jacob.

7 Lift up your heads, O ye gates;
And be ye lifted up, ye everlasting doors:
And the King of glory will come in.

8 Who is the King of glory?
Jehovah strong and mighty,
Jehovah mighty in battle.

9 Lift up your heads, O ye gates;
Yea, lift them up, ye everlasting doors:
And the King of glory will come in.

10 Who is this King of glory?
Jehovah of hosts,
He is the King of glory.

This is the final psalm of the three, and as in Psalm xxii, the words so far exceed the possibility of exhaustion by any circumstances originating them as to create an opinion unanimously in favour of their Messianic application. In this song the Saviour Who through suffering triumphed; the Shepherd Who through pilgrimage leads His own, is seen ascending to the place of power and authority.

The **first** movement recognizes the sovereignty of Jehovah over the created world and its inhabitants (vers. 1, 2). There is then a question asked which recognizes a need. The hill of the Lord, which is the place of authority (see Ps. ii. 6) is vacant, and the question is asked, "Who shall ascend into it?" The answer declares the need for purity of conduct and character.

Suddenly there breaks forth the antiphonal chanting of angels. Some are accompanying the King as He approaches the place of power. Others wait, guarding the entrance. The first company claims entrance for Him. The second assembly challenges His right. The answer tells of might inherent, and of victory in battle; and through the lifted portals we see Him pass, and know Him for "Jehovah of hosts." He has passed through psalm xxii, and is exercising the office of psalm xxiii; and after, He is seen claiming the authority of psalm xxiv.

PSALM 25

Jehovah Besought for Deliverance

UNTO thee, O Jehovah, do I lift up my soul.
2 O my God, in thee have I trusted,
Let me not be put to shame;
Let not mine enemies triumph over me.
3 Yea, none that wait for thee shall be put to shame:
They shall be put to shame that deal treacherously without cause.
4 Show me thy ways, O Jehovah; Teach me thy paths.
5 Guide me in thy truth, and teach me;
For thou art the God of my salvation;
For thee do I wait all the day.

6 Remember, O Jehovah, thy tender mercies and thy lovingkindnesses;
For they have been ever of old.
7 Remember not the sins of my youth, nor my transgressions:
According to thy lovingkindness remember thou me,
For thy goodness' sake, O Jehovah.
8 Good and upright is Jehovah:
Therefore will he instruct sinners in the way.
9 The meek will he guide in justice;
And the meek will he teach his way.
10 All the paths of Jehovah are lovingkindness and truth

Unto such as keep his covenant
and his testimonies.

11 For thy name's sake, O Jehovah,
Pardon mine iniquity, for it is
great.

12 What man is he that feareth
Jehovah?
Him shall he instruct in the way
that he shall choose.

13 His soul shall dwell at ease;
And his seed shall inherit the
land.

14 The friendship of Jehovah is
with them that fear him;
And he will show them his
covenant.

15 Mine eyes are ever toward Jehovah;
For he will pluck my feet out of
the net.

16 Turn thee unto me, and have
mercy upon me;

For I am desolate and afflicted.

17 The troubles of my heart are
enlarged:
Oh bring thou me out of my
distresses.

18 Consider mine affliction and my
travail;
And forgive all my sins.

19 Consider mine enemies, for they
are many;
And they hate me with cruel
hatred.

20 Oh keep my soul, and deliver
me:
Let me not be put to shame, for
I take refuge in thee.

21 Let integrity and uprightness
preserve me,
For I wait for thee.

22 Redeem Israel, O God,
Out of all his troubles.

The sob of a great sorrow sounds throughout this psalm. The circumstances of its writing were those of desolation, affliction, distress, travail, as the latter part especially shows. Yet the main content is one full of help to all who are in sorrow. It is far more than a wail saddening all who read it. It is the voice of hope and confidence, and tells of succour and of strength.

There are three movements in it. The first (vers. 1–7), and last (vers. 16–22) are prayers uttered out of great need. The central (vers. 8–15) is contemplation and declaration of the goodness of God. Thus structurally the psalm is beautiful. Its central glory is a revelation of God's goodness and patience (vers. 8–10). Then a sob at the heart of everything (ver. 11). Immediately an account of the blessedness of the man who trusts. The opening verses contain the prayer of a distressed soul, whose thought of God is revealed in the central portion. The closing verses are the earnest cry of that soul to such a

God, and in such confidence the details of the experience of
suffering are named.

PSALM 26

Jehovah Worshipped. Conditions

JUDGE me, O Jehovah, for I
have walked in mine integrity:
I have trusted also in Jehovah
without wavering.
2 Examine me, O Jehovah, and
prove me;
Try my heart and my mind.
3 For thy lovingkindness is before
mine eyes;
And I have walked in thy truth.
4 I have not sat with men of falsehood;
Neither will I go in with dis-
semblers.
5 I hate the assembly of evil-
doers,
And will not sit with the wicked.
6 I will wash my hands in in-
nocency:
So will I compass thine altar,
O Jehovah;

7 That I may make the voice of
thanksgiving to be heard,
And tell of all thy wondrous
works.
8 Jehovah, I love the habitation
of thy house,
And the place where thy glory
dwelleth.
9 Gather not my soul with sinners,
Nor my life with men of blood;
10 In whose hands is wickedness,
And their right hand is full of
bribes.
11 But as for me, I will walk in
mine integrity:
Redeem me, and be merciful
unto me.
12 My footh standeth in an even
place:
In the congregations will I bless
Jehovah.

The central word of the song may be said to be, "So will I
compass Thine altar, O Jehovah" (ver. 6). On either side
conditions of worship are described. First the conditions of
personal life necessary to worship (vers. 1–6). Afterwards the
true exercise of worship is described (vers. 7, 8). Then the
psalm becomes a prayer for preparation (vers. 9–11); and
ends with the declaration of assurance (ver. 12).

As to conditions of personal life fitting for worship, they
may be described as complete separation from evil ways and
evil persons. Fellowship with Jehovah is only possible when
there is no fellowship with the wicked. Moreover, the Judge

must be Jehovah Himself. To Him the singer makes his appeal. In this fact there is great solemnity and great comfort. Jehovah's standards are high, but they are ever far more reasonable than those of men. The exercise of worship at its highest is that of praise, issuing from delight in the dwelling-place and glory of God. The prayer for preparation explains the opening words. In its light they are seen to be of the nature of appeal to Jehovah's decision rather than boasting in His presence. The final prayer for preparation is, "Redeem me and be merciful unto me." Such a prayer is immediately answered, and this the last verse makes plain.

PSALM 27

Jehovah Worshipped. Experience

JEHOVAH is my light and my salvation;
Whom shall I fear?
Jehovah is the strength of my life;
Of whom shall I be afraid?
2 When evil-doers came upon me to eat up my flesh,
Even mine adversaries and my foes, they stumbled and fell.
3 Though a host should encamp against me,
My heart shall not fear:
Though war should rise against me,
Even then will I be confident.
4 One thing have I asked of Jehovah, that will I seek after:
That I may dwell in the house of Jehovah all the days of my life,
To behold the beauty of Jehovah,
And to inquire in his temple.

5 For in the day of trouble he will keep me secretly in his pavilion:
In the covert of his tabernacle will he hide me;
He will lift me up upon a rock.
6 And now shall my head be lifted up above mine enemies round about me;
And I will offer in his tabernacle sacrifices of joy;
I will sing, yea, I will sing praises unto Jehovah.

7 Hear, O Jehovah, when I cry with my voice:
Have mercy also upon me, and answer me.
8 *When thou saidst,* Seek ye my face; my heart said unto thee,
Thy face, Jehovah, will I seek.
9 Hide not thy face from me;
Put not thy servant away in anger:

Thou hast been my help;
Cast me not off, neither forsake
me, O God of my salvation.
10 When my father and my mother
forsake me,
Then Jehovah will take me up.
11 Teach me thy way, O Jehovah;
And lead me in a plain path,
Because of mine enemies.
12 Deliver me not over unto the
will of mine adversaries:

For false witnesses are risen up
against me,
And such as breathe out cruelty.
13 *I had fainted,* unless I had believed to see the goodness of
Jehovah
In the land of the living
14 Wait for Jehovah:
Be strong and let thy heart take
courage;
Yea, wait thou for Jehovah.

The real significance of this psalm is that of the experience
of worship. It is somewhat strange that the remarkable contrast between the first (vers. 1–6) and second (vers. 7–14)
parts has given rise to the view that two men have written the
psalm, or if one person is the author, he must have written
them at different times. The psalm reveals the true attitude
and exercise of the worshipping soul. Praise and prayer follow each other in their true order. First the offering of praise
due to the consciousness of Jehovah. Then pouring out of the
heart's need to the One worshipped. The conception of God
revealed in the first half makes possible the abandon of the
petitions in the second half. The God Who is light, and salvation and strength, Who hides in His pavilion, and lifts the
soul on to the rock is the very One Whose face a man, forsaken of father and mother, pursued by adversaries, and slan-
dered by enemies, will most easily appeal to. This is the
meaning of the injunction of the final verse. When hosannas
languish on our tongues it is because we do not begin with
Jehovah. To see Him first in the hour of communion, and to
praise Him, is to be able without reserve to pour out all the
story of our sorrow in His ear, and to know that when the
soul beseeches Him not to cast off, it may affirm in confidence,
"Jehovah will take me up."

PSALM 28

Jehovah Appealed to and Worshipped

UNTO thee, O Jehovah, will I
call:
My rock, be not thou deaf unto
me;
Lest, if thou be silent unto me,
I become like them that go down
into the pit.
2 Hear the voice of my supplications, when I cry unto thee,
When I lift up my hands toward
thy holy oracle.
3 Draw me not away with the
wicked,
And with the workers of iniquity;
That speak peace with their
neighbors,
But mischief is in their hearts.
4 Give them according to their
work, and according to the
wickedness of their doings:
Give them after the operation of
their hands;
Render to them their desert.

5 Because they regard not the
works of Jehovah,
Nor the operation of his hands,
He will break them down and not
build them up.
6 Blessed be Jehovah,
Because he hath heard the voice
of my supplications.
7 Jehovah is my strength and my
shield;
My heart hath trusted in him,
and I am helped:
Therefore my heart greatly rejoiceth;
And with my song will I praise
him.
8 Jehovah is their strength.
And he is a stronghold of salvation to his anointed.
9 Save thy people, and bless thine
inheritance:
Be their shepherd also, and bear
them up for ever.

The affinity between this psalm and the previous one is
evident, and its placing by the editor here was in all likelihood
due to that fact. In psalm xxvii in true order, praise prepares
for, and issues in prayer, the whole ending in an appeal to
"wait on Jehovah." The next psalm opens, "Unto Thee, O
Jehovah, will I call." This is not to suggest that the song was
written by the same person, or immediately. It rather affords
an illustration of a song written by one who acted upon the
principle enjoined.

The cry of need is a very urgent one. The peril is so great
that death threatens. Unless Jehovah help, there is no help.
That the danger arose from enemies is evident from his cry to
Jehovah for justice. Suddenly the prayer becomes a song of

praise, an act of adoration. The prayer is heard, help is granted, the song begins. That this psalm, with its inverted order of prayer and praise, follows closely upon that in which the order is that of praise and prayer, is encouraging. The true order is praise and prayer. If the heart is not strong enough for this, let it learn how to praise by speaking first in prayer of its sorrow. The one thing impossible in the matter of worship is to compress it within the narrow limits of stated formulae.

PSALM 29

Jehovah in the Majesty of the Storm

ASCRIBE unto Jehovah, O ye sons of the mighty,
Ascribe unto Jehovah glory and strength.
2 Ascribe unto Jehovah the glory due unto his name;
Worship Jehovah in holy array.

3 The voice of Jehovah is upon the waters:
The God of glory thundereth,
Even Jehovah upon many waters.
4 The voice of Jehovah is powerful;
The voice of Jehovah is full of majesty.
5 The voice of Jehovah breaketh the cedars;
Yea, Jehovah breaketh in pieces the cedars of Lebanon.
6 He maketh them also to skip like a calf;

Lebanon and Sirion like a young wild-ox.
7 The voice of Jehovah cleaveth the flames of fire.
8 The voice of Jehovah shaketh the wilderness;
Jehovah shaketh the wilderness of Kadesh.
9 The voice of Jehovah maketh the hinds to calve,
And strippeth the forests bare:
And in his temple everything saith, Glory.

10 Jehovah sat *as King* at the Flood;
Yea, Jehovah sitteth as King for ever.
11 Jehovah will give strength unto his people;
Jehovah will bless his people with peace.

This is a wonderful picture of a storm, viewed from the standpoint of one who is supremely conscious of Jehovah. The great name occurs oftener in this psalm than in any other in this first book, being found no less than eighteen times. Therein is discovered the key to the whole movement. Once the name suggestive of wonder-working might is used, "The God of glory thundereth." For the rest this God is seen to be Jehovah of the trusting soul. From this outlook all the sublimity and majesty are seen under the control of love, and the singer finds occasion for the highest form of praise in the presence of a storm which otherwise might have filled the heart with terror.

The storm is described in the central part of the song (vers. 3–9). To the description there is a prelude calling upon "the sons of God" to praise (vers. 1, 2). In the epilogue (vers. 10, 11), the storm seems to have subsided, and the psalmist sings of the one supreme impression produced. Over all the flood Jehovah sat as King. The deductions are simple and yet full of beauty. Jehovah always sits as King. During the storm He will give strength to His people. Following it He shall give them peace.

PSALM 30

Jehovah Delivering from Affliction

I WILL extol thee, O Jehovah; for thou hast raised me up,
And hast not made my foes to rejoice over me.
2 O Jehovah my God,
I cried unto thee, and thou hast healed me.
3 O Jehovah, thou hast brought up my soul from Sheol;
Thou has kept me alive, that I should not go down to the pit.
4 Sing praise unto Jehovah, O ye saints of his,
And give thanks to his holy memorial *name.*

5 For his anger is but for a moment;
His favor is for a lifetime:
Weeping may tarry for the night,
But joy *cometh* in the morning.
6 As for me, I said in my prosperity,
I shall never be moved.
7 Thou, Jehovah, of thy favor hadst made my mountain to stand strong:
Thou didst hide thy face; I was troubled.

8 I cried to thee, O Jehovah;
   And unto Jehovah I made supplication:
9 What profit is there in my
   blood, when I go down to the
   pit?
   Shall the dust praise thee? shall
   it declare thy truth?
10 Hear, O Jehovah, and have
   mercy upon me:

Jehovah, be thou my helper.
11 Thou hast turned for me my
   mourning into dancing;
   Thou hast loosed my sackcloth,
   and girded me with gladness;
12 To the end that my glory may
   sing praise to thee, and not be
   silent.
   O Jehovah my God, I will give
   thanks unto thee for ever.

This is a song of praise for deliverance (vers. 1–5) and a meditation on the deliverance and its lessons (vers. 6–12a); with a final note of praise (ver. 12b). The phrases descriptive of the trouble are such as to leave little room for doubt that the singer had been sick, and nigh unto death: "Thou hast raised me up," "Thou hast healed me," "Thou hast brought up my soul from Sheol." Moreover, he believed that the sickness was a Divine chastisement, and through it and his deliverance he had found the method of Jehovah:—

"His anger is but for a moment."
"Weeping may tarry for a night."

The issue of such experience is of the highest, "life," "joy in the morning." The review is full of suggestiveness. Days of prosperity had issued in self-satisfaction. Jehovah hid His face. That was the moment of His anger, and that the night of weeping! There was the return to Jehovah in the cry of anguish. The answer was immediate; mourning became dancing, sackcloth was exchanged for gladness. What was all this for? "To the end that my glory may sing praise to Thee, and not be silent." Self-satisfaction cannot praise Jehovah. Therefore, it must be corrected by discipline. The final note of praise shows that through affliction and by deliverance the lesson has been learned.

PSALM 31

Jehovah the Refuge of the Afflicted

IN THE, O Jehovah, do I take
refuge;
Let me never be put to shame:
Deliver me in thy righteousness.
2 Bow down thine ear unto me;
deliver me speedily:
Be thou to me a strong rock,
A house of defence to save me.
3 For thou art my rock and my
fortress;
Therefore for thy name's sake
lead me and guide me.
4 Pluck me out of the net that
they have laid privily for me;
For thou art my stronghold.
5 Into thy hand I commend my
spirit:
Thou has redeemed me, O Jehovah, thou God of truth.
6 I hate them that regard lying
vanities;
But I trust in Jehovah.
7 I will be glad and rejoice in thy
loving kindness;
For thou hast seen my affliction:
Thou hast known my soul in ad-
versities;
8 And thou hast not shut me up
into the hand of the enemy;
Thou hast set my feet in a large
place.
9 Have mercy upon me, O Jehovah, for I am in distress:
Mine eye wasteth away with
grief, yea, my soul and my
body.
10 For my life is spent with sorrow,
And my years with sighing:
My strength faileth because of
mine iniquity,
And my bones are wasted away.

11 Because of all mine adversaries
I am become a reproach,
Yea, unto my neighbors exceedingly,
And a fear to mine acquaintance:
They that did see me without
fled from me.
12 I am forgotten as a dead man
out of mind:
I am like a broken vessel.
13 For I have heard the defaming
of many,
Terror on every side:
While they took counsel together against me,
They devised to take away my
life.
14 But I trusted in thee, O Jehovah:
I said, Thou art my God.
15 My times are in thy hand:
Deliver me from the hand of
mine enemies, and from them
that persecute me.
16 Make thy face to shine upon
thy servant:
Save me in thy loving-kindness.
17 Let me not be put to shame, O
Jehovah; for I have called
upon thee:
Let the wicked be put to shame,
let them be silent in Sheol.
18 Let the lying lips be dumb,
Which speak against the righteous insolently,
With pride and contempt.
19 Oh how great is thy goodness,
Which thou hast laid up for
them that fear thee,

Which thou hast wrought for
them that take refuge in thee,
Before the sons of men!

20 In the covert of thy presence
wilt thou hide them from the
plottings of man:
Thou wilt keep them secretly in
a pavilion from the strife of
tongues.

21 Blessed be Jehovah;
For he hath showed me his marvellous lovingkindness in a
strong city.

22 As for me, I said in my haste,

I am cut off from before thine
eyes:
Nevertheless thou heardest the
voice of my supplications,
When I cried unto thee.

23 Oh love Jehovah, all ye his
saints:
Jehovah preserveth the faithful,
And plentifully rewardeth him
that dealeth proudly.

24 Be strong, and let your heart
take courage,
All ye that hope in Jehovah.

In this great song of trust struggling through tears to triumph, we have a fine example of an experience often repeated
in the history of the children of faith. There are three divisions. In the first (vers. 1–8) the double sense of trust and
trial is clearly manifest. In the second (vers. 9–18) for a time
the trial seems almost to have overcome the trust, so keen is
the consciousness thereof. In the last (vers. 19–24), trust has
completely triumphed, and the sense of the singer is that of
perfect safety in the pavilion of Jehovah. In the first, in the
midst of a sense of sobs, the soul of the singer valiantly affirms
its confidence, and pleads for help. In the second, the affirmation of trust is in a past tense, and the present is one of trial
and tears. In the last, trust is a condition which needs no
formal declaration, but sings itself out in victory and gladness.

In this song we find the seasons of the soul as we all know
them sooner or later. First autumn with its winds and gathering clouds, yet having sunlight, and a golden fruitage, even
though the breath of death is everywhere (vers. 1–8). Then
follows winter, chill and lifeless, full of sobs and sighing (vers.
9–13). After that the spring, with its hope and expectation,
its sweeping rains, and bursting sun-gleams (vers. 14–18). At
last the glad and golden summer (vers. 19–24). We need them
all to complete our year!

PSALM 32

Jehovah and the Backsliding Soul

BLESSED is he whose transgression is forgiven,
Whose sin is covered.

2 Blessed is the man unto whom Jehovah imputeth not iniquity,
And in whose spirit there is no guile.

3 When I kept silence, my bones wasted away
Through my groaning all the day long.

4 For day and night thy hand was heavy upon me:
My moisture was changed *as* with the drought of summer.

5 I acknowledged my sin unto thee,
And mine iniquity did I not hide:
I said, I will confess my transgressions unto Jehovah;
And thou forgavest the iniquity of my sin.

6 For this let every one that is godly pray unto thee in a time when thou mayest be found:
Surely when the great waters overflow they shall not reach unto him.

7 Thou art my hiding-place; thou wilt preserve me from trouble;
Thou wilt compass me about with songs of deliverance.

8 I will instruct thee and teach thee in the way which thou shalt go:
I will counsel thee with mine eye upon thee.

9 Be ye not as the horse, or as the mule, which have no understanding;
Whose trappings must be bit and bridle to hold them in,
Else they will not come near unto thee.

10 Many sorrows shall be to the wicked;
But he that trusteth in Jehovah, lovingkindness shall compass him about.

11 Be glad in Jehovah, and rejoice, ye righteous;
And shout for joy, all ye that are upright in heart.

This is known as the second of the penitential psalms. It is the song of a man who is rejoicing in the assurance of restoration. Opening with an outburst of praise, which reveals the experimental knowledge of the happiness of forgiveness (vers. 1, 2), it proceeds to describe the bitterness of the soul's experience while sin is unconfessed (vers. 3, 4). Then the way of restoration by confession, and the readiness of Jehovah to forgive, are declared (ver. 5). On the basis of such restoration the soul has access to God, and the assurance of His succour in trouble (vers. 6, 7). The message of Jehovah to His child is then sung, in which the promise of guidance is made, and the condition of submission is stated (vers. 8, 9). All ends with an affirmation of the safety of such as trust in Jehovah, and a call to men to praise Him.

Among all the psalms there is none which touches deeper things in the life of the soul, or more perfectly reveals the methods of Jehovah in the matters of sin, sorrow and guidance. He is ready to pardon, able to deliver, and willing to guide.

PSALM 33

Jehovah the Mighty Deliverer

REJOICE in Jehovah, O ye righteous:
Praise is comely for the upright.

2 Give thanks unto Jehovah with the harp:
Sing praises unto him with the psaltery of ten strings.

3 Sing unto him a new song;
Play skilfully with a loud noise.

4 For the word of Jehovah is right:
And all his work is *done* in faithfulness.

5 He loveth righteousness and justice:
The earth is full of the lovingkindness of Jehovah.

6 By the word of Jehovah were the heavens made,
And all the host of them by the breath of his mouth.

7 He gathereth the waters of the sea together as a heap:
He layeth up the deeps in storehouses.

8 Let all the earth fear Jehovah:
Let all the inhabitants of the world stand in awe of him.

9 For he spake, and it was done;
He commanded, and it stood fast.

10 Jehovah bringeth the counsel of the nations to nought;
He maketh the thoughts of the peoples to be of no effect.

11 The counsel of Jehovah standeth fast for ever,
The thoughts of his heart to all generations.

12 Blessed is the nation whose God is Jehovah,
The people whom he hath chosen for his own inheritance.

13 Jehovah looketh from heaven;
He beholdeth all the sons of men;

14 From the place of his habitation he looketh forth
Upon all the inhabitants of the earth,

15 He that fashioneth the hearts of
  them all,
  That considereth all their works.
16 There is no king saved by the
  multitude of a host:
  A mighty man is not delivered
  by great strength.
17 A horse is a vain thing for
  safety;
  Neither doth he deliver any by
  his great power.
18 Behold, the eye of Jehovah is
  upon them that fear him,
  Upon them that hope in his lovingkindness;

19 To deliver their soul from death,
  And to keep them alive in famine.
20 Our soul hath waited for Jehovah:
  He is our help and our shield.
21 For our heart shall rejoice in
  him,
  Because we have trusted in his
  holy name.
22 Let thy lovingkindness, O Jehovah, be upon us,
  According as we have hoped in
  thee.

This is a triumphant song of praise, opening with a call
to vocal and instrumental music. "Rejoice," "praise," "give
thanks," "sing praises," "sing," "play"—thus all modes of
expression are appealed to. The praise proceeds, and the
greatness and goodness of Jehovah are sung in general terms
(vers. 4–11). The whole of the facts are summarized, His
word is right, His work is faithful (ver. 4). His character is
perfect, combining light—"righteousness and judgment": and
love—"lovingkindness" (ver. 5). He is the Creator, full of
power so that men should worship (vers. 6–9). He is the
active King, overruling all the affairs of men (vers. 10, 11).

The song then praises Jehovah as the God of the chosen
people (vers. 12–19). He chose them, and in their interest
watches all the sons of men (vers. 12–15). His watchfulness
of His own is a greater security than armies or horses (vers.
16–19). The song ends with an affirmation of trust, an assurance of joy, and a prayer for mercy (vers. 20–22). There is a
lilt and a lift about this psalm which is of the very essence of
gladness. It is indeed a song of deliverance (xxxii. 7).

PSALM 34

Jehovah the Constant Succourer

I WILL bless Jehovah at all times:
His praise shall continually be in my mouth.

2 My soul shall make her boast in Jehovah:
The meek shall hear thereof, and be glad.

3 Oh magnify Jehovah with me
And let us exalt his name together.

4 I sought Jehovah, and he answered me,
And delivered me from all my fears.

5 They looked unto him, and were radiant:
And their faces shall never be confounded.

6 This poor man cried, and Jehovah heard him,
And saved him out of all his troubles.

7 The angel of Jehovah encampeth round about them that fear him,
And delivereth them.

8 Oh taste and see that Jehovah is good:
Blessed is the man that taketh refuge in him.

9 Oh fear Jehovah, ye his saints;
For there is no want to them that fear him.

10 The young lions do lack, and suffer hunger;
But they that seek Jehovah shall not want any good thing.

11 Come, ye children, hearken unto me:
I will teach you the fear of Jehovah.

12 What man is he that desireth life,
And loveth *many* days, that he may see good?

13 Keep thy tongue from evil,
And thy lips from speaking guile.

14 Depart from evil, and do good;
Seek peace, and pursue it.

15 The eyes of Jehovah are toward the righteous.
And his ears are *open* unto their cry.

16 The face of Jehovah is against them that do evil,
To cut off the remembrance of them from the earth.

17 *The righteous* cried, and Jehovah heard,
And delivered them out of all their troubles.

18 Jehovah is nigh unto them that are of a brmoken heart,
And saveth such as are of a contrite spirit.

19 Many are the afflictions of the righteous;
But Jehovah delivereth him out of them all.

20 He keepeth all his bones:
Not one of them is broken.

21 Evil shall slay the wicked;
And they that hate the righteous shall be condemned.

22 Jehovah redeemeth the soul of his servants;
And none of them that take refuge in him shall be condemned.

In this psalm praise is personal. After the chorus of the last we have a solo full of feeling. It tells of the goodness of Jehovah, and that in order that others may know and be helped. The opening declares this. The song is to be perpetual, and the meek are to be made glad thereby. Then there is the desire to draw others into the same attitude of praise. It is good to go through simply to find the things Jehovah has done. "He answered me." "Delivered me from all my fears." "They . . . were irradiated." "Jehovah heard him and saved him." "His eyes are toward . . . His ears are open." "Jehovah heard . . . and delivered them." "Jehovah is nigh." "Jehovah delivereth." "He keepeth." "Jehovah redeemeth." This is not an exhaustive list, for on the side of human reception many more things are said. It is a song which tells of the nearness, the tender sensitiveness, the ready help, the mighty power of Jehovah on behalf of all such as trust Him. It is, moreover, rich in its lack of selfishness. The singer is eager for others to hear, to test, to praise, and he takes time to sing to the children, that they also may know the secret of life.

PSALM 35

Jehovah Besought for Help Against Enemies

STRIVE thou, O Jehovah, with them that strive with me:
Fight thou against them that fight against me.

2 Take hold of shield and buckler,
And stand up for my help.

3 Draw out also the spear, and stop the way against them that pursue me:
Say unto my soul, I am thy salvation.

4 Let them be put to shame and brought to dishonor that seek after my soul:

Let them be turned back and confounded that devise my hurt.

5 Let them be as chaff before the wind,
And the angel of Jehovah driving *them* on.

6 Let their way be dark and slippery,
And the angel of Jehovah pursuing them.

7 For without cause have they hid for me their net *in* a pit;

Without cause have they digged *a pit* for my soul.

8 Let destruction come upon him unawares;
And let his net that he hath hid catch himself:
With destruction let him fall therein.

9 And my soul shall be joyful in Jehovah:
It shall rejoice in his salvation.

10 All my bones shall say, Jehovah, who is like unto thee,
Who deliverest the poor from him that is too strong for him,
Yea, the poor and the needy from him that robbeth him?

11 Unrighteous witnesses rise up;
They ask me of things that I know not.

12 They reward me evil for good,
To the bereaving of my soul.

13 But as for me, when they were sick, my clothing was sack-cloth:
I afflicted my soul with fasting;
And my prayer returned into mine own bosom.

14 I behaved myself as though it had been my friend or my brother:
I bowed down mourning, as one that bewaileth his mother.

15 But in mine adversity they rejoiced, and gathered themselves together:
The abjects gathered themselves together against me, and I knew *it* not;
They did tear me, and ceased not:

16 Like the profane mockers in feasts,
They gnashed upon me with their teeth.

17 Lord, how long wilt thou look on?
Rescue my soul from their destructions,
My darling from the lions.

18 I will give thee thanks in the great assembly:
I will praise thee among much people.

19 Let not them that are mine enemies wrongfully rejoice over me;
Neither let them wink with the eye that hate me without a cause.

20 For they speak not peace;
But they devise deceitful words against them that are quiet in the land.

21 Yea, they opened their mouth wide against me;
They said, Aha, aha, our eye hath seen it.

22 Thou hast seen it, O Jehovah; keep not silence:
O Lord, be not far from me.

23 Stir up thyself, and awake to the justice *due* unto me,
Even unto my cause, my God and my Lord.

24 Judge me, O Jehovah my God, according to thy righteousness;
And let them not rejoice over me.

25 Let them not say in their heart, Aha, so would we have it:
Let them not say, We have swallowed him up.

26 Let them be put to shame and confounded together that rejoice at my hurt:
Let them be clothed with shame and dishonor that magnify themselves against me.

27 Let them shout for joy, and be
glad, that favor my righteous
cause:
Yea, let them say continually,
Jehovah be magnified,

Who hath pleasure in the prosperity of his servant.
28 And my tongue shall talk of thy righteousness
And of thy praise all the day long.

There is a sob and an agony in this song. The singer is sore beset with enemies. They are striving with him, fighting against him. They are plotting against him, treacherously spreading a net for his feet. He cries out to Jehovah for help, vowing that he will offer praise for deliverance (vers. 1–10). The sob touches deeper depths. The cruelty and oppression are being shown by those whom he has in the past befriended. In their time of trouble he had mourned with them. In the day of his halting they have taken advantage of weakness still further to wound.

Again he cries for rescue by the Lord, and promises to praise Him publicly (vers. 11–18). And again the same prayer is offered. The foes are not only cruel and treacherous; they are full of bitterness, and taunt and mock the suffering man, and in his agony he cries out for help, for the third time promising to praise Him (vers. 19–28). Before we criticize the singer for his attitude towards his foes, let us imagine ourselves in his place. In no sense is the level of spiritual realization in this psalm equal to that in many others. One of the greatest values of the collection is its revelation of how under all circumstances the soul may turn to God.

PSALM 36

Jehovah Forgotten and Recognized. A Contrast

THE transgression of the wicked saith within my heart,
There is no fear of God before his eyes.

2 For he flattereth himself in his own eyes,
That his iniquity will not be found out and be hated.

3 The words of his mouth are iniquity and deceit:
He hath ceased to be wise *and*
to do good.
4 He deviseth iniquity upon his
bed;
He setteth himself in a way that
is not good;
He abhorreth not evil.
5 Thy lovingkindness, O Jehovah,
is in the heavens;
Thy faithfulness *reacheth* unto
the skies.
6 Thy righteousness is like the
mountains of God;
Thy judgments are a great
deep:
O Jehovah, thou preservest
man and beast.
7 How precious is thy lovingkindness, O God!
And the children of men take
refuge under the shadow of
thy wings.
8 They shall be abundantly satisfied with the fatness of thy
house;
And thou wilt make them drink
of the river of thy pleasures.
9 For with thee is the fountain of
life:
In thy light shall we see light,
10 Oh continue thy lovingkindness
unto them that know thee,
And thy righteousness to the
upright in heart.
11 Let not the foot of pride come
against me.
And let not the hand of the
wicked drive me away.
12 There are the workers of iniquity fallen:
They are thrust down, and shall
not be able to rise.

The antithetical nature of this psalm is self-evident. In the first part (vers. 1–4) the wickedness of the wicked is described as to its reason and expression. The one and only reason of transgression is that the fear of God is lost. All evil results therefrom. In contrast to this, the advantages of the remembrance of Jehovah are set forth first by a description of certain facts concerning Him.

One can easily imagine that the psalm was written on some natural height from which the singer looked out upon a far-stretching scene in the outstanding features of which he saw symbols of truth concerning his God. Note the sweep of vision. The heavens, the skies or clouds, the mountains, the great deep, the river, and over all, the light. There is a fine fitness in the interpretation of suggestiveness. The encompassing blue speaks of lovingkindness; the passing clouds in the mystery of their orderliness, of His faithfulness; the mountains suggest His righteousness from which rivers of pleasure flow to mingle in the deep of His judgments. Of all the abundant and varying life He is the Source or Fountain; and the sunshine of His face is the light on everything. All ends with a prayer for the continued safety of the Divine care and protection.

PSALM 37

Jehovah the Confidence of His People

FRET not thyself because of evil-doers,
Neither be thou envious against them that work unrighteousness.

2 For they shall soon be cut down like the grass,
And wither as the green herb.

3 Trust in Jehovah, and do good;
Dwell in the land, and feed on his faithfulness.

4 Delight thyself also in Jehovah;
And he will give thee the desires of thy heart.

5 Commit thy way unto Jehovah;
Trust also in him, and he will bring it to pass.

6 And he will make thy righteousness to go forth as the light,
And thy justice as the noonday.

7 Rest in Jehovah, and wait patiently for him:
Fret not thyself because of him who prospereth in his way,
Because of the man who bringeth wicked devices to pass.
Cease from anger, and forsake wrath:
Fret not thyself, *it tendeth* only to evil-doing.

9 For evil-doers shall be cut off;
But those that wait for Jehovah, they shall inherit the land.

10 For yet a little while, and the wicked shall not be:
Yea, thou shalt diligently consider his place, and he shall not be.

11 But the meek shall inherit the land,
And shall delight themselves in the abundance of peace.

12 The wicked plotteth against the just,
And gnasheth upon him with his teeth.

13 The Lord will laugh at him;
For he seeth that his day is coming.

14 The wicked have drawn out the sword, and have bent their bow,
To cast down the poor and needy,
To slay such as are upright in the way.

15 Their sword shall enter into their own heart,
And their bows shall be broken.

16 Better is a little that the righteous hath
Than the abundance of many wicked.

17 For the arms of the wicked shall
   be broken;
   But Jehovah upholdeth the
   righteous.
18 Jehovah knoweth the days of
   the perfect;
   And their inheritance shall be
   for ever.
19 They shall not be put to shame
   in the time of evil;
   And in the days of famine they
   shall be satisfied.
20 But the wicked shall perish,
   And the enemies of Jehovah
   shall be as the fat of lambs:
   They shall consume; in smoke
   shall they consume away.
21 The wicked borroweth, and pay-
   eth not again;
   But the righteous dealeth graciously, and giveth.
22 For such as are blessed of him
   shall inherit the land;
   And they that are cursed of him
   shall be cut off.
23 A man's goings are established
   of Jehovah;
   And he delighteth in his way.
24 Though he fall, he shall not be
   utterly cast down;
   For Jehovah upholdeth him
   with his hand.
25 I have been young, and now am
   old;
   Yet have I not seen the righteous forsaken,
   Nor his seed begging bread.
26 All the day long he dealeth graciously, and lendeth;
   And his seed is blessed.
27 Depart from evil, and do good;
   And dwell for evermore.
28 For Jehovah loveth justice,
   And forsaketh not his saints;

They are preserved for ever:
But the seed of the wicked shall
   be cut off.
29 The righteous shall inherit the
   land,
   And dwell therein for ever.
30 The mouth of the righteous
   talketh of wisdom,
   And his tongue speaketh justice.
31 The law of his God is in his
   heart;
   None of his steps shall slide.
   The wicked watcheth the righteous,
   And seeketh to slay him.
33 Jehovah will not leave him in
   his hand,
   Nor condemn him when he is
   judged.
34 Wait for Jehovah, and keep his
   way,
   And he will exalt thee to inherit
   the land:
   When the wicked are cut off,
   thou shalt see it.
35 I have seen the wicked in great
   power,
   And spreading himself like a
   green tree in its native soil.
36 But one passed by, and, lo, he
   was not:
   Yea, I sought him, but he could
   not be found.
37 Mark the perfect man, and behold the upright;
   For there is a *happy* end to the
   man of peace.
38 As for transgressors, they shall
   be destroyed together:
   The end of the wicked shall be
   cut off.
39 But the salvation of the righteous is of Jehovah:

He is their stronghold in the time of trouble.

40 And Jehovah helpeth them, and rescueth them:

He rescueth them from the wicked, and saveth them, Because they have taken refuge in him.

This psalm stands in striking contrast to Psalm **xxxv**. While it is perfectly true that Jehovah patiently bears with, and ministers consolation to the fretful souls who pour out their complaint in His ear; it is nevertheless a low level on which to live for the man of faith. The other psalm was full of fretfulness. This has as its keynote, "Fret not."

The underlying problem is that of the prosperity of evil men. It is an astonishment and a perplexity still, troubling many a tried and trusting heart. The psalmist first declares that all such prosperity is short-lived, and then tells the secrets of quietness, in spite of the problem. There are first positive injunctions. They may be grouped thus: "Trust in Jehovah"; "Delight in Jehovah"; "Commit thy way unto Jehovah"; "Rest in Jehovah."

Then again the fundamental injunction is twice repeated, "Fret not." It is wrong; it is harmful; it is needless. Let the trusting wait. Events will justify the action. The prosperity of wickedness cannot last. It is the meek and trusting soul who finally possesses the land, and enters into peace.

Continuing, the psalmist works out his contrast into greater detail. The prosperity of the wicked has within it the elements of its own destruction, and cannot last (vers. 12–20). This is all stated by way of contrast. The little of the righteous is better than the abundance of many wicked. This is by no means out of date. It is only necessary to wait long enough, and to watch, to know that the principle is abiding. Ill-gotten gains, and the triumph of wickedness are alike doomed by inherent evil to sure and certain destruction. Then the other side is stated in great fulness (vers. 21–31). The way established by Jehovah is sure. There may be failure, but there is restoration. With the more complex civilization in the midst of which we live, perhaps sometimes the righteous have been driven to beg; but even now such cases are surely rare, and after some varied experience I should want to subject the begging one to somewhat severe cross-examination before accepting his testimony as against that of the psalmist. Even if it be granted, the underlying principle remains, that the bread of charity is to be chosen in preference to the wealth of wickedness.

In verses 32–40 we have the final contrast of this psalm. The first statement is that of the safety of the righteous against the machinations of the wicked. Jehovah never abandons His own to the malice of evil men. It is true that the wicked may flourish for a time, but suddenly he passes out of sight, and without leaving any trace. Look on to the issues if you would see the true meaning of things! The upright comes into peace at last, because Jehovah helps them, rescues them, saves them. The way in which this psalm has appealed to men, and continues to do so, is a proof of how prone the heart is to rebel against the seeming prosperity of the wicked, and also a demonstration of the conviction of men that it is better to trust in Jehovah than to achieve any kind of success by other means. Faith does falter and demand some explanation. It finds all it asks when resolutely it obeys the injunctions to trust, delight, commit, rest, wait!

PSALM 38

Jehovah Appealed to in Penitence

O JEHOVAH, rebuke me not in thy wrath;
Neither chasten me in thy hot displeasure.
2 For thine arrows stick fast in me,
And thy hand presseth me sore.

3 There is no soundness in my flesh because of thine indignation;
Neither is there any health in my bones because of my sin.
4 For mine iniquities are gone over my head:

As a heavy burden they are too heavy for me.

5 My wounds are loathsome and corrupt,
Because of my foolishness.

6 I am pained and bowed down greatly;
I go mourning all the day long.

7 For my loins are filled with burning;
And there is no soundness in my flesh.

8 I am faint and sore bruised:
I have groaned by reason of the disquietness of my heart.

9 Lord, all my desire is before thee;
And my groaning is not hid from thee.

10 My heart throbbeth, my strength faileth me:
As for the light of mine eyes, it also is gone from me.

11 My lovers and my friends stand aloof from my plague;
And my kinsmen stand afar off.

12 They also that seek after my life lay snares *for me;*
And they that seek my hurt speak mischievous things,
And meditate deceits all the day long.

13 But I, as a deaf man, hear not;
And I am as a dumb man that openeth not his mouth.

14 Yea, I am as a man that heareth not,
And in whose mouth are no reproofs.

15 For in thee, O Jehovah, do I hope:
Thou wilt answer, O Lord my God.

16 For I said, Lest they rejoice over me:
When my foot slippeth, they magnify themselves against me.

17 For I am ready to fall,
And my sorrow is continually before me.

18 For I will declare mine iniquity;
I will be sorry for my sin.

19 But mine enemies are lively, *and* are strong;
And they that hate me wrongfully are multiplied.

20 They also that render evil for good
Are adversaries unto me, because I follow the thing that is good.

21 Forsake me not, O Jehovah:
O my God, be not far from me.

22 Make haste to help me,
O Lord, my salvation.

This is the third of what are known as the penitential psalms. The circumstances of the singer were most distressing. He was suffering from some terrible physical malady; was deserted by his friends, and persecuted by his enemies. The deepest bitterness of his soul was caused by his overwhelming sense of his moral pollution. He recognizes that all his sufferings were the rebukes and chastisements of Jehovah for his sin. This sense of sin crushed him, and in his distress he cried out to Jehovah. The use of the Divine names and titles in this psalm is interesting. The first cry for help is to Jehovah. When he would utter his complaint concerning the desertion of friends, and persecution of foes, he addresses himself to the Lord, as the supreme Being. In his final appeal he both begins and closes with Jehovah, Lord and God. All the foundations seem to have given way beneath his feet, and with deep contrition and desperate endeavour he strives to take hold of God in all the facts of His Being. In this he was right, for so desperate a case demands the help, the government, the might of God. Blessed be His name for ever, all are at our disposal.

PSALM 39

Jehovah the Hope of the Afflicted

I SAID, I will take heed to my ways,
That I sin not with my tongue:
I will keep my mouth with a bridle,
While the wicked is before me.

2 I was dumb with silence, I held my peace, even from good;
And my sorrow was stirred.

3 My heart was hot within me;
While I was musing the fire burned;
Then spake I with my tongue:

4 Jehovah, make me to know mine end,
And the measure of my days, what it is;
Let me know how frail I am.

5 Behold, thou hast made my days *as* handbreadths;
And my life-time is as nothing before thee:
Surely every man at his best estate is altogether vanity.

6 Surely every man walketh in a vain show;
Surely they are disquieted in vain:
He heapeth up *riches*, and knoweth not who shall gather them.

7 And now, Lord, what wait I for?
My hope is in thee.

8 Deliver me from all my transgressions:
Make me not the reproach of the foolish.

9 I was dumb, I opened not my mouth;
Because thou didst it.

10 Remove thy stroke away from me:
I am consumed by the blow of thy hand.

11 When thou with rebukes dost correct man for iniquity,

Thou makest his beauty to consume away like a moth:
Surely every man is vanity.
12 Hear my prayer, O Jehovah,
and give ear unto my cry;
Hold not thy peace at my tears:
For I am a stranger with thee,

A sojourner, as all my fathers
were.
13 Oh spare me, that I may re-
cover strength,
Before I go hence, and be no
more.

Again the circumstances are those of sorrow and affliction.
The attitude of the sufferer is one of true dignity. If the psalm
be taken in connection with the preceding one, it marks an
advance, perhaps a gain out of that experience. Then we saw
a man crying out for Jehovah and His help. Here is a man still
in circumstances of trial, and acutely conscious of them, but
he has found the secret place of communion, and this conditions his attitudes. Towards his foes there is maintained a
great silence, the secret of which he presently declares, "I was
dumb, I opened not my mouth because Thou didst it." Yet
the things he sees strangely stir him, and at last he breaks the
silence.

Here again the result of his knowledge of Jehovah is seen in
that he speaks of Him, and not to his enemies. Thus he sets
the strange prosperity of the wicked in relation to God. All
the apparent success is seen to be nothing worth, and this sorrowful man makes his personal appeal to Jehovah for help
and succour.

PSALM 40

Jehovah Worshipped in Praise and Prayer

I WAITED patiently for Jehovah;
And he inclined unto me, and
heard my cry.
2 He brought me up also out of a
horrible pit, out of the miry
clay;
And he set my feet upon a rock,
and established my goings.

3 And he hath put a new song in
my mouth, even praise unto
our God:
Many shall see it, and fear,
And shall trust in Jehovah.
4 Blessed is the man that maketh
Jehovah his trust,
And respecteth not the proud,
nor such as turn aside to lies.

5 Many, O Jehovah my God, are
the wonderful works which
thou hast done,
And thy thoughts which are to
us-ward:
They cannot be set in order
unto thee;
If I would declare and speak of
them,
They are more than can be
numbered.

6 Sacrifice and offering thou has
no delight in;
Mine ears hast thou opened:
Burnt-offering and sin-offering
hast thou not required.

7 Then said I, Lo, I am come;
In the roll of the book it is written of me:

8 I delight to do thy will, O my
God;
Yea, thy law is within my heart.

9 I have proclaimed glad tidings
of righteousness in the great
assembly;
Lo, I will not refrain my lips,
O Jehovah, thou knowest.

10 I have not hid thy righteousness
within my heart;
I have declared thy faithfulness
and thy salvation;
I have not concealed thy lovingkindness and thy truth from
the great assembly.

11 Withhold not thou thy tender
mercies from me, O Jehovah;

Let thy lovingkindness and thy
truth continually preserve
me.

12 For innumerable evils have compassed me about;
Mine iniquities have overtaken
me, so that I am not able to
look up;
They are more than the hairs of
my head;
And my heart hath failed me.

13 Be pleased, O Jehovah, to deliver me:
Make haste to help me, O Jehovah.

14 Let them be put to shame and
confounded together
That seek after my soul to destroy it:
Let them be turned backward
and brought to dishonor
That delight in my hurt.

15 Let them be desolate by reason
of their shame
That say unto me, Aha, aha.

16 Let all those that seek thee rejoice and be glad in thee:
Let such as love thy salvation
say continually, Johovah be
magnified.

17 But I am poor and needy;
Yet the Lord thinketh upon me:
Thou art my help and my de-
liverer;
Make no tarrying, O my God.

Again we find in this psalm the perfect structure manifest in
Psalm xxxvii. Praise prepares for prayer. The experience has
mounted higher than in the preceding song (xxxix). The circumstances are still those of affliction, but a new consciousness
of Jehovah, resulted from having "waited patiently" for Him,
inspires a lofty song of praise (vers. 1–10). This gives the soul

a great freedom to pour out its complaint (vers. 11–16), after which, in conclusion, there follows an affirmation of faith, and a final prayer (ver. 17).

The patient waiting resulted in the singer's sense that Jehovah was bending over him, and listening to his cry. The result is a new song which is rightly interpreted at its deepest in the words of the hymn:—

"Glory to Thee for all the grace
I have not tasted yet."

This is expressed in recognition of the activity of Jehovah God, and the certainty that His one purpose for His people is that they should delight in His will, and proclaim Him to others.

Then follows the prayer. Sorrow and sin have oppressed the heart beyond the power of its endurance. In distress, and yet in confidence, appeal is made to Jehovah. The final word of confidence is very full of beauty, "The Lord thinketh upon me."

PSALM 41

Jehovah Recognized as Rewarding Compassion

BLESSED is he that considereth the poor:
Jehovah will deliver him in the day of evil.

2 Jehovah will preserve him and keep him alive,
And he shall be blessed upon the earth;
And deliver not thou him unto the will of his enemies.

3 Jehovah will support him upon the couch of languishing:
Thou makest all his bed in his sickness.

4 I said, O Jehovah, have mercy upon me:

Heal my soul; for I have sinned against thee.

5 Mine enemies speak evil against me, *saying,*
When will he die, and his name perish?

6 And if he come to see *me,* he speaketh falsehood;
His heart gathereth iniquity to itself:
When he goeth abroad, he telleth it.

7 All that hate me whisper together against me;
Against me do they devise my hurt.

8 An evil disease, *say they*, cleaveth fast unto him;
And now that he lieth he shall rise up no more.

9 Yea, mine own familiar friend, in whom I trusted,
Who did eat of my bread,
Hath lifted up his heel against me.

10 But thou, O Jehovah, have mercy upon me, and raise me up,
That I may requite them.

11 By this I know that thou delightest in me,
Because mine enemy doth not triumph over me.

12 And as for me, thou upholdest me in mine integrity,
And settest me before thy face for ever.

13 Blessed be Jehovah, the God of Israel,
From everlasting and to everlasting.
Amen, and Amen.

This whole song depends for interpretation upon its opening beatitude. The man who is considerate towards the weak, that is compassionate, is blessed. His blessings are then described. Let emphasis be placed in reading upon "him" and "he," and "his," in verses 1–3. It will then be seen that all these things come to the man at first described, namely, the compassionate man.

Then the psalmist confesses his sin. In the light of the beatitude the sin is seen to have been that of lack of compassion, and this is the secret of the bitter hatred of his enemies which he proceeds to describe. Returning to his cry for mercy, his words are to be carefully noted (ver. 10). What is the meaning of "requite"? Almost all expositors agree in treating it as a word indicating revenge, and then attempt to explain it away. The word may certainly be translated recompense, and is far oftener used to indicate a kind action than a vindictive one. If that be so here, the consistency of the argument is apparent. He has failed in compassion, therefore his enemies and even his friend are against him. He asks for Jehovah's mercy, that being raised up he may treat his enemies differently. The Messianic reference is not destroyed. The wrong of those who harmed the Christ is greater because they acted without cause. Even then His prayer, "Father, forgive," harmonizes with this interpretation. His raising up by God was for blessing on men.

BOOK II.

PSALMS 42–72

BOOK II. PSALMS 42–72

DOXOLOGY

"Blessed be the Lord God, the God of Israel,
Who only doeth wondrous things;
And blessed be His glorious Name for ever;
And let the whole earth be filled with His glory. Amen, and Amen." Ps. 72–18, 19.

A. THE TITLE.	B. THE RELATION.	C. THE QUALITY.	D. THE QUANTITY.	E. THE EXTENT.
"Jehovah Elohim." The Essential. Helper Supreme.	"The God of Israel." "Who only doeth wondrous things."	"Blessed." The Person. His Name. "Amen, and Amen."	"For ever."	"The whole earth filled with His Glory."

The Divine Name.

The dominant name in this book is "God." It occurs in every psalm at least twice, and in one as many as 26 times. It is written in the singular (El) 16 times, and in the plural (Elohim) 198 times. "Jehovah" is found 32 times. From 15 psalms it is absent altogether. The general title "Lord" (Adonahy) occurs 19 times scattered through 12 of the psalms.

In addition, the title "Jah," is used once.

The Dominant Thought.

In the second book the dominant thought is that of the might of God realized by His people, and manifest through them. The worship is that of Jehovah, as the wonder-working God.

ANALYSIS

A. MIGHTY DELIVERANCE. 42 to 51		B. MIGHTY DEFENCE. 52 to 60		C. MIGHTY DOMINION. 61 to 72	
I. Exile.	43, 44	I. The Enemy.	53 to 55	I. The Need.	61 to 64
i. The Desire.	42	i. The godless One.	52, 53	i. Assurance.	61
ii. The Prayer.	43	ii. The Cry of Distress.	54, 55	ii. Patience.	63
iii. The Despair.	44			iii. Confidence.	63
				iv. Certainty.	54
II. Hope.	45 to 49	II. The Defender.	56 to 60	II. The Answer.	65 to 68
i. The King.	45	i. Hope.	56, 57	i. Praise for Might.	65
ii. The Refuge.	46	ii. Prayer.	53 to 60	ii. Praise for Deliverance.	66
iii. The Victor.	47			iii. Universal Praise.	67
iv. The Defender.	48			iv. The Arising of God.	68
v. The Life-Giver.	49				
III. Restoration.	1–51			III. The Process.	69 to 72
i. The Act of God.	50			i. The Suffering Witness.	69
ii. The Attitude of Man.	51			ii. The Cry for Help.	70
				iii. The Cry for Confidence.	71
				iv. The King and the King-dom.	72

PSALM 42

God Remembered in Exile

AS the hart panteth after the
water brooks,
So panteth my soul after thee,
O God.
2 My soul thirsteth for God, for
the living God:
When shall I come and appear
before God?
3 My tears have been my food
day and night,
While they continually say unto
me, Where is thy God?
4 These things I remember and
pour out my soul within me,
How I went with the throng,
and led them to the house of
God,
With the voice of joy and
praise, a multitude keeping
holyday.
5 Why art thou cast down, O my
soul?
And why art thou disquieted
within me?
Hope thou in God; for I shall
yet praise him
For the help of his countenance.
6 O my God, my soul is cast down
within me:
Therefore do I remember thee
from the land of the Jordan,
And the Hermons, from the hill
Mizar.
7 Deep calleth unto deep at the
noise of thy waterfalls:
All thy waves and thy billows
are gone over me.
8 Yet Jehovah will command his
lovingkindness in the day-
time;
And in the night his song shall
be with me,
Even a prayer unto the God of
my life.
9 I will say unto God my rock,
Why hast thou forgotten me?
Why go I mourning because of
the oppression of the enemy?
10 As with a sword in my bones,
mine adversaries reproach me,
While they continually say unto
me, Where is thy God?
11 Why art thou cast down, O my
soul?
And why art thou disquieted
within me?
Hope thou in God; for I shall
yet praise him,
Who is the help of my countenance, and my God.

This is the song of an exile, and moreover, of an exile among
enemies who have no sympathy with his religious convictions.
He cries out after God with all the intensity of one who knows
God, and cares supremely for the honour of His name. His
greatest grief is their mocking enquiry after his God. By contrast he remembers being in the midst of worshipping multi-

tudes, their leader and companion. In the midst of his grief he appeals to his own soul in the language of hope and confidence. A great conflict goes on within, for he affirms, "My soul is cast down."

Notice carefully the heroism of the man. He makes his trouble and disquietude the occasion of remembering God. Out of the place of his exile he turns his thoughts to God. The result is not a deadening of his sense of sorrow, but rather a setting of it in right relationship to God. Trouble has come in cataracts and waves and billows, but they are all God's own. "Thy cataracts ... Thy waves ... Thy billows." When sorrow is set in this relationship, there is a consciousness of love in the day time; there is in the night a song and a prayer. The trouble is still there, the oppression and reproach of the enemy, but courage and hope continue also, and the conviction of coming deliverance. It is a wonderful psalm, and has been the song of many an afflicted yet trusting soul.

PSALM 43

God Leading the Exile Home

JUDGE me, O God, and plead my cause against an ungodly nation:
Oh deliver me from the deceitful and unjust man.
2 For thou art the God of my strength; why hast thou cast me off?
Why go I mourning because of the oppression of the enemy?
3 Oh send out thy light and thy truth; let them lead me:
Let them bring me unto thy holy hill,
And to thy tabernacles.
4 Then will I go unto the altar of God,
Unto God my exceeding joy;
And upon the harp will I praise thee, O God, my God.
5 Why art thou cast down, O my soul?
And why art thou disquieted within me?
Hope thou in God; for I shall yet praise him,
Who is the help of my countenance, and my God.

This psalm is either a part of the previous one, or is closely connected with it. It breathes the same note of confidence, ending with practically the same words as the two parts of the former. It reaches a higher plane in that it only refers to sorrow and mourning in order to protest against them in the light of certainty of God's deliverance.

From prayer for that deliverance, which he has twice in the previous psalm declared to be certain, he passes to affirmation of how, following the leading of God's light and truth, he will go up to worship. Notice the procession to praise as he describes it. To the hill; to the tabernacles; to the altar; and then the act of praise. Not yet has the answer come. The darkness and the mystery are still about him, but the shining way is seen; and again the soul is forbidden to despair, and hope is encouraged in God.

PSALM 44

God the Author of Good and Evil

WE have heard with our ears, O God,
Our fathers have told us,
What work thou didst in their days,
In the days of old.

2 Thou didst drive out the nations with thy hand;
But them thou didst plant:
Thou didst afflict the peoples;
But them thou didst spread abroad.

3 For they gat not the land in possession by their own sword,
Neither did their own arm save them;
But thy right hand, and thine arm, and the light of thy countenance,
Because thou wast favorable unto them.

4 Thou art my King, O God:

Command deliverance for Jacob.

5 Through thee will we push down our adversaries:
Through thy name will we tread them under that rise up against us.

6 For I will not trust in my bow,
Neither shall my sword save me.

7 But thou hast saved us from our adversaries,
And hast put them to shame that hate us.

8 In God have we made our boast all the day long,
And we will give thanks unto thy name for ever.

9 But now thou hast cast us off, and brought us to dishonor,
And goest not forth with our hosts.

20 Thou makest us to turn back
   from the adversary;
   And they that hate us take spoil
   for themselves.
11 Thou hast made us like sheep
   appointed for food,
   And hast scattered us among
   the nations.
12 Thou sellest thy people for
   nought,
   And hast not increased *thy
   wealth* by their price.
13 Thou makest us a reproach to
   our neighbors,
   A scoffing and a derision to
   them that are round about us.
14 Thou makest us a byword
   among the nations,
   A shaking of the head among
   the peoples.
15 All the day long is my dishonor
   before me,
   And the shame of my face hath
   covered me,
16 For the voice of him that reproacheth and blasphemeth,
   By reason of the enemy and the
   avenger.
17 All this is come upon us; yet
   have we not forgotten thee,
   Neither have we dealt falsely in
   thy covenant.

18 Our heart is not turned back,
   Neither have our steps declined
   from thy way,
19 That thou hast sore broken us
   in the place of jackals,
   And covered us with the shadow
   of death.
20 If we have forgotten the name
   of our God,
   Or spread forth our hands to a
   strange god;
21 Will not God search this out?
   For he knoweth the secrets of
   the heart.
22 Yea, for thy sake are we killed
   all the day long;
   We are accounted as sheep for
   the slaughter.
23 Awake, why sleepest thou, O
   Lord?
   Arise, cast *us* not off for ever.
24 Wherefore hidest thou thy face,
   And forgettest our affliction and
   our oppression?
25 For our soul is bowed down to
   the dust:
   Our body cleaveth unto the
   earth.
26 Rise up for our help,
   And redeem us for thy lovingkindness' sake.

The final meaning of this psalm is discovered in its last four verses. It is a prayer for deliverance from circumstances of defeat. Its strength of appeal lies in its recognition of the government of God. He is the Author of good and evil. Of course evil is used here in the sense of disaster and calamity. He sings of the God of good first (vers. 1-8). There is a double recognition of this. History attests it. The testimony of the fathers affirms it. They had originally come into possession of the land by the act of God (vers. 1-3). Then there is personal recognition of it. Trust is to be reposed in nothing save God (vers. 4–8). The word "But" indicates a change. The day is one of disaster, and this is recognized as the act of God. "Thou hast cast us off." "Thou makest us to turn back," and so on (vers. 9–16).

Yet there has not been apostasy. Nay, rather it had been a pathway of suffering for the sake of God and His name (vers. 17–22). Light is thrown upon this by Paul's use of the words in Romans viii. 36. Then follows the plea for help and deliverance. It is a perfectly honest and reasonable plea, yet the wonderful advance of Christian experience upon the highest in the old economy is nowhere more plainly shown than here. The apostle of the new covenant makes no appeal for deliverance, but rather declares that in all these things we are more than conquerors, and affirms that nothing can separate us from the love of God.

PSALM 45

God Gladdening the King and His Bride

MY heart overfloweth with a goodly matter;
I speak the things which I have made touching the king:
My tongue is the pen of a ready writer.

2 Thou art fairer than the children of men;
Grace is poured into thy lips:
Therefore God hath blessed thee for ever.

3 Gird thy sword upon thy thigh, O mighty one,
Thy glory and thy majesty.

4 And in thy majesty ride on prosperously,
Because of truth and meekness *and* righteousness:
And thy right hand shall teach thee terrible things.

5 Thine arrows are sharp;
The peoples fall under thee;
They are in the heart of the king's enemies.

6 Thy throne, O God, is for ever and ever:
A sceptre of equity is the sceptre of thy kingdom.

7 Thou hast loved righteousness, and hated wickedness:
Therefore God, thy God, hath anointed thee
With the oil of gladness above thy fellows.

8 All thy garments *smell of* myrrh, and aloes, *and* cassia;

Out of ivory palaces stringed instruments have made thee
glad.

9 Kings' daughters are among thy
honorable women:
At thy right hand doth stand
the queen in gold of Ophir.

10 Hearken, O daughter, and consider, and incline thine ear;
Forget also thine own people,
and thy father's house:

11 So will the king desire thy
beauty;
For he is thy lord; and reverence thou him.

12 And the daughter of Tyre *shall
be there* with a gift;
The rich among the people shall
entreat thy favor.

13 The king's daughter within *the
palace* is all glorious:

Her clothing is in wrought with
gold.

14 She shall be led unto the king in
broidered work:
The virgins her companions that
follow her
Shall be brought unto thee.

15 With gladness and rejoicing
shall they be led:
They shall enter into the king's
palace.

16 Instead of thy fathers shall be
thy children,
Whom thou shalt make princes
in all the earth.

17 I will make thy name to be
remembered in all genera-
tions:
Therefore shall the peoples give
thee thanks for ever and ever.

Whether this psalm has, or had a local application, or is wholly idealistic, cannot be certainly determined. It matters very little, for it is one of the songs which inevitably is Messianic in its deepest and fullest meaning. After an introduction which speaks of the fullness of his heart, the singer addresses the king, telling of the glory of his person, the perfection of his rule, and the beauty of his bride (vers. 1–9).

He then turns to the bride, and in view of her high calling counsels her to forget her own people, and surrender herself wholly to her husband (vers. 10–12). If the king in mind was Solomon, and the bride the daughter of Pharaoh, the suggestiveness of the song becomes the more remarkable. He then describes the queen gloriously arrayed for her marriage (vers. 13–15), and ends by words of promised blessing to the king.

If the inclusive truth of this psalm be larger than we are able to grasp, there is a personal application full of value and full of beauty. It is as we see the glory of the Lord that we become ready to renounce all our own people and possessions, that we may be wholly to His praise, and so become the instruments through whom the royal race is propagated, and the glory of the King made known among the generations and the peoples.

PSALM 46

God the Refuge of His People

GOD is our refuge and strength,
  A very present help in trouble.

2 Therefore will we not fear, though the earth do change,
And though the mountains be shaken into the heart of the seas;

3 Though the waters thereof roar and be troubled,
Though the mountains tremble with the swelling thereof.

4 There is a river, the streams whereof make glad the city of God,
The holy place of the tabernacles of the Most High.

5 God is in the midst of her; she shall not be moved:
God will help her, and that right early.

6 The nations raged, the kingdoms were moved:

He uttered his voice, the earth melted.

7 Jehovah of hosts is with us;
The God of Jacob is our refuge.

8 Come, behold the works of Jehovah,
What desolations he hath made in the earth.

9 He maketh wars to cease unto the end of the earth;
He breaketh the bow, and cutteth the spear in sunder;
He burneth the chariots in the fire.

10 Be still, and know that I am God:
I will be exalted among the nations, I will be exalted in the earth.

11 Jehovah of hosts is with us;
The God of Jacob is our refuge.

Comment on this great song of confidence seems almost unnecessary, so powerfully has it taken hold upon the heart of humanity, and so perfectly does it set forth the experience of trusting souls in all ages, in circumstances of tempest shock.

The system of the song is worth noting. It is divided into three parts. The first (vers. 1-3) is the challenge of confidence. The second (vers. 4-7) tells the secret of confidence.

The third (vers. 8–11) declares the vindication of confidence.

The challenge announces confidence in God as refuge and strength, and very present help, and defies fear even in the midst of the wildest upheavals. In days when tempests shake loose all solid things, and the restless waters roar and surge till mountains shake, the soul is confident.

The secret of the confidence is the consciousness of the nearness of God. He is a river of gladness in the midst of the city. What matters the tumult around?

The vindication of confidence is to be found in observing His activity in all surrounding things, from this place of safety and strength within the ctiy. The twice repeated refrain (vers. 7, 11) is full of beauty as it reveals the twofold conception of God which is the deepest note in the music. He is the King of all hosts. He is the God of the individual. Scholars believe, and with every reason, that the refrain should also occur between verses 3 and 4. This certainly perfects the literary form, and adds to the beauty of the psalm.

PSALM 47

God Reigning over the Nations

OH clap your hands, all ye peoples;
Shout unto God with the voice of triumph.

2 For Jehovah Most High is terrible;
He is a great King over all the earth.

3 He subdueth peoples under us,
And nations under our feet.

4 He chooseth our inheritance for us,
The glory of Jacob whom he loved.

5 God is gone up with a shout,
Jehovah with the sound of a trumpet.

6 Sing praises to God, sing praises:
Sing praises unto our King, sing praises.

7 For God is the King of all the earth:
Sing ye praises with understanding.

8 God reigneth over the nations:
God sitteth upon his holy throne.

9 The princes of the peoples are gathered together
To be the people of the God of Abraham;

| For the shields of the earth belong unto God: | He is greatly exalted. |

This is a song of the sovereignty of God. In the Hebrew ceremonial it was pre-eminently the song of the New Year, being repeated seven times ere the sounding of the trumpets which announced the feast.

It opens with an appeal to the peoples to unite in His adoration as the one supreme Ruler. The singer has a true sense of the real mission of the chosen as the appointed rulers of the peoples. Their song is called for, and therefore it is plain that their subjugation is looked upon as beneficent to them as well as to Israel. The appeal is renewed to praise the uplifted and enthroned King.

A prophetic vision of the ultimate recognition of the throne of God concludes the psalm. It has a wide outlook. Not the one nation only, but all the princes are seen submissive to His rule, and so become the people of the God of Abraham. This is the true note of rejoicing. Not merely is the safety of the one city the cause of gladness, but the gathering together under the one all-beneficent reign of God, of all the peoples. This is rejoicing in hope of the glory of God, far more spacious and perfect than any satisfaction in personal deliverance or safety. If our joy is to be all it ought to be, we must have this larger outlook upon the purposes of God.

PSALM 48

God Reigning over His Own

GREAT is Jehovah, and greatly to be praised,
In the city of our God, in his holy mountain.
2 Beautiful in elevation, the joy of the whole earth,
Is mount Zion, *on* the sides of the north,
The city of the great King.
3 God hath made himself known in her palaces for a refuge.
4 For, lo, the kings assembled themselves,
They passed by together.
5 They saw it, then were they amazed;

They were dismayed, they hasted away.

6 Trembling took hold of them there,
Pain, as of a woman in travail.

7 With the east wind
Thou breakest the ships of Tarshish.

8 As we have heard, so have we seen
In the city of Jehovah of hosts, in the city of our God:
God will establish it for ever.

9 We have thought on thy lovingkindness, O God,
In the midst of thy temple.

10 As is thy name, O God,
So is thy praise unto the ends of the earth:

Thy right hand is full of righteousness.

11 Let mount Zion be glad,
Let the daughters of Judah rejoice,
Because of thy judgments.

12 Walk about Zion, and go round about her;
Number the towers thereof;

13 Mark ye well her bulwarks;
Consider her palaces:
That ye may tell it to the generation following.

14 For this God is our God for ever and ever:
He will be our guide *even* unto death.

In Psalm xlvi the dominant note was of confidence because of the government of God in the midst of His people. This is a song describing the experience resulting from such government. It is the anthem of a deliverance wrought for the city against an alliance of hostile kings. The beauty and glory of the city remain, notwithstanding the attack of the foes. The intervention of God was of such a nature that the attack failed ere it positively began. "The kings assembled themselves, they passed by together." They were seized with weakness and fear, and fled. So God had delivered, and the deliverance is a reason for new confidence that the city will be established for ever.

The singer urges the inhabitants to examine well the city that the wonder of its preservation may fill the heart with praise, and be the foundation for faith in all the years to come. We may seem to have lost something in the reading of this psalm, because we cannot place it historically with any certainty. Yet it is so true to a constantly recurring experience of the saints that it has become a song of constant use.

Threatening perils massed against us suddenly waver and pass away smitten by unseen hands, and deliverance is wrought when we had seen nothing but destruction. Verily great is Jehovah, and greatly to be praised as the God of deliverance.

PSALM 49

God the Source of Immortality

HEAR this, all ye peoples;
    Give ear, all ye inhabitants
    of the world,
2 Both low and high,
    Rich and poor together.
3 My mouth shall speak wisdom;
    And the meditation of my heart
    shall be of understanding.
4 I will incline mine ear to a para-
    ble:
    I will open my dark saying upon
    the harp.
5 Wherefore should I fear in the
    days of evil,
    When iniquity at my heels com-
    passeth me about?
6 They that trust in their wealth,
    And boast themselves in the
    multitude of their riches;
7 None *of them* can by any means
    redeem his brother,
    Nor give to God a ransom for
    him
8 (For the redemption of their
    life is costly,
    And it faileth for ever),
9 That he should still live alway,
    That he should not see corrup-
    tion.
10 For he shall see it. Wise men
    die;
    The fool and the brutish alike
    perish,
    And leave their wealth to others.

11 Their inward thought is, *that*
    their houses *shall continue* for
    ever.
    And their dwelling-places to all
    generations:
    They call their lands after their
    own names.
12 But man *being* in honor abideth
    not:
    He is like the beasts that perish.
13 This their way is their folly:
    Yet after them men approve
    their sayings.
14 They are appointed as a flock
    for Sheol;
    Death shall be their shepherd:
    And the upright shall have do-
    minion over them in the
    morning;
    And their beauty shall be for
    Sheol to consume,
    That there be no habitation for
    it.
15 But God will redeem my soul
    from the power of Sheol;
    For he will receive me.
16 Be not thou afraid when one is
    made rich,
    When the glory of his house is
    increased:
17 For when he dieth he shall carry
    nothing away;

His glory shall not descend after him.

18 Though while he lived he blessed his soul
(And men praise thee, when thou doest well to thyself),

19 He shall go to the generation of his fathers;
They shall never see the light.

20 Man that is in honor, and understandeth not,
Is like the beasts that perish.

This is the song of a principle, and the psalmist commences by calling peoples of all castes and classes to give attention. It denies the power of material wealth, and affirms that of uprightness. There are two things which wealth cannot do. It can neither help a man to escape death, nor can it ensure the life of the one possessing it. The passion of the heart for immortality is manifest in the building of houses and the naming of the land. It is all useless. They are no more able to secure personal immortality thus than are the beasts which perish.

Yet there is a mastery over Sheol and death. It is to be found in uprightness. The declaration:—

"The upright shall have dominion over them in the morning," is very difficult to explain if it does not contain the light of hope beyond the grave. The morning is certainly something beyond Sheol and death, and the hope of the upright is in God's deliverance from Sheol. The teaching of the song is simple and sublime, present and perpetual. Right is mightier than wealth. It reaches farther, and accomplishes more. Wealth passes away empty-handed. Righteousness sings, even in death, of redemption, and a morning of dominion.

PSALM 50

God Manifesting Himself Through His People

THE Mighty One, God, Jehovah, hath spoken,
And called the earth from the rising of the sun unto the going down thereof.

2 Out of Zion, the perfection of beauty,
God hath shined forth.

3 Our God cometh, and doth not keep silence:

A fire devoureth before him,
And it is very tempestuous
round about him.

4 He calleth to the heavens above,
And to the earth, that he may
judge his people:

5 Gather my saints together unto
me,
Those that have made a covenant with me by sacrifice.

6 And the heavens shall declare
his righteousness;
For God is judge himself.

7 Hear, O my people, and I will
speak;
O Israel, and I will testify unto
thee:
I am God, *even* thy God.

8 I will not reprove thee for thy
sacrifices;
And thy burnt-offerings are continually before me.

9 I will take no bullock out of thy
house,
Nor he-goats out of thy folds.

10 For every beast of the forest is
mine,
And the cattle upon a thousand
hills.

11 I know all the birds of the
mountains;
And the wild beasts of the field
are mine.

12 If I were hungry, I would not
tell thee;
For the world is mine, and the
fulness thereof.

13 Will I eat the flesh of bulls,
Or drink the blood of goats?

14 Offer unto God the sacrifice of
thanksgiving;
And pay thy vows unto the
Most High;

15 And call upon me in the day of
trouble:
I will deliver thee, and thou shalt
glorify me.

16 But unto the wicked God saith,
What hast thou to do to declare
my statutes,
And that thou hast taken my
covenant in thy mouth,

17 Seeing that thou hatest instruction,
And castest my words behind
thee?

18 When thou sawest a thief, thou
consentedst with him,
And has been partaker with
adulterers.

19 Thou givest thy mouth to evil,
And thy tongue frameth deceit.

20 Thou sittest and speakest
against thy brother;
Thou slanderest thine own
mother's son.

21 These things hast thou done,
and I kept silence;
Thou thoughtest that I was altogether such a one as thyself:
But I will reprove thee, and set
them in order before thine
eyes.

22 Now consider this, ye that forget God,
Lest I tear you in pieces, and
there be none to deliver:

23 Whoso offereth the sacrifice of
thanksgiving glorifieth me;
And to him that ordereth his
way *aright*
Will I show the salvation of
God.

The singer addresses himself in the name of God to the whole earth that it may hear and learn a lesson of importance. The call is made in the first verse. The final appeal is in verses 22 and 23. The lesson is that forgetfulness of God issues in gravest peril, while the remembrance which worships ensures the blessing of salvation.

Between the call to attention and the final appeal the psalmist sings of the relation between God and His own (vers. 2–15); and then of the attitude of God to the wicked. As to the former they are to be the medium of His praise. God shined forth out of Zion. In order to this the saints are to be gathered to Him that through them He may be manifested in power and righteousness. Their gathering is to be not on the ground of any sacrifice they can bring of things already belonging to God, but wholly on the basis of praise and trust. The wicked can have no part in such manifestation of God, and therein lies their chief sin and failure. This is a thought of most searching power. Our most heinous sin is not the act of wrong done, but the fact that such wrong incapacitates us from fulfilling our highest function of glorifying God, and showing forth His praise.

PSALM 51

God the Saviour of the Sinful

HAVE mercy upon me, O God,
according to thy lovingkindness:
According to the multitude of thy tender mercies blot out my transgressions.
2 Wash me thoroughly from mine iniquity,
And cleanse me from my sin.
3 For I know my transgressions;
And my sin is ever before me.

4 Against thee, thee only, have I sinned,
And done that which is evil in thy sight;
That thou mayest be justified when thou speakest,
And he clear when thou judgest.
5 Behold, I was brought forth in iniquity;
And in sin did my mother conceive me.

6 Behold thou desirest truth in the inward parts;
And in the hidden part thou wilt make me to know wisdom.

7 Purify me with hyssop, and I shall be clean:
Wash me, and I shall be whiter than snow.

8 Make me to hear joy and gladness,
That the bones which thou hast broken may rejoice.

9 Hide thy face from my sins,
And blot out all mine iniquities.

10 Create in me a clean heart, O God;
And renew a right spirit within me.

11 Cast me not away from thy presence;
And take not thy holy Spirit from me.

12 Restore unto me the joy of thy salvation;
And uphold me with a willing spirit.

13 Then will I teach transgressors thy ways;

And sinners shall be converted unto thee.

14 Deliver me from blood-guiltiness, O God, thou God of my salvation;
And my tongue shall sing aloud of thy righteousness.

15 O Lord, open thou my lips;
And my mouth shall show forth thy praise.

16 For thou delightest not in sacrifice; else would I give it:
Thou hast no pleasure in burnt-offering.

17 The sacrifices of God are a broken spirit:
A broken and contrite heart, O God, thou wilt not despise.

18 Do good in thy good pleasure unto Zion:
Build thou the walls of Jerusalem.

19 Then wilt thou delight in the sacrifices of righteousness,
In burnt-offering and whole burnt-offering:
Then will they offer bullocks upon thine altar.

This is the first of a number of psalms (eighteen) to which titles are prefaced, which connect them with David, eight out of the number having historic references. There is a remarkable fitness in every case between the incident thus indicated and the psalm following; but whether the placing is accurate or not, is open to question.

This is indeed one of the great penitential psalms, being the fourth in the seven which are usually so described. It opens with a general cry for pardon, which comes out of a deep sense of sin, and an equally profound desire for forgiveness. In the first three verses sin is described as "transgression," "iniquity," "sin"; and the mercy sought as to "blot out," "wash," "cleanse." The penitent soul cries for forgiveness upon the basis of having confessed. Suddenly the intensity of conviction deepens, as the act of sin is traced back to its reason in the pollution of the nature. This leads to a deeper cry. As the first was for pardon, the second is for purity, for cleansing of heart, and renewal of spirit.

The prayer passes on to seek for the things which follow such cleansing, the maintenance of fellowship, and the consciousness of joy. Looking on in hope, the song anticipates that service of thanksgiving and praise which will issue from such pardon and purity.

PSALM 52

God the Destroyer of the Sinful

WHY boastest thou thyself in mischief, O mighty man?
The lovingkindness of God *endureth* continually.

2 Thy tongue deviseth very wickedness,
Like a sharp razor, working deceitfully.

3 Thou lovest evil more than good,
And lying rather than to speak righteousness.

4 Thou lovest all devouring words,
O thou deceitful tongue.
God will likewise destroy thee for ever;
He will take thee up, and pluck thee out of thy tent,
And root thee out of the land of the living.

6 The righteous also shall see *it*, and fear,
And shall laugh at him, *saying*,

7 Lo, this is the man that made not God his strength,
But trusted in the abundance of his riches,
And strengthened himself in his wickedness.

8 But as for me, I am like a green olive-tree in the house of God:
I trust in the lovingkindness of God for ever and ever.

9 I will give thee thanks for ever, because thou hast done it;
And I will hope in thy name, for it is good, in the presence of thy saints.

In this song the attitude of God toward the wicked man who is a tyrant is manifest. The mighty man who boasts himself in mischief is first put in striking contrast to God Whose mercy endureth continually.

There follows a description of the mischief in which such a man makes his boast. One is reminded of James' description of the tongue, and its fearful power, as the psalmist describes the mischief of evil speech, growing out of an evil nature. The God of mercy destroys the mischief-maker, and thus demonstrates His mercifulness. God's dealings with such a man are to be seen by the righteous, and they are to understand that the reason thereof is to be discovered in the fact that this man was godless.

Suddenly the singer puts his position into contrast with the end of the man, because he is in contrast with the attitude of the man. Instead of being rooted up, he is like a tree in the house of God. Instead of trusting in the abundance of riches, he trusts in the mercy of God. The contrast of the same reveals the abiding truth of the unchangeableness of God. All that seems to be different in His dealing with man is due to difference existing in man's attitude towards Him.

PSALM 53

God Disappointed in Man

THE fool hath said in his heart,
    There is no God.
Corrupt are they, and have done abominable iniquity;
There is none that doeth good.
2 God looked down from heaven upon the children of men,
To see if there were any that did understand,
That did seek after God.
3 Every one of them is gone back; they are together become filthy;
There is none that doeth good, no, not one.

4 Have the workers of iniquity no knowledge,
Who eat up my people as they eat bread,
And call not upon God?
5 There were they in great fear, where no fear was;
For God hath scattered the bones of him that encampeth against thee:
Thou hast put them to shame, because God hath rejected them.
6 Oh that the salvation of Israel were come out of Zion!

When God bringeth back the captivity of his people,	Then shall Jacob rejoice, *and* Israel shall be glad.

This psalm, with slight variations, is found in Book I (Ps. xiv). Its introduction a second time necessarily leads us to notice the differences. In all probability the editor incorporated it into this book because of these very changes. They are first the substitution of "God" for "Jehovah" four times. Perhaps for liturgical use in some special circumstances in which the desire was to express the praise of God as the wonder-working God, the change was made. All that was true of Jehovah's knowledge of men (see Ps. xiv), is true also of God's attitude toward men as the Wonder-Worker. Not only as Helper, but as the supreme One, He looks upon men. Not only do the workers of iniquity fail to discover Him as the Helper, they do not call upon Him as the mighty One. The other main change is to be found in verse 5, for the exposition of which see note on Psalm xiv.

PSALM 54

God the Helper of the Oppressed

SAVE me, O God, by thy name,
And judge me in thy might.
2 Hear my prayer, O God;
Give ear to the words of my mouth.
3 For strangers are risen up against me,
And violent men have sought after my soul:
They have not set God before them.
4 Behold, God is my helper:

The Lord is of them that uphold my soul.
5 He will requite the evil unto mine enemies:
Destroy thou them in thy truth.
6 With a freewill-offering will I sacrifice unto thee:
I will give thanks unto thy name, O Jehovah, for it is good.
7 For he hath delivered me out of all trouble;
And mine eye hath seen *my desire* upon mine enemies.

The burden of the psalm is expressed in the first two verses. Its reason is described in verse 3, which assurance is the song of what remains. Taking the second and third sections first, they deal with the sorrow of the soul, and the succour which comes from God.

The sorrow is that of opposition and persecution by those who are godless. The description of this is preceded by the prayer which cries for salvation by the name of God, and judgment in His might. There is no touch of despair manifest. Over against the strangers risen up against him he sets God Who is his Helper. Over against the violent men who seek after his soul he sets the Lord Who upholds the soul. The issue is perfect confidence that God will requite the evil and destroy the enemy. Already, though perhaps yet in the midst of the peril, he sings the song of deliverance, as though it were already realized. The central sentence of the song is "God is mine helper." Wherever man is conscious of this fact, he is superior to all the opposition of his enemies, and so is able in the midst of the most difficult circumstances to sing the song of deliverance.

PSALM 55

God the Deliverer of the Betrayed

GIVE ear to my prayer, O God; And hide not thyself from my supplication.

2 Attend unto me, and answer me:
I am restless in my complaint, and moan,

3 Because of the voice of the enemy,
Because of the oppression of the wicked;
For they cast iniquity upon me,
And in anger they persecute me.

4 My heart is sore pained within me:
And the terrors of death are fallen upon me.

5 Fearfulness and trembling are come upon me,
And horror hath overwhelmed me.

6 And I said, Oh that I had wings like a dove!
Then would I fly away, and be at rest.

7 Lo, then would I wander far off,
I would lodge in the wilderness.

8 I would haste me to a shelter
From the stormy wind and tempest.

9 Destroy, O Lord, *and* divide their tongue;
For I have seen violence and strife in the city.

10 Day and night they go about it upon the walls thereof:
Iniquity also and mischief are in the midst of it.

11 Wickedness is in the midst thereof:
Oppression and guile depart not from its streets.

12 For it was not an enemy that reproached me;
Then I could have borne it:
Neither was it he that hated me that did magnify himself against me;
Then I would have hid myself from him:

13 But it was thou, a man mine equal,
My companion, and my familiar friend.

14 We took sweet counsel together;
We walked in the house of God with the throng.

15 Let death come suddenly upon them,
Let them go down alive into Sheol;
For wickedness is in their dwelling, in the midst of them.

16 As for me, I will call upon God;
And Jehovah will save me.

17 Evening, and morning, and at noonday, will I complain, and moan;
And he will hear my voice.

18 He hath redeemed my soul in peace from the battle that was against me;
For they were many *that strove* with me.

19 God will hear, and answer them.
Even he that abideth of old,
The men who have no changes,
And who fear not God.

20 He hath put forth his hands against such as were at peace with him:
He hath profaned his covenant.

21 His mouth was smooth as butter,
But his heart was war:
His words were softer than oil,
Yet were they drawn swords.

22 Cast thy burden upon Jehovah, and he will sustain thee:
He will never suffer the righteous to be moved.

23 But thou, O God, wilt bring them down into the pit of destruction:
Bloodthirsty and deceitful men shall not live out half their days;
But I will trust in thee.

This is the outcry of a man of faith in sore peril. The emotional nature is moved to its very centre, and tides of deep feeling surge through his soul. He has been cruelly betrayed by his familiar friend who would seem to have been at the head of a conspiracy against him.

It is really a revelation of how fellowship with God leads ultimately to the victory of faith. There are three movements manifest. The first is that of fear. Appeal is made to God out of a consciousness of fearfulness, trembling, horror. So terrible is this fear that he would fain fly away and escape it all (vers. 1–8). The troubled heart then breaks forth into fury. So mean is the method of the foe that the anger of the man is aroused, and he cries for vengeance against the oppressor (vers. 9–15). He then appeals to God, and at once declares that he is delivered. The wrong of the wicked is no less, but calmly stated in the light of God it is a burden to be cast upon Him, and the conviction of His deliverance is created. Fear only leads to desire for flight. Fury only emphasizes the consciousness of wrong. Faith alone creates courage.

PSALM 56

God the Tender Friend of the Oppressed

BE merciful unto me, O God; for man would swallow me up:
All the day long he fighting oppresseth me.
2 Mine enemies would swallow me up all the day long;
For they are many that fight proudly against me.
3 What time I am afraid, I will put my trust in thee.
4 In God (I will praise his word), In God have I put my trust, I will not be afraid;
What can flesh do unto me?
5 All the day long they wrest my words:
All their thoughts are against me for evil.
6 They gather themselves together, they hide themselves.
They mark my steps, Even as they have waited for my soul.
7 Shall they escape by iniquity?

In anger cast down the peoples, O God.
8 Thou numberest my wanderings:
Put thou my tears into thy bottle;
Are they not in thy book?
9 Then shall mine enemies turn back in the day that I call:
This I know, that God is for me.
10 In God (I will praise *his* word), In Jehovah (I will praise *his* word),
11 In God have I put my trust, I will not be afraid;
What can man do unto me?
12 Thy vows are upon me, O God:
I will render thank-offerings unto thee.
13 For thou has delivered my soul from death:
Hast thou not *delivered* by feet from falling,
That I may walk before God In the light of the living?

The keynote of this psalm is the concluding declaration of the previous one, "I will trust in Thee." Here again are evident the same circumstances of oppression (vers. 5–7).

The song opens and closes with praise. The opening (vers. 1–4) is a prayer for deliverance which culminates in a note of praise. Notice how it ascends. First the singer declares that in the hour of fear he will trust. Then he declares he will trust and not be afraid. The closing movement is wholly one of praise. The tenderness of God is exquisitely stated. To Him wanderings are known, and by Him tears are preserved. Against all adversaries God is for him. Then again the high note of trust cancelling fear, is struck, and the psalm ends with a sacrifice of praise. It is a gracious thing to know God well enough to be able resolutely to trust Him when fear possesses the heart. It is a much finer thing to trust Him so completely as to have no fear. Both ways lead homeward, but the former is low level travelling, while the latter is high level.

PSALM 57

God the Refuge in Calamity

BE merciful unto me, O God, be merciful unto me;
For my soul taketh refuge in thee:
Yea, in the shadow of thy wings will I take refuge,
Until *these* calamities be overpast.

2 I will cry unto God Most High,
Unto God that performeth *all* things for me.

3 He will send from heaven, and save me,
When he that would swallow me up reproacheth;
God will send forth his lovingkindness and his truth.

4 My soul is among lions;
I lie among them that are set on fire,
Even the sons of men, whose teeth are spears and arrows,
And their tongue a sharp sword.

5 Be thou exalted, O God, above the heavens;
Let thy glory *be* above all the earth.

6 They have prepared a net for my steps;
My soul is bowed down:
They have digged a pit before me;
They are fallen into the midst thereof themselves.

7 My heart is fixed, O God, my
heart is fixed:
I will sing, yea, I will sing
praises.
8 Awake up, my glory, awake,
psaltery and harp:
I myself will awake right early.
9 I will give thanks unto thee, O
Lord, among the peoples:

I will sing praises unto thee
among the nations.
10 For thy lovingkindness is great
unto the heavens,
And thy truth unto the skies.
11 Be thou exalted, O God, above
the heavens;
Let thy glory be above all the
earth.

Yet again the theme is the same, but the triumph of trust is
even more conspicuous. Compare the opening here with that
of the previous song. The cry is the same, but the reason is
different. There it was a cry born of the consciousness of the
enemy. Here it is born of the vision of God, and of trust in
Him. Compare also the wish of Psalm lv. 6 with the experience in this case. There the desire was for the inefficient
wings of a dove for flight. Here the sense is of the sufficient
wings of God for refuge until calamities are past. Now the
cry is one of real need, for the opposition is stated in terms as
pointed as ever, but it is a song of confidence all the while. In
the psalm that speaks of fear and flight the heart is "sore
pained." Now in trust it is "fixed," and a rush of praise is the
issue.

Faith does not free us from trial, but it does enable us to
triumph over it. Moreover, faith lifts us high above the purely
personal sense of pain, and creates a passion for the exaltation
of God among the nations. The heart at leisure from itself is
always the heart fixed in God.

PSALM 58

God the God of Vengeance

DO ye indeed in silence speak
righteousness?
Do ye judge uprightly, O ye
sons of men?

2 Nay, in heart ye work wickedness;
Ye weigh out the violence of
your hands in the earth.

3 The wicked are estranged from the womb:
They go astray as soon as they are born, speaking lies.
4 Their poison is like the poison of a serpent:
They are like the deaf adder that stoppeth her ear,
5 Which hearkeneth not to the voice of charmers,
Charming never so wisely.
6 Break their teeth, O God, in their mouth:
Break out the great teeth of the young lions, O Jehovah.
7 Let them melt away as water that runneth apace:
When he aimeth his arrows, let them be as though they were cut off.

8 *Let them be* as a snail which melteth and passeth away,
Like the untimely birth of a woman, that hath not seen the sun.
9 Before your pots can feel the thorns,
He will take them away with a whirlwind, the green and the burning alike.
10 The righteous shall rejoice when he seeth the vengeance:
He shall wash his feet in the blood of the wicked;
11 So that men shall say, Verily there is a reward for the righteous:
Verily there is a God that judgeth in the earth.

This is a fine setting forth of the certainty of the judgment of God against wickedness. The psalmist declares its reason (vers. 1–5), its process (vers. 6–9), and its effect (vers. 10, 11).

The whole psalm will be misunderstood save as we carefully note its opening questions. The reason of the judgment is not personal wrong. It is rather the failure of the rulers to administer justice. They are silent when they should speak. Their judgments are not upright. Evil in heart, they lie in word, and poison like serpents, and no charming wins them. The process of judgment is described in the form of prayer, which fact shows the sympathy of the singer with the God Who is for ever against the oppressor. The terms are fierce and terrible, but not more so than is the wrath and stroke of God against such evil men. The effect of the Divine judgment is to be the rejoicing of the righteous, the destruction of the wicked, and His vindication among men. It is a sickly sentimentality and a wicked weakness that has more sympathy with the corrupt oppressors than with the anger of God.

PSALM 59

God the High Tower of the Oppressed

DELIVER me from mine enemies, O my God:
Set me on high from them that rise up against me.

2 Deliver me from the workers of iniquity,
And save me from the bloodthirsty men.

3 For, lo, they lie in wait for my soul;
The mighty gather themselves together against me;
Not for my transgression, nor for my sin, O Jehovah.

4 They run and prepare themselves without *my* fault:
Awake thou to help me, and behold.

5 Even thou, O Jehovah God of hosts, the God of Israel,
Arise to visit all the nations:
Be not merciful to any wicked transgressors.

6 They return at evening, they howl like a dog,
And go round about the city.

7 Behold, they belch out with their mouth;
Swords are in their lips:
For who, *say they*, doth hear?

8 But thou, O Jehovah, wilt laugh at them;
Thou wilt have all the nations in derision.

9 *Because of* his strength I will give heed unto thee;
For God is my high tower.

10 My God with his lovingkindness will meet me:
God will let me see *my desire* upon mine enemies.

11 Slay them not, lest my people forget:
Scatter them by thy power, and bring them down,
O Lord our shield.

12 *For* the sin of their mouth, *and* the words of their lips,
Let them even be taken in their pride,
And for cursing and lying which they speak.

13 Consume them in wrath, consume them, so that they shall be no more:
And let them know that God ruleth in Jacob,
Unto the ends of the earth.

14 And at evening let them return, let them howl like a dog,
And go round about the city.

15 They shall wander up and down for food,
And tarry all night if they be not satisfied.

16 But I will sing of thy strength;
Yea, I will sing aloud of thy lovingkindness in the morning:
For thou hast been my high tower,
And a refuge in the day of my distress.

17 Unto thee, O my strength, will I sing praises:
For God is my high tower, the God of my mercy.

Again we have a song from the midst of circumstances of peril. The singer is the object of determined, stealthy, and malignant opposition. It is divided into two parts, both ending with the same declaration, "God is my high tower."

The first (vers. 1–9) describes the danger. Without any reason, and with the most relentless determination, his enemies are attempting to encompass his destruction. He announces his determination to wait on his Strength, and declares that God is his high Tower.

The second part is a prayer that God will deal with these foes. Not that they may be slain, but rather that they may be consumed in their own sinning. He then announces his determination to sing praises to his Strength, and the note of the praise is that of prayer. God is his high Tower! There is perhaps no more beautiful description of what God is to His tried people. The phrase suggests at once strength and peace. A tower against which all the might of the foe hurls itself in vain. A high tower so that the soul taking refuge therein is lifted far above the turmoil and the strife, and enabled to view from a vantage ground of perfect safety the violence which is futile, and the victory of God.

PSALM 60

God the Hope of His People

O GOD, thou hast cast us off, thou hast broken us down;
Thou hast been angry; oh restore us again.

2 Thou hast made the land to tremble; thou hast rent it:
Heal the breaches thereof; for it shaketh.

3 Thou hast showed thy people hard things:
Thou hast made us to drink the wine of staggering.

4 Thou hast given a banner to them that fear thee,
That it may be displayed because of the truth.

5 That thy beloved may be delivered,
Save with thy right hand, and answer us.

6 God hath spoken in his holiness: I will exult;
I will divide Shechem, and mete out the valley of Succoth.

7 Gilead is mine, and Manasseh is
  mine;
  Ephraim also is the defence of
  my head;
  Judah is my sceptre.
8 Moab is my washpot;
  Upon Edom will I cast my
  shoe:
  Philistia, shout thou because of
  me.
9 Who will bring me into the
  strong city?

  Who hath led me unto Edom?
10 Hast not thou, O God, cast us
  off?
  And thou goest not forth, O
  God, with our hosts.
11 Give us help against the adversary;
  For vain is the help of man.
12 Through God we shall do valiantly;
  For he it is that will tread down
  our adversaries.

This is a song out of the midst of defeat. It may be divided
into three parts. The first is a recognition of the cause of such
defeat, ending with a prayer (vers. 1–5). The second expresses
the answer of God in the soul of the singer (vers. 6–8). In the
third there is a note of helplessness, a cry of need and a cry of
confidence. In the midst of an evidently disastrous defeat the
singer recognizes the government of God. His appeal for help
is based upon his recognition of the true vocation of the
people. They bear a banner for the display of truth. Note the
"Selah" at this point, suggesting especial attention to this fact.
For the sake of that banner the cry is raised for deliverance.

Then he tells of the answer, but the supreme note is "God
hath spoken in His holiness." All the fine imagery which describes triumph follows that declaration. Victory is only possible in holiness. Defeat is ever the issue of sin. All human aid
is helpless when God has abandoned the people. The song
ends with a cry for help and the declaration of personal
assurance.

PSALM 61

God the Hope of Man

HEAR my cry, O God;
  Attend unto my prayer.
2 From the end of the earth will I
  call unto thee, when my heart
  is overwhelmed:

  Lead me to the rock that is
  higher than I.
3 For thou hast beer a refuge for
  me,
  A strong tower from the enemy.

4 I will dwell in thy tabernacle for ever:
I will take refuge in the covert of thy wings.

6 For thou, O God, hast heard my vows:
Thou hast given *me* the heritage of those that fear thy name.

6 Thou wilt prolong the king's life;
His years shall be as many generations.

7 He shall abide before God for ever:
Oh prepare lovingkindness and truth, that they may preserve him.

8 So will I sing praise unto thy name for ever,
That I may daily perform my vows.

In this song there is the same undertone of confidence as in the last. Here, however, it is rather the voice of one man than that of the people. The reference to the king in verse 6, although in the third person, makes it likely that it was written by David, under the stress of some circumstances of trial, most probably at some period of exile from his city.

His longing is for restoration to God rather than to circumstances. All through there seems to breathe a sense of perfect confidence in God, together with a consciousness of present need, and a longing desire for a return to past experience. There is no uncertainty in his mind concerning God's help of him in days that are gone. The very height of the psalm as a prayer is reached when he cries, "O prepare lovingkindness and truth, that they may preserve him." There has been some difficulty as to the word "prepare." Perhaps it ought not to be there. In that case we have an affirmation rather than a petition, which may read, "lovingkindness and truth shall continually guard him." The one impression made by the reading of the psalm is that of the singer's sense that in the midst of trouble his hope is still in God.

PSALM 62

God the Only Hope of Man

MY soul waiteth in silence for
God only:
From him *cometh* my salvation.
2 He only is my rock and my salvation:
He is my high tower; I shall not
be greatly moved.
3 How long will ye set upon a
man,
That ye may slay *him,* all of
you,
Like a leaning wall, like a tot-
tering fence?
4 They only consult to thrust him
down from his dignity;
They delight in lies;
They bless with their mouth,
but they curse inwardly.
5 My soul, wait thou in silence
for God only;
For my expectation is from him.
6 He only is my rock and my salvation:
He is my high tower; I shall not
be moved.

7 With God is my salvation and
my glory:
The rock of my strength, and
my refuge, is in God.
8 Trust in him at all times, ye
people;
Pour out your heart before him:
God is a refuge for us.
9 Surely men of low degree are
vanity, and men of high degree are a lie:
In the balances they will go up;
They are together lighter than
vanity.
10 Trust not in oppression,
And become not vain in robbery:
If riches increase, set not your
heart *thereon.*
11 God hath spoken once,
Twice have I heard this,
That power belongeth unto God.
12 Also unto thee, O Lord, belongeth lovingkindness;
For thou renderest to every man
according to his work.

In this psalm the principle of the last is yet more emphat-
ically expressed. It opens with the declaration, "My soul
waiteth only *upon* God," and then proceeds in three stanzas
to set forth this fact.

The first opens with the words we have already quoted, and
is an affirmation of confidence made in the presence of enemies. Indeed it is addressed to them, declaring the relation
of defence which God bears to him; and appealing to them
against their malicious onslaught. The sense of his enemies is
with him as is evidenced in his words, "I shall not be greatly
moved."

In the second stanza he addresses first his own soul, and then appeals to the people, most probably those over whom he rules. To himself he repeats what he has said to his enemies, as to the relation of God to him; and this time, with his eye fixed upon God, he reaches a higher level of confidence, and says, "I shall not be moved."

Finally, he puts the false helps upon which men depend into contrast with the only Help of man, Who is God Himself. The false helps are "men of low degree," "men of high degree," "oppression," "robbery," "riches," and the weakness and uselessness of all are declared.

PSALM 63

God the Perfect Hope of Man

O God, thou are my God; earnestly will I seek thee:
My soul thirsteth for thee, my flesh longeth for thee,
In a dry and weary land, where no water is.

2 So have I looked upon thee in the sanctuary,
To see thy power and thy glory.

3 Because thy lovingkindness is better than life,
My lips shall praise thee.

4 So I will bless thee while I live:
I will lift up my hands in thy name.

5 My soul shall be satisfied as with marrow and fatness;
And my mouth shall praise thee with joyful lips;

6 When I remember thee upon my bed,

And meditate on thee in the night-watches.

7 For thou hast been my help,
And in the shadow of thy wings will I rejoice.

8 My soul followeth hard after thee:
Thy right hand upholdeth me.

9 But those that seek my soul, to destroy it,
Shall go into the lower parts of the earth.

10 They shall be given over to the power of the sword:
They shall be a portion for foxes.

11 But the king shall rejoice in God:
Every one that sweareth by him shall glory;
For the mouth of them that speak lies shall be stopped.

Here the conviction which has been the inspiration of the two previous psalms reaches a consummation of expression.

The song can hardly be divided, for it runs on in a continuous outpouring of praise. The surrounding circumstances are still those of difficulty and sadness, and yet the statement of these things at the beginning and at the close constitutes a background, throwing up into clearer relief the sure confidence of the soul in God.

Beginning with the affirmation, "O God, Thou art my God," the singer declares his thirst in a dry land for the same visions of God which in former days he had seen in the sanctuary. Immediately the song ascends to higher levels. The past is the inspiration of the present. Over all diverse and difficult circumstances it rises in triumph because it knows God. Happy indeed is the soul who is able to make sorrow the occasion of a song, and darkness the opportunity for shining. Two things are necessary for such triumph as this. These are indicated in the opening words of the psalm. First, there must be the consciousness of personal relationship, "O God, Thou art my God"; and secondly, there must be earnest seeking after God, "Early will I seek Thee." Relationship must be established. Fellowship must be cultivated.

PSALM 64

God the Defence of the Persecuted

HEAR my voice, O God, in my
complaint:
Preserve my life from fear of
the enemy.
2 Hide me from the secret counsel
of evil-doers,
From the tumult of the workers
of iniquity;
3 Who have whet their tongue
like a sword,
And have aimed their arrows,
even bitter words,

4 That they may shoot in secret
places at the perfect:
Suddenly do they shoot at
him, and fear not.
5 They encourage themselves in
an evil purpose;
They commune of laying snares
privily;
They say, Who will see them?
6 They search out iniquities;
We have accomplished, *say they,*
a diligent search:

And the inward thought and the heart of every one is deep.

7 But God will shoot at them;
With an arrow suddenly shall they be wounded.

8 So they shall be made to stumble, their own tongue being against them:
All that see them shall wag the head.

9 And all men shall fear;
And they shall declare the work of God,
And shall wisely consider of his doing.

10 The righteous shall be glad in Jehovah, and shall take refuge in him;
And all the upright in heart shall glory.

This is a cry of distress, and yet not of despair. The singer is beset by wily enemies who plan and plot against him with malicious and persistent determination. In great detail he describes their method. It is that of secret counsel and studied cruelty. They have one object, that of harming the righteous by shooting at him from secret places. They strengthen themselves by declaring that none can see them. This is his distress. The warfare is unequal. His foes are not in the open but under cover.

At verse 7 we have the beginning of his account of the reason why his distress is not despair. Over against their evil determination to shoot at the righteous is the fact that God shall shoot at them. That is the security of the trusting soul. In New Testament times the truth is expressed differently, but the principle abides, "If God be for us, who can be against us?" The practical application of this to the righteous is that there is no need for them to attempt to take vengeance on their enemies. Their one care is to trust in God. Such trust will issue in gladness, and the inevitable vindication of their faith. In order to this we ever need to pray as the psalmist does, not so much for deliverance from enemies as for deliverance from fear of them.

PSALM 65

God the God of Harvest

PRAISE waiteth for thee, O
God, in Zion;
And unto thee shall the vow be
performed.
2 O thou that hearest prayer,
Unto thee shall all flesh come.
3 Iniquities prevail against me:
As for our transgressions, thou
wilt forgive them.
4 Blessed is the man whom thou
choosest, and causest to approach *unto thee,*
That he may dwell in thy
courts:
We shall be satisfied with the
goodness of thy house,
Thy holy temple.
5 By terrible things thou wilt answer us in righteousness,
O God of our salvation,
Thou that art the confidence of
all the ends of the earth,
And of them that are afar off
upon the sea:
6 Who by his strength setteth fast
the mountains,
Being girded about with might;
7 Who stilleth the roaring of the
seas,
The roaring of their waves,
And the tumult of the peoples.
8 They also that dwell in the ut-

termost parts are afraid at
thy tokens:
Thou makest the outgoings of
the morning and evening to
rejoice.
9 Thou visitest the earth, and
waterest it,
Thou greatly enrichest it;
The river of God is full of
water:
Thou providest them grain,
when thou hast so prepared
the earth.
10 Thou waterest its furrows abundantly;
Thou settlest the ridges thereof:
Thou makest it soft with showers;
Thou blessest the springing
thereof.
11 Thou crownest the year with
thy goodness;
And thy paths drop fatness.
12 They drop upon the pastures of
the wilderness;
And the hills are girded with
joy.
13 The pastures are clothed with
flocks;
The valleys also are covered
over with grain;
They shout for joy, they also
sing.

This is a great song of worship. The occasion would seem to
be that of a harvest festival. The people are assembled for
praise (vers. 1–4). God's particular goodness in the harvest is
celebrated (vers. 5–8).

With reference to the assembling of the people the marginal

reading is full of beauty. "There shall be silence before Thee and praise." The same thought is present, though obscure in the text, "Praise *waiteth* for Thee." It is the true attitude of worship. Reverent silence preparing for, and issuing in, adoring praise. There is always a difficulty in the way of worship, "Iniquities prevail." Yet these are not final hindrances, for God purges away transgressions. The way into the silence of praise is described. God chooses, and causes to approach. The man so conducted dwells in the courts of God, and is satisfied with the goodness of His house.

That is a fine description of worship in its expression, its method, its experience. The greatness of the power of God is the subject of the worshipper's song, and that power is at the disposal of those who worship. Then, finally, is sung the song of harvest. This is beautiful as a description of God's part therein. Man's toil is not described. It is taken for granted, and is his prayer. God's answer is that of co-operation by which harvest comes in joy and singing.

PSALM 66

God the Object of Worship

MAKE a joyful noise unto God,
all the earth:

2 Sing forth the glory of his
name:
Make his praise glorious.

3 Say unto God, How terrible are
thy works!
Through the greatness of thy
power shall thine enemies submit themselves unto thee.

4 All the earth shall worship thee,
And shall sing unto thee;
They shall sing to thy name,

5 Come, and see the works of
God;

He is terrible in his doing toward the children of men.

6 He turned the sea into dry land;
They went through the river on
foot:
There did we rejoice in him.

7 He ruleth by his might for ever;
His eyes observe the nations:
Let not the rebellious exalt
themselves.

8 Oh bless our God, ye peoples,
And make the voice of his praise
to be heard;

9 Who holdeth our soul in life,
And suffereth not our feet to be
moved.

10 For thou, O God, hast proved us:
Thou hast tried us, as silver is tried.

11 Thou broughtest us into the net;
Thou layedst a sore burden upon our loins.

12 Thou didst cause men to ride over our heads;
We went through fire and through water;
But thou broughtest us out into a wealthy place.

13 I will come into thy house with burnt-offerings;
I will pay thee my vows,

14 Which my lips uttered,
And my mouth spake, when I was in distress.

15 I will offer unto thee burnt-offerings of fatlings,
With the incense of rams;
I will offer bullocks with goats.

16 Come, and hear, all ye that fear God,
And I will declare what he hath done for my soul.

17 I cried unto him with my mouth,
And he was extolled with my tongue.

18 If I regard iniquity in my heart,
The Lord will not hear:

19 But verily God hath heard;
He hath attended to the voice of my prayer.

20 Blessed be God,
Who hath not turned away my prayer,
Nor his lovingkindness from me.

This is one of the most beautiful of the songs of worship. It is divided into two parts by a change from the use of the plural pronoun (vers. 1–12) to the use of the singular (vers. 13–20).

In the first part appeal is made to all the earth to worship God because of what He has shown Himself to be on behalf of His people. This is a recognition of the true function of the people of God, that of revealing God to the outside nations in such a way as to constrain them to worship.

In the second half the worship becomes individual and personal, and yet the same purpose is manifest in the appeal to others to hear. In this case those called upon to hear are such as fear God. Thus the testimony of the individual is for the strengthening of the faith of God's own, in order that they may be more perfectly equipped for their testimony to those without.

In the story of God's dealing with His people there is a recognition of His government through all the differing experiences of their history. By deliverance and by distress, by triumph and trial, He has conducted them to a wealthy place. Very full of comfort is the individual realization, following as it does this larger experience. In the economy of God the lonely man is not lost in the multitude, and the solo of his praise is as precious as is the chorus of their worship.

PSALM 67

God the Governor of the Nations

GOD be merciful unto us, and bless us,
And cause his face to shine upon us;
2 That thy way may be known upon earth,
Thy salvation among all nations.
3 Let the peoples praise thee, O God;
Let all the peoples praise thee.
4 Oh let the nations be glad and sing for joy;
For thou wilt judge the peoples with equity,
And govern the nations upon earth.
5 Let the peoples praise thee, O God;
Let all the peoples praise thee.
6 The earth hath yielded its increase:
God, even our own God, will bless us.
7 God will bless us;
And all the ends of the earth shall fear him.

In this psalm there is a fine merging of prayer and praise. Its dominant note is that of prayer. It is prayer, moreover, on the highest level. It asks for personal blessing, but its deepest passion is that all peoples may be blessed, and led to praise. If it was a harvest festival song, as the first part of verse 6 would indicate, then the local occasion is graciously submerged in a far wider outlook. The singer, even more remarkably than in the preceding psalm, recognizes the true function of the holy nation. The word "that" with which verse 2 opens, is of the utmost importance—that God's "way may be known upon earth," and His "saving health among all nations," is the ultimate purpose of His heart, and the mission of His people.

In order to this the singer prays for blessing *on* and *through* them; *on* them, "God be merciful unto us and bless us"; *through* them, "Cause His face to shine with us." The central desire of the prayer is uttered at its centre (vers. 3–5); and the method is again indicated at its close (vers. 6, 7). This is not asking in order to consume gifts upon personal lusts. It is rather a passion which is self-emptied and therefore pure. Such praying hastens the Kingdom.

PSALM 68

God the Strength of His People

LET God arise, let his enemies be scattered;
Let them also that hate him flee before him.

2 As smoke is driven away, so drive them away:
As wax melteth before the fire,
So let the wicked perish at the presence of God.

3 But let the righteous be glad; let them exult before God:
Yea, let them rejoice with gladness.

4 Sing unto God, sing praises to his name:
Cast up a highway for him that rideth through the deserts;
His name is Jehovah, and exult ye before him.

5 A father of the fatherless, and a judge of the widows,
Is God in his holy habitation.

6 God setteth the solitary in families:
He bringeth out the prisoners into prosperity;
But the rebellious dwell in a parched land.

7 O God, when thou wentest forth before thy people,
When thou didst march through the wilderness;

8 The earth trembled,
The heavens also dropped *rain* at the presence of God:
Yon Sinai *trembled* at the presence of God, the God of Israel.

9 Thou, O God, didst send a plentiful rain,
Thou didst confirm thine inheritance, when it was weary.

10 Thy congregation dwelt therein:
Thou, O God, didst prepare of thy goodness for the poor.

11 The Lord giveth the word:
The women that publish the tidings are a great host.

12 Kings of armies flee, they flee;
And she that tarrieth at home divideth the spoil.

13 When ye lie among the sheepfolds,
It is as the wings of a dove covered with silver,

And her pinions with yellow gold.

14 When the Almighty scattered kings therein,
It was as when it snoweth in Zalmon.

15 A mountain of God is the mountain of Bashan;
A high mountain is the mountain of Bashan.

16 Why look ye askance, ye high mountains,
At the mountain which God hath desired for his abode?
Yea, Jehovah will dwell in it for ever.

17 The chariots of God are twenty thousand, even thousands upon thousands:
The Lord is among them, as in Sinai, in the sanctuary.

18 Thou hast ascended on high, thou hast led away captives;
Thou hast received gifts among men,
Yea, among the rebellious also, that Jehovah God might dwell with them.

19 Blessed be the Lord, who daily beareth our burden,
Even the God who is our salvation.

20 God is unto us a God of deliverances;
And unto Jehovah the Lord belongeth escape from death.

21 But God will smite through the head of his enemies,
The hairy scalp of such a one as goeth on still in his guiltiness.

22 The Lord said, I will bring again from Bashan,

I will bring them again from the depths of the sea;

23 That thou mayest crush them, dipping thy foot in blood,
That the tongue of thy dogs may have its portion from thine enemies.

24 They have seen thy goings, O God,
Even the goings of my God, my King, into the sanctuary.

25 The singers went before, the minstrels followed after,
In the midst of the damsels, playing with timbrels.

26 Bless ye God in the congregations,
Even the Lord, ye that are of the fountain of Israel.

27 There is little Benjamin their ruler,
The princes of Judah and their council,
The princes of Zebulun, the princes of Naphtali.

28 Thy God hath commanded thy strength:
Strengthen, O God, that which thou hast wrought for us.

29 Because of thy temple at Jerusalem
Kings shall bring presents unto thee.

30 Rebuke the wild beast of the reeds,
The multitude of the bulls, with the calves of the peoples,
Trampling under foot the pieces of silver:
He hath scattered the peoples that delight in war.

31 Princes shall come out of Egypt;
Ethiopia shall haste to stretch out her hands unto God.

32 Sing unto God, ye kingdoms of
    the earth;
    Oh sing praises unto the Lord;
33 To him that rideth upon the
    heaven of heavens, which are
    of old;
    Lo, he uttereth his voice, a
    mighty voice.
34 Ascribe ye strength unto God:

His excellency is over Israel,
And his strength is in the skies.
35 O God, *thou art* terrible out of
    thy holy places:
    The God of Israel, he giveth
    strength and power unto *his*
    people.
Blessed be God.

If appeal may be made to the consciousness of the saints,
there is no doubt that this is one of the grandest of the psalms.
There is a sweep and majesty about it which takes hold upon
heart and mind and will. It sings the praise of the God of
deliverances. It opens with a song of pure praise (vers. 1–6).
This is then justified by a review of His past dealings with
His people (vers. 7–18). Finally, it affirms the present activity
of God, and declares confidence in His future succour (vers.
19–35).

In the first six verses there is a wonderful description of
God in His majesty and meekness, in His might and mercy.
The contrasts are remarkable. He scatters His enemies. He
is a Father of the fatherless. The wicked perish at His presence. He sets the solitary in families. There is no sense of
contradiction. Rather the unity of the apparently dissimilar
things is at once felt. His righteousness is the strength of His
mercy. His might is the ability of His help. The righteous
need have no fear of His strength, but rather rejoice in it,
trust in it, and co-operate with it by casting up a highway for
Him.

The next section of the psalm (vers. 7–18) is a description
of God's dealing with His people Israel from their deliverance
from Egypt to their establishment in the land, and the found-
ing of their city. The might of His going forth is referred to,
and the effect it produced is described. The giving of the constitution and law at Sinai is remembered.

Then His preparation of the land for His people and their settlement therein is spoken of, together with the song of the women who thus have found their homes. And still the song moves on to describe how God scattered kings before His people, and moved right onward until in majesty He had entered and possessed the hill of His city, the centre of His earthly government. It is a fine setting of history in its relation to the activity of God. It is this view of God enthroned and governing which gives courage to the heart, and inspires the songs of victory. The same twofold fact of the Divine method is apparent here as in the first part of the psalm. His might causes kings to flee, but the issue is the comfort and sustenance of the men. He goes forth in all the resistless majesty of His great hosts, referred to as chariots numbering thousands upon thousands, and the result is captivity of captivity, and the provision of gifts even among the rebellious.

Yet the song does not wholly depend upon past history for its strength. The last section (vers. 19–35) deals with the present activity of God. He is a present God, and in the days of the singer gives evidence of His power and pity. There is a great force in the emphasis on present consciousness in the opening of the third part of the psalm:—

"Blessed be the Lord, Who daily beareth our burden,
Even the God Who is our salvation, Selah.
God is unto us a God of deliverances."

The Selah calls a halt in the presence of present facts, and prepares for the confident affirmation which immediately succeeds.

This opens the way for a prophecy of coming deliverance uttered as an anthem of faith. The appeal of the song to the people of God in all ages in their hours of difficulty is easily understood. It expresses the one and only consciousness which is equal to making a day of darkness and difficulty the occasion of illumination and song. A history seen in the light of

God's throne and an experience of His present succour combine to flash a light upon the darkest day and the most difficult circumstances, which will compel confidence and create thanksgiving.

PSALM 69

God the Succourer of the Sorrowful

SAVE me, O God;
For the waters are come in unto my soul.

2 I sink in deep mire, where there is no standing:
I am come into deep waters, where the floods overflow me.

3 I am weary with my crying; my throat is dried:
Mine eyes fail while I wait for my God.

4 They that hate me without a cause are more than the hairs of my head:
They that would cut me off, being mine enemies wrongfully, are mighty:
That which I took not away I have to restore.

5 O God, thou knowest my foolishness;
And my sins are not hid from thee.

6 Let not them that wait for thee be put to shame through me, O Lord Jehovah of hosts:
Let not those that seek thee be brought to dishonor through me, O God of Israel.

7 Because for thy sake I have borne reproach;
Shame hath covered my face.

8 I am become a stranger unto my brethren,
And an alien unto my mother's children.

9 For the zeal of thy house hath eaten me up;
And the reproaches of them that reproach thee are fallen upon me.

10 When I wept, *and chastened* my soul with fasting,
That was to my reproach.

11 When I made sackcloth my clothing,
I became a byword unto them.

12 They that sit in the gate talk of me;
And *I am* the song of the drunkards.

13 But as for me, my prayer is unto thee, O Jehovah, in an acceptable time:
O God, in the abundance of thy lovingkindness,
Answer me in the truth of thy salvation.

14 Deliver me out of the mire, and let me not sink:
Let me be delivered from them that hate me, and out of the deep waters.

15 Let not the waterflood overwhelm me,
Neither let the deep swallow me up;
And let not the pit shut its mouth upon me.

16 Answer me, O Jehovah; for thy
lovingkindness is good:
According to the multitude of
thy tender mercies turn thou
unto me.
17 And hide not thy face from thy
servant;
For I am in distress; answer me
speedily.
18 Draw nigh unto my soul, and
redeem it:
Ransom me because of mine
enemies.
19 Thou knowest my reproach, and
my shame, and my dishonor:
Mine adversaries are all before
thee.
20 Reproach hath broken my
heart; and I am full of heaviness:
And I looked for some to take
pity, but there was none;
And for comforters, but I found
none.
21 They gave me also gall for my
food;
And in my thirst they gave me
vinegar to drink.
22 Let their table before them become a snare;
And when they are in peace, *let
it become* a trap.
23 Let their eyes be darkened, so
that they cannot see;
And make their loins continually
to shake.
24 Pour out thine indignation upon
them,
And let the fierceness of thine
anger overtake them.
25 Let their habitation be desolate;
Let none dwell in their tents.

26 For they persecute him whom
thou hast smitten;
And they tell of the sorrow of
those whom thou hast
wounded.
27 Add iniquity unto their iniquity;
And let them not come into thy
righteousness.
28 Let them be blotted out of the
book of life,
And not be written with the
righteous.
29 But I am poor and sorrowful:
Let thy salvation, O God, set
me up on high.
30 I will praise the name of God
with a song,
And will magnify him with
thanksgiving.
31 And it will please Jehovah better than an ox,
Or a bullock that hath horns
and hoofs.
32 The meek have seen it, and are
glad:
Ye that seek after God, let your
heart live.
33 For Jehovah heareth the needy,
And despiseth not his prisoners.
34 Let heaven and earth praise
him,
The seas, and everything that
moveth therein.
35 For God will save Zion, and
build the cities of Judah;
And they shall abide there, and
have it in possession.
36 The seed also of his servants
shall inherit it;
And they that love his name
shall dwell therein.

There is perhaps no psalm in the whole psalter in which the sense of sorrow is profounder or more intense. The soul of the singer pours itself out in unrestrained abandonment to the overwhelming and terrible grief which consumes it. The first half is occupied wholly with a statement of the terrible consciousness. There is first a cry of distress, piercing and passionate (vers. 1–6). The circumstances described are those of helpless whelming in waters and in mire. Yet the chief agony is that God seems to be neglectful of the cry, and a fear fills the heart lest others should be harmed through what they see of the hopelessness and helplessness of his suffering.

In the next movement the singer declares that this suffering has come in the path of loyalty to God (vers. 7–12). Whatever the circumstances giving rise to the song it is evident that the singer had been brought into them because of his zeal for God. Following this declaration the cry for succour is repeated with new emphasis and passion (vers. 13–18). This part of the psalm affords a revelation of the condition into which the men of faith are sometimes brought. Yet it contains suggestion of a sorrow profounder than any experienced save by One. Nothing can be conceived more overwhelming than the strange and inexplicable suffering resulting from loyalty to God and zeal for His honour. Undeserved reproach is the most stupendous grief possible to the sensitive soul. Yet even throughout this whole movement expressive of such intense grief there is an undertone of confidence in God.

In the presence of that God Whose lovingkindness the singer has declared to be good, he continues to pour out his complaint. He knows that God is acquainted with it, and therefore with the greater freedom describes it. In detail he speaks of the brutality of his enemies, and wails over his poverty of comforters and helps. The only reply that men made to his appeal to them for help was to give him such things as would aggravate his suffering.

Suddenly the song becomes a passionate cry for vengeance. It is a false view of things which criticizes this cry as being unworthy of a man familiar with God. It is really the expression of a righteous desire for judgment against essential wrong. The method which he has described as being used by his adversaries, violated the essential and fundamental order of the Divine Kingdom. For the sake of that order and the vindication of God there must be a place for retribution and vengeance. The passion passes, and a prayer follows which merges into praise, and culminates in a great affirmation of confidence in God.

The whole psalm expresses depths which few of us can fathom. It can only be appreciated as an unveiling of sorrow and suffering at its very profoundest depths, and therefore is rightly considered to be prophetic and Messianic. As far as we can enter into its teaching it suggests to us that a cry to God in sorrow which is honest in its expression invariably merges in the economy of His grace into a song of praise.

PSALM 70

God the Hope of the Despairing

*M*AKE haste, O God, to deliver me;
Make haste to help me, O Jehovah.

2 Let them be put to shame and confounded
That seek after my soul:
Let them be turned backward and brought to dishonor
That delight in my hurt.

3 Let them be turned back by reason of their shame
That say, Aha, aha.

4 Let all those that seek thee rejoice and be glad in thee;
And let such as love thy salvation say continually,
Let God be magnified.

5 But I am poor and needy;
Make haste unto me, O God:
Thou are my help and my deliverer;
O Jehovah, make no tarrying.

This short psalm is a rushing sob of anxious solicitude. There is little of restfulness in it. Enemies are engaged in cruel persecution and mockery. It seems as though the singer felt that the strain was becoming too much for him, and in fear lest he should be overcome he cries aloud for God to hasten to his deliverance. The faith of the singer is evident in that he cries to God, and evidently has no room in his heart for question as to God's ability to keep him. The only question is as to whether help will arrive in time.

It is not the highest type of faith which is revealed, but we are profoundly thankful to find such a song in this great book of religious poetry. Rightly or wrongly, we often come to such places of doubt. No doubt exists either as to God's ability or as to His interest in love for us, but is He not trying us beyond the power of our endurance? He is not, but for moments of terrible tension it seems as though He were. Then here is a psalm for such days or hours. Let us take it and use it, knowing that He would far rather have in our song an expression of an honest questioning than any affectation of a confidence not possessed. Moreover, He would rather have from us such a song than silence.

PSALM 71

God the Confidence of Old Age

IN thee, O Jehovah, do I take refuge:
Let me never be put to shame.
2 Deliver me in thy righteousness, and rescue me:
Bow down thine ear unto me, and save me.
3 Be thou to me a rock of habitation, whereunto I may continually resort:
Thou hast given commandment to save me;
For thou art my rock and my fortress.
4 Rescue me, O my God, out of the hand of the wicked,
Out of the hand of the unrighteous and cruel man.
5 For thou art my hope, O Lord Jehovah:
Thou art my trust from my youth.
6 By thee have I been holden up from the womb;
Thou art he that took me out of my mother's bowels:
My praise shall be continually of thee.
7 I am as a wonder unto many;
But thou art my strong refuge.
8 My mouth shall be filled with thy praise,

And with thy honor all the day.

9 Cast me not off in the time of old age;
Forsake me not when my strength faileth.

10 For mine enemies speak concerning me;
And they that watch for my soul take counsel together,

11 Saying, God hath forsaken him:
Pursue and take him; for there is none to deliver.

12 O God, be not far from me; O my God, make haste to help me.

13 Let them be put to shame *and* consumed that are adversaries to my soul;
Let them be covered with reproach and dishonor that seek my hurt.

14 But I will hope continually,
And will praise thee yet more and more.

15 My mouth shall tell of thy righteousness,
And of thy salvation all the day;
For I know not the numbers *thereof.*

16 I will come with the mighty acts of the Lord Jehovah:
I will make mention of thy righteousness, even of thine only.

17 O God, thou hast taught me from my youth;

And hitherto have I declared thy wondrous works.

18 Yea, even when I am old and grayheaded, O God, forsake me not,
Until I have declared thy strength unto *the next* generation,
Thy might to every one that is to come.

19 Thy righteousness also, O God, is very high;
Thou who hast done great things,
O God, who is like unto thee?

20 Thou, who hast showed us many and sore troubles,
Wilt quicken us again,
And wilt bring us up again from the depths of the earth.

21 Increase thou my greatness,
And turn again and comfort me.

22 I will also praise thee with the psaltery,
Even thy truth, O my God:
Unto thee will I sing praises with the harp,
O thou Holy One of Israel.

23 My lips shall shout for joy when I sing praises unto thee;
And my soul, which thou hast redeemed.

24 My tongue also shall talk of thy righteousness all the day long;
For they are put to shame, for they are confounded, that seek my hurt.

This is pre-eminently a song of the aged, and like old age it is reminiscent. The singer passes from memory to hope, and from experience to praise. No very definite division is possible. Generally speaking, it may be noticed that the first part expresses need, and is principally prayer; while the second half affirms confidence, and is principally praise.

The song opens with a prayer for deliverance (vers. 1–8). This is not so much a cry out of present distress as a prayer that in the event of trouble he may be able to resort to God. The old man is discovered in that the first three verses are almost a direct quotation from a previous psalm (xxxi), perhaps one of his own. His experience of God from birth is his confidence that he will be heard now. This leads the song on in prayer that he may still be helped in age, for he still has adversaries (vers. 9–13). Here again are quotations from earlier psalms which the marginal references will aid the reader in discovering. The singer then rises to higher levels as he tells of his confidence in God, and asks that he may be helped to declare God to the succeeding generation. The psalm is a song of sunset, and it is full of beauty. There are storm clouds on the western sky. Some are spent, and some still threaten; but on all is a light which transfigures them.

PSALM 72

God the King of the King

GIVE the king thy judgments,
O God,
And thy righteousness unto the king's son.

2 He will judge thy people with righteousness,
And thy poor with justice.

3 The mountains shall bring peace to the people,
And the hills, in righteousness.

4 He will judge the poor of the people,
He will save the children of the needy,
And will break in pieces the oppressor.

5 They shall fear thee while the sun endureth,
And so long as the moon, throughout all generations.

6 He will come down like rain upon the mown grass,
As showers that water the earth.

7 In his days shall the righteous flourish,
And abundance of peace, till the moon be no more.

8 He shall have dominion also from sea to sea,
And from the River unto the ends of the earth.

9 They that dwell in the wilderness shall bow before him;
And his enemies shall lick the dust.

10 The kings of Tarshish and of the isles shall render tribute:
The kings of Sheba and Seba shall offer gifts.

11 Yea, all kings shall fall down before him;
All nations shall serve him.

12 For he will deliver the needy when he crieth,
And the poor, that hath no helper.

13 He will have pity on the poor and needy,
And the souls of the needy he will save.

14 He will redeem their soul from oppression and violence;
And precious will their blood be in his sight:

15 And they shall live; and to him shall be given of the gold of Sheba:

And men shall pray for him continually;
They shall bless him all the day long.

16 There shall be abundance of grain in the earth upon the top of the mountains;
The fruit thereof shall shake like Lebanon:
And they of the city shall flourish like grass of the earth.

17 His name shall endure for ever;
His name shall be continued as long as the sun:
And men shall be blessed in him;
All nations shall call him happy.

18 Blessed be Jehovah God, the God of Israel,
Who only doeth wondrous things:

19 And blessed be his glorious name for ever;.
And let the whole earth be filled with his glory.
Amen, and Amen.

This is a great psalm of the Theocracy. Incidentally the whole perfect order is revealed. God high over all, enthroned and in all actively governing. The king, appointed by God and gaining his guidance from Him, so reigning over his own people as to succour the needy, spoil the oppressor, and secure the prosperity of the righteous; and so reigning that the beneficial influence of the kingship and kingdom are felt over all the earth. Submission to him is followed by the deliverance of the poor and helpless, and universal peace and prosperity.

This is the Kingdom for which the world still waits. It is a perfect order which has never yet been recognized and obeyed. This was surely all in the view of Jesus when He taught us to pray for the coming of the Kingdom. The one King has come, and men would not have Him to reign. Therefore, notwithstanding all the best and highest efforts of man without Him, the needy are still oppressed, and peace and prosperity are postponed. The song of this psalm is to us a prophecy of hope. We have seen the King, and we know the perfect Kingdom must come, for God cannot be defeated. The psalm and the second book end with the doxology which we have already considered.

BOOK III.

PSALMS 73–89

BOOK III. PSALMS 73–89

DOXOLOGY

"Blessed be the Lord for evermore. Amen, and Amen." Ps. 89–52.

A. THE TITLE.	B. THE QUALITY.	C. THE QUANTITY.
"Jehovah." The essential Helper. (See first Doxology.)	"Blessed." "Amen, and Amen."	"For evermore."

The Divine Name.

The dominant name in this book is still "God." It occurs once at least in every psalm, and in one as many as 15 times. It is written in the singular (El) 20 times, and in the plural (Elohim) 60 times.

"Jehovah" is found in the book 44 times. It is only absent from two psalms, and occurs in one 10 times.

The Dominant Thought.

In the third book the dominant thought is that of the worship of God under all circumstances. Both names are used throughout, although that of God predominates. While this is so, the final doxology speaks of Jehovah, showing that the thought is that of worship rendered to God because He is the essential Helper.

ANALYSIS

PSALM 73

God the Good of His People

SURELY God is good to Israel,
  Even to such as are pure in
  heart.
2 But as for me, my feet were almost gone;
  My steps had well nigh slipped.
3 For I was envious at the arrogant,
  When I saw the prosperity of
  the wicked.
4 For there are no pangs in their
  death;
  But their strength is firm.
5 They are not in trouble as *other*
  men,
  Neither are they plagued like
  other men.
6 Therefore pride is as a chain
  about their neck;
  Violence covereth them as a
  garment.
7 Their eyes stand out with fatness:
  They have more than heart
  could wish.
8 They scoff, and in wickedness
  utter oppression:
  They speak loftily.
9 They have set their mouth in
  the heavens,
  And their tongue walketh
  through the earth.
10 Therefore his people return
  hither:
  And waters of a full *cup* are
  drained by them.
11 And they say, How doth God
  know?
  And is there knowledge in the
  Most High?
12 Behold, these are the wicked;

And, being alway at ease, they
  increase in riches.
13 Surely in vain have I cleansed
  my heart,
  And washed my hands in inno-
  cency;
14 For all the day long have I been
  plagued,
  And chastened every morning.
15 If I had said, I will speak thus;
  Behold, I had dealt treacherously with the generation of
  my children.
16 When I thought how I might
  know this,
  It was too painful for me;
17 Until I went into the sanctuary
  of God,
  And considered their latter end.
18 Surely thou settest them in
  slippery places:
  Thou castest them down to destruction.
19 How are they become a desolation in a moment!
  They are utterly consumed with
  terrors.
20 As a dream when one awaketh,
  So, O Lord, when thou awakest
  thou wilt despise their image.
21 For my soul was grieved,
  And I was pricked in my heart:
22 So brutish was I, and ignorant;
  I was *as* a beast before thee.
23 Nevertheless I am continually
  with thee:
  Thou hast holden my right
  hand.
24 Thou wilt guide me with thy
  counsel,

And afterward receive me to glory.

25 Whom have I in heaven *but thee?*
And there is none upon earth that I desire besides thee.

26 My flesh and my heart faileth;
But God is the strength of my heart and my portion for ever.

27 For, lo, they that are far from thee shall perish:
Thou hast destroyed all them that play the harlot, *departing* from thee.

28 But it is good for me to draw near unto God:
I have made the Lord Jehovah my refuge,
That I may tell of all thy works.

The marginal reading, "Only good is God to Israel" indicates the real value of this song. Israel has no other good, and needs no other. Yet it is not always easy to realize this, and the psalmist tells how he nearly stumbled in view of the prosperity of the wicked, and how he was restored. The first half describes the perplexing vision of the prosperity of the wicked. The whole psalm was written in the light of the conviction expressed in the last half, but it describes first the things which startled and perplexed the soul. The wicked prosper in life, and death itself seems to have no terror for them. They are satisfied and more than satisfied, and because of these things men deny the knowledge of God, and turn their feet into the way of wickedness, affirming the uselessness of right doing to procure benefits.

This is all very true to human life as we know it. Evil often appears both pleasant and prosperous, and the struggling saint is tempted to think it is hardly worth while. That was the temptation of the singer. His feet were almost gone; his feet had wellnigh slipped. The psalmist then tells the story of how he was delivered. He attempted to unravel the mystery, and find out why men succeeded, and were satisfied without God. It was too painful, that is, too difficult for him. He could not solve the riddle. At last he found the true viewpoint. He went into the sanctuary of God. Then everything changed. He ceased to look at the present only. He saw the end of the wicked.

PSALM 74

God as Silent and Inactive

O GOD, why hast thou cast *us* off for ever?
Why doth thine anger smoke against the sheep of thy pasture?

2 Remember thy congregation, which thou hast gotten of old,
Which thou hast redeemed to be the tribe of thine inheritance;
And mount Zion, wherein thou hast dwelt.

3 Lift up thy feet unto the perpetual ruins,
All the evil that the enemy hath done in the sanctuary.

4 Thine adversaries have roared in the midst of thine assembly;
They have set up their ensigns for signs.

5 They seemed as men that lifted up
Axes upon a thicket of trees.

6 And now all the carved work thereof
They break down with hatchet and hammers.

7 They have set thy sanctuary on fire;
They have profaned the dwelling-place of thy name *by casting it* to the ground.

8 They said in their heart,
Let us make havoc of them altogether:
They have burned up all the synagogues of God in the land.

9 We see not our signs:
There is no more any prophet;

A more spacious outlook, taking in the whole issue of things, corrected all the false seeming of the near vision. Yet the sanctuary was also the place where the nearest things were seen most accurately, because seen in relation to the large things.

Again he remembered and recognized his own wrong done, in misjudging God; but was able to affirm God's presence and care; and out of the consciousness the song of praise is born. There is only one viewpoint to be trusted, and that is the sanctuary of God. From the secret place of the Most High we see things as God sees them. This corrects the finite vision and opinion by the infinite facts. To see the issue of the near is to understand the real meaning of the near, and this is ever to bring to the heart of the trusting a thanksgiving and a song.

Neither is there among us any that knoweth how long.

10 How long, O God, shall the adversary reproach?
Shall the enemy blaspheme thy name for ever?

11 Why drawest thou back thy hand, even thy right hand?
Pluck it out of thy bosom *and* consume *them.*

12 Yet God is my King of old,
Working salvation in the midst of the earth.

13 Thou didst divide the sea by thy strength:
Thou brakest the heads of the sea-monsters in the waters.

14 Thou brakest the heads of leviathan in pieces;
Thou gavest him to be food to the people inhabiting the wilderness.

15 Thou didst cleave fountain and flood:
Thou driedst up mighty rivers.

16 The day is thine, the night also is thine:
Thou hast prepared the light and the sun.

17 Thou hast set all the borders of the earth:

Thou hast made summer and winter.

18 Remember this, that the enemy hath reproached, O Jehovah,
And that a foolish people hath blasphemed thy name.

19 Oh deliver not the soul of thy turtle-dove unto the wild beast:
Forget not the life of thy poor for ever.

20 Have respect unto the covenant;
For the dark places of the earth are full of the habitations of violence.

21 Oh let not the oppressed return ashamed:
Let the poor and needy praise thy name.

22 Arise, O God, plead thine own cause:
Remember how the foolish man reproacheth thee all the day.

23 Forget not the voice of thine adversaries:
The tumult of those that rise up against thee ascendeth continually.

This is a great complaint, but it is a complaint of faith. Hardly a gleam of light is to be found throughout. The singer sits in the midst of national desolation and pours out his soul to God in passionate appeal for His help, and protest against His silence and inactivity. This is not the song of an atheist, but the wail of a believer. He has a past experience of God's power and a present conviction thereof. The signs of that power are in day and night, in summer and winter. The one place from which He seems to be absent is the place of his people's distress.

The ground of the singer's plea is not the distress of these people finally. It is rather that the enemy reproaches the name of Jehovah, and blasphemes it. In that central complaint the name Jehovah, which is ever suggestive of the essential Helper, emerges, and there only, in the psalm. The master consciousness of the moment is that of God the mighty One, but there is that deeper knowledge of Him as the Helper of the needy. Again we are thankful that such a psalm has a place here, for it is so true to much human experience. When the heart is hot and restless, and it seems as though God had forsaken His own, he is a wise man who turns to Him in song, even though the song be only a complaint.

PSALM 75

God Speaking and Active

WE give thanks unto thee, O God;
We give thanks, for thy name is near:
Men tell of thy wondrous works.

2 When I shall find the set time,
I will judge uprightly.

3 The earth and all the inhabitants thereof are dissolved:
I have set up the pillars of it.

4 I said unto the arrogant, Deal not arrogantly;
And to the wicked, Lift not up the horn:

5 Lift not up your horn on high;
Speak not with a stiff neck.

6 For neither from the east, nor from the west,
Nor yet from the south, *cometh* lifting up.

7 But God is the judge:
He putteth down one, and lifteth up another.

8 For in the hand of Jehovah there is a cup, and the wine foameth;
It is full of mixture, and he poureth out of the same:
Surely the dregs thereof, all the wicked of the earth shall drain them, and drink them.

9 But I will declare for ever,
I will sing praises to the God of Jacob.

10 All the horns of the wicked also will I cut off;
But the horns of the righteous shall be lifted up.

If this, and the former psalm were written by different men and at different periods, then the spiritual sense of the editor is most clearly revealed in their juxtaposition in this book. This is a complete and remarkable answer to that.

In form the song is dramatic. It opens with a chorus which is an ascription of praise (ver. 1). This is answered directly by God Himself. He declares that in the set time He judges. All the appearances of the hour may be perplexing, but the heart may know that He knows, and only waits the right moment to act. Chaos may characterize the outlook, but order enwraps it all, for He has set up the pillars (vers. 2, 3).

Then the solo of the confident soul breaks forth, and addressing the wicked, charges them not to be confident, because God is the Judge. He holds in His hand the cup of judgment. Ultimately He abases the wicked, and lifts up the righteous. Therefore the singer's song is ceaseless. In experience, such a song as this always succeeds an honest declaration of perplexity made directly to God by a tried but trusting soul. The prophecy of Habakkuk is another perfect illustration of the fact.

PSALM 76

God the God of Victory

IN Judah is God known:
His name is great in Israel.
2 In Salem also is his tabernacle,
And his dwelling-place in Zion.
3 There he brake the arrows of the bow;
The shield, and the sword, and the battle.
4 Glorious art thou *and* excellent,
From the mountains of prey.
5 The stouthearted are made a spoil,
They have slept their sleep;
And none of the men of might have found their hands.
6 At thy rebuke, O God of Jacob,

Both chariot and horse are cast into a dead sleep.
7 Thou, even thou, art to be feared;
And who may stand in thy sight when once thou art angry?
8 Thou didst cause sentence to be heard from heaven;
The earth feared, and was still,
9 When God arose to judgment,
To save all the meek of the earth.
10 Surely the wrath of man shall praise thee:
The residue of wrath shalt thou gird upon thee.

11 Vow and pay unto Jehovah
   your God:
   Let all that are round about
   him bring presents unto him
   that ought to be feared.

12 He will cut off the spirit of
   princes:
   He is terrible to the kings of
   the earth.

The singer celebrates a great victory, recognizing it as the
work of God. The song has three movements. In the first
God is seen as the defence of the people (vers. 1–3). In the
second His victory over their enemies is declared (vers. 4–9).
In the third the truth is summarized, and appeal is made to
His people and the surrounding nations as to their proper
attitude toward Him (vers. 10–12). The national life gathers
around Him. He is known by the nation; His dwelling place
is in their city. The attack made upon them has been broken
by the One Who dwells in the midst of them.

The issue of His judgment is manifest in the blotting out of
the enemy. They have ceased to be, having been put to the
sleep of death. God's judgments are purposeful, He arose to
save the meek, and they are resistless; the enemies are no
more. So perfect is His government that by judgment He
compels evil to serve His purpose, making the wrath of men
to praise Him.

To such a God there should be allegiance sworn and rendered by His people, and the surrounding peoples should
submit with gifts. While the weapons of our warfare are
spiritual, God is the same in might, and while He is in the
midst, our defence is sure. No weapon formed against the
trusting people can prosper.

PSALM 77

God the Healer of Sorrows

I WILL cry unto God with my
   voice,
   Even unto God with my voice;
   and he will give ear unto me.

2 In the day of my trouble I
   sought the Lord:
   My hand was stretched out in
   the night, and slacked not;

My soul refused to be comforted.

3 I remember God, and am disquieted:
I complain, and my spirit is overwhelmed.

4 Thou holdest mine eyes watching:
I am so troubled that I cannot speak.

5 I have considered the days of old,
The years of ancient times.

6 I call to remembrance my song in the night:
I commune with mine own heart;
And my spirit maketh diligent search.

7 Will the Lord cast off for ever?
And will he be favorable no more?

8 Is his lovingkindness clean gone for ever?
Doth his promise fail for evermore?

9 Hath God forgotten to be gracious?
Hath he in anger shut up his tender mercies?

10 And I said, This is my infirmity;
But I *will remember* the years of the right hand of the Most High.

11 I will make mention of the deeds of Jehovah;

For I will remember thy wonders of old.

12 I will meditate also upon all thy work,
And muse on thy doings.

13 Thy way, O God, is in the sanctuary:
Who is a great god like unto God?

14 Thou art the God that doest wonders:
Thou hast made known thy strength among the peoples.

15 Thou hast with thine arm redeemed thy people,
The sons of Jacob and Joseph.

16 The waters saw thee, O God;
The waters saw thee, they were afraid:
The depths also trembled.

17 The clouds poured out water;
The skies sent out a sound:
Thine arrows also went abroad.

18 The voice of thy thunder was in the whirlwind;
The lightnings lightened the world:
The earth trembled and shook.

19 Thy way was in the sea,
And thy paths in the great waters,
And thy footsteps were not known.

20 Thou leddest thy people like a flock,
By the hand of Moses and Aaron.

This is a song of the healing of sorrow. It opens with the declaration of determination to cry to God, and then proceeds to explain the reason of this determination. Verse 10 is the pivot upon which the whole psalm turns, from a description of an experience of darkness and sorrow, to one of gladness and praise.

The first part tells the story of sorrow overwhelming the soul. The second gives a song which is the outcome of a vision which has robbed sorrow of its sting. In the first part, a great infirmity overshadows the sky, and there is no song. In the second, a great song pours itself out, and sorrow is forgotten. The difference is that between a man brooding over trouble, and a man seeing high above it the enthroned God. In the first half, self is predominant. In the second, God is seen in His glory. A very simple method with the psalm makes this perfectly clear. In verses 1 to 9 there are twenty-two occurrences of the personal pronoun in the first person, and eleven references to God by name, title, and pronoun. In the second there are only three personal references and four and twenty mentions of God. The message of the psalm is that to brood upon sorrow is to be broken and disheartened, while to see God is to sing on the darkest day. Once come to know that our years are of His right hand, and there is light everywhere, and the song ascends.

PSALM 78

God the God of Patience

GIVE ear, O my people, to my law:
Incline your ears to the words of my mouth.
2 I will open my mouth in a parable;
I will utter dark sayings of old,
3 Which we have heard and known,
And our fathers have told us.
4 We will not hide them from their children,
Telling to the generation to come the praises of Jehovah,
And his strength, and his wondrous works that he hath done.
5 For he established a testimony in Jacob,
And appointed a law in Israel,
Which he commanded our fathers,
That they should make them known to their children;
6 That the generation to come might know *them*, even the children that should be born;

Who should arise and tell *them*
  to their children,
7 That they might set their hope
  in God,
  And not forget the works of
  God,
  But keep his commandments,
8 And might not be as their fathers,
  A stubborn and rebellious generation,
  A generation that set not their
  heart aright,
  And whose spirit was not sted-
  fast with God.
9 The children of Ephraim, being
  armed and carrying bows,
  Turned back in the day of battle.
10 They kept not the covenant of
  God,
  And refused to walk in his law;
11 And they forgat his doings,
  And his wondrous works that he
  had showed them.
12 Marvellous things did he in the
  sight of their fathers,
  In the land of Egypt, in the
  field of Zoan.
13 He clave the sea, and caused
  them to pass through;
  And he made the waters to
  stand as a heap.
14 In the day-time also he led them
  with a cloud,
  And all the night with a light of
  fire.
15 He clave rocks in the wilderness,
  And gave them drink abundantly as out of the depths.
16 He brought streams also out of
  the rock,
  And caused waters to run down
  like rivers.

17 Yet went they on still to sin
  against him,
  To rebel against the Most High
  in the desert.
18 And they tempted God in their
  heart
  By asking food according to
  their desire.
19 Yea, they spake against God;
  They said, Can God prepare a
  table in the wilderness?
20 Behold, he smote the rock, so
  that waters gushed out,
  And streams overflowed;
  Can he give bread also?
  Will he provide flesh for his
  people?
21 Therefore Jehovah heard, and
  was wroth;
  And a fire was kindled against
  Jacob,
  And anger also went up against
  Israel;
22 Because they believed not in
  God,
  And trusted not in his salvation.
23 Yet he commanded the skies
  above,
  And opened the doors of
  heaven;
24 And he rained down manna
  upon them to eat,
  And gave them food from
  heaven.
25 Man did eat the bread of the
  mighty:
  He sent them food to the full.
26 He caused the east wind to blow
  in the heavens;
  And by his power he guided the
  south wind.
27 He rained flesh also upon them
  as the dust,
  And winged birds as the sand of
  the seas:

28 And he let it fall in the midst of
    their camp,
  Round about their habitations.
29 So they did eat, and were well
    filled;
  And he gave them their own de-
    sire.
30 They were not estranged from
    that which they desired,
  Their food was yet in their
    mouths,
31 When the anger of God went up
    against them,
  And slew of the fattest of them,
  And smote down the young men
    of Israel.
32 For all this they sinned still,
  And believed not in his won-
    drous works.
33 Therefore their days did he con-
    sume in vanity,
  And their years in terror.
34 When he slew them, then they
    inquired after him;
  And they returned and sought
    God earnestly.
35 And they remembered that God
    was their rock,
  And the Most High God their
    redeemer.
36 But they flattered him with
    their mouth,
  And lied unto him with their
    tongue.
37 For their heart was not right
    with him,
  Neither were they faithful in his
    covenant.
38 But he, being merciful, forgave
    their iniquity, and destroyed
    them not:
  Yea, many a time turned he his
    anger away,
  And did not stir up all his
    wrath.

39 And he remembered that they
    were but flesh,
  A wind that passeth away, and
    cometh not again.
40 How oft did they rebel against
    him in the wilderness,
  And grieve him in the desert!
41 And they turned again and
    tempted God,
  And provoked the Holy One of
    Israel.
42 They remembered not his hand,
  Nor the day when he redeemed
    them from the adversary;
43 How he set his signs in Egypt,
  And his wonders in the field of
    Zoan,
44 And turned their rivers into
    blood,
  And their streams, so that they
    could not drink.
45 He sent among them swarms of
    flies, which devoured them;
  And frogs, which destroyed
    them.
46 He gave also their increase unto
    the caterpillar,
  And their labor unto the locust.
47 He destroyed their vines with
    hail,
  And their sycomore-trees with
    frost.
48 He gave over their cattle also
    to the hail,
  And their flocks to hot thunder-
    bolts.
49 He cast upon them the fierce-
    ness of his anger,
  Wrath, and indignation, and
    trouble,
  A band of angels of evil.
50 He made a path for his anger;
  He spared not their soul from
    death,

But gave their life over to the pestilence,

51 And smote all the first-born in Egypt,
The chief of their strength in the tents of Ham.

52 But he led forth his own people like sheep,
And guided them in the wilderness like a flock.

53 And he led them safely, so that they feared not;
But the sea overwhelmed their enemies.

54 And he brought them to the border of his sanctuary,
To this mountain, which his right hand had gotten.

55 He drove out the nations also before them,
And allotted them for an inheritance by line,
And made the tribes of Israel to dwell in their tents.

56 Yet they tempted and rebelled against the Most High God,
And kept not his testimonies;

57 But turned back, and dealt treacherously like their fathers:
They were turned aside like a deceitful bow.

58 For they provoked him to anger with their high places,
And moved him to jealousy with their graven images.

59 When God heard *this*, he was wroth,
And greatly abhorred Israel;

60 So that he forsook the tabernacle of Shiloh,
The tent which he placed among men;

61 And delivered his strength into captivity,

And his glory into the adversary's hand.

62 He gave his people over also unto the sword,
And was wroth with his inheritance.

63 Fire devoured their young men;
And their virgins had no marriage-song.

64 Their priests fell by the sword;
And their widows made no lamentation.

65 Then the Lord awaked as one out of sleep,
Like a mighty man that shouteth by reason of wine.

66 And he smote his adversaries backward:
He put them to a perpetual reproach.

67 Moreover he refused the tent of Joseph,
And chose not the tribe of Ephraim,

68 But chose the tribe of Judah,
The mount Zion which he loved.

69 And he built his sanctuary like the heights,
Like the earth which he hath established for ever.

70 He chose David also his servant,
And took him from the sheepfolds:

71 From following the ewes that have their young he brought him,
To be the shepherd of Jacob his people, and Israel his inheritance.

72 So he was their shepherd according to the integrity of his heart,
And guided them by the skilfulness of his hands.

This title indicates the supreme quantity of this psalm. Throughout all its measures, over against the repeated failure of His people, the persistent patience of God is set forth in bold relief. The purpose of the psalm however, is that of warning the people of God against unfaithfulness, by the story of past failure.

The first eight verses declare the purpose of the singer, after announcing his determination. The things of the past are to be recounted for the sake of the children. Notice very carefully the statement of the latter part of this introduction. It declares the institution in Israel of a method for dealing with the children. The words "testimony" and "law" (ver. 5), do not here refer to the Mosaic economy, but to a specific arrangement for the transmission of that law. This arrangement was that of instructing the children. The value of such instruction was that the new generation should be safeguarded in its hope, its memory, its conduct. There is nothing in which the Christian family life to-day is in graver peril than in its neglect on the part of the parents to give children systematic instruction in the things of faith. The stories of God's dealings in the past, and of the principles of relationship to Him, are at once the most wonderful and most valuable we can tell our children.

The singer then proceeded with the work of "telling . . . the praises of the Lord." Verses 9–31 recites the disloyalty of the people in spite of the goodness of God, and thus explains the reason of the Divine chastisement. The prophetic writings (especially Hosea) show that Ephraim became the leader in the rebellion and disloyalty which cursed the nation; and so, figuratively, and as standing for the rest, Ephraim is here addressed.

The description is figurative. The people armed and equipped, were guilty of cowardice. They turned back because they forgot God. Then follows a poetic description of the way in which God delivered them from Egypt, and led them in the wilderness. These facts of the guidance of God make their cowardice sinful. This goodness is further traced in His dealing with them step by step. The reading of it shows the waywardness and wickedness of the persistent unbelief of the people, but more remarkable is the fact of God's methods with them. Provision and punishment are alike evidences of His love and faithfulness.

Still the same story runs on in verses 32–55. Here however the fickleness of their obedience is specially set forth. "They believed not . . . He slew them . . . They enquired after Him . . . They lied to Him." This is typical of the whole movement. Yet God's patience was always manifest. With infinite tenderness He bore with them, and waited for them; forgave them, and pitied them. In spite of all, they continued to rebel, and the reason was that they did not remember His hand.

The singer then sang anew of the things they had forgotten, of God's signs in Egypt, of His leading them out, and of His bringing them into possession. It would seem almost past belief to us as we read that a people so led could forget. Yet is not this sin of forgetfulness with us perpetually? In some day of danger and perplexity we become so occupied with the immediate peril as to utterly fail to think of past deliverances. Such forgetfulness is of the nature of unbelief in its worst form. It wrongs God, and paralyses our own power. It is even more evil for us to fail to interpret to our children the Divine activity in past history, and in our own lives, for the men and women who face life lacking such instruction are without one of the most valuable forces in its battle.

Even when, in spite of their infidelity, God brought them into possession, they tempted and provoked God. Then came His seven dealings with them, which are described. These dealings are also systematic, and as He refused and chose, it was ever with purposes of blessing in His heart. It is indeed a great song of God's patience, and there is no story more fruitful if man will but learn it. It is questionable whether any of us could escape the charges made here against the people of God; and it is certain that we might all survey our lives, and sing just such a song of determined patience and persistence on the part of God. We need to be very careful however, lest we dwell upon this story of patience in such a way as to translate it into an excuse for continuity in unfaithfulness on our part. This is the most deadly of all heresies; and if we are tempted to trespass upon the loving methods of God, let us not forget that the psalm is also the story of severe punishment; and moreover, God was compelled ultimately to cast away from all privilege the people who failed to respond to the methods of His gentleness and patience.

PSALM 79

God the Hope of the Distressed

O GOD, the nations are come into thine inheritance;
Thy holy temple have they defiled;
They have laid Jerusalem in heaps.
2 The dead bodies of thy servants have they given to be food unto the birds of the heavens.
The flesh of thy saints unto the beasts of the earth.
3 Their blood have they shed like water round about Jerusalem;
And there was none to bury them.
4 We are become a reproach to our neighbors,
A scoffing and derision to them that are round about us.

5 How long, O Jehovah? wilt thou be angry for ever?
Shall thy jealousy burn like fire?
6 Pour out thy wrath upon the nations that know thee not,
And upon the kingdoms that call not upon thy name.
7 For they have devoured Jacob,
And laid waste his habitation.
8 Remember not against us the iniquities of our forefathers:
Let thy tender mercies speedily meet us;
For we are brought very low.
9 Help us. O God of our salvation, for the glory of thy name;
And deliver us, and forgive our sins, for thy name's sake.
10 Wherefore should the nations say, Where is their God?

Let the avenging of the blood of thy servants which is shed Be known among the nations in our sight.

11 Let the sighing of the prisoner come before thee: According to the greatness of thy power preserve thou those that are appointed to death;

12 And render unto our neighbors sevenfold into their bosom Their reproach, wherewith they have reproached thee, O Lord.

13 So we thy people and sheep of thy pasture Will give thee thanks for ever; We will show forth thy praise to all generations.

This is a cry of distress. The conditions described are those of overwhelming national calamity. The country and the city of God are overrun and spoiled by ruthless enemies. The people have been slain and left without burial. Out of the midst of these circumstances the psalmist prays to God for pardon, help, and deliverance.

There is no present note of praise in the psalm, but there is an undertone of confidence in God. This is the quality of these old songs of the men of faith which makes them living and powerful in an age utterly different from the one in which they were written. A careful perusal of this song will show three things as most evidently forming the deepest conviction of the singer's hope. First there is the sense that all the calamity which has overtaken them is the result of their own sin. Behind this is a great idea of the power and goodness of God. These things need not have been had they been faithful, for God is strong and tender. Again there is the passion for the glory of the Divine Name,

"Help us, O God of our salvation, for the glory of Thy name; And deliver us, and purge away our sins, for Thy name's sake. Wherefore should the heathen say, Where is their God?"

Finally, the very fact of the song is a revelation of the underlying confidence in God. In distress the heart seeks its way back to some hiding-place, and finds it in the Name of God, Who, by suffering is dealing with them.

PSALM 80

God the Restorer of His People

GIVE ear, O Shepherd of Israel,
Thou that leadest Joseph
like a flock;
Thou that sittest *above* the
cherubim, shine forth.

2 Before Ephraim and Benjamin
and Manasseh, stir up thy
might,
And come to save us.

3 Turn us again, O God;
And cause thy face to shine, and
we shall be saved.

4 O Jehovah God of hosts,
How long wilt thou be angry
against the prayer of thy people?

5 Thou hast fed them with the
bread of tears,
And given them tears to drink
in large measure.

6 Thou makest us a strife unto
our neighbors;
And our enemies laugh among
themselves.

7 Turn us again, O God of hosts;
And cause thy face to shine, and
we shall be saved.

8 Thou broughtest a vine out of
Egypt:
Thou didst drive out the na-
tions, and plantedst it.

9 Thou preparedst *room* before it,
And it took deep root, and filled
the land.

10 The mountains were covered
with the shadow of it,
And the boughs thereof were
like cedars of God.

11 It sent out its branches unto the
sea,
And its shoots unto the River.

12 Why hast thou broken down its
walls,
So that all they that pass by
the way do pluck it?

13 The boar out of the wood doth
ravage it,
And the wild beasts of the field
feed on it.

14 Turn again, we beseech thee, O
God of hosts:
Look down from heaven, and
behold, and visit this vine,

15 And the stock which thy right
hand planted,
And the branch that thou madest strong for thyself.

16 It is burned with fire, it is cut
down:
They perish at the rebuke of
thy countenance.

17 Let thy hand be upon the man
of thy right hand,
Upon the son of man whom
thou madest strong for thyself.

18 So shall we not go back from
thee:
Quicken thou us, and we will
call upon thy name.

19 Turn us again, O Jehovah God
of hosts;
Cause thy face to shine, and we
shall be saved.

Again we have a song out of the midst of distress. There is
far more light and colour about it than in the previous one.

The circumstances do not seem to be any more favourable than those described before. There is this difference however, between the two psalms. The first is mainly occupied with the disastrous conditions; this one begins with a prayer which is a recognition of the past relationship of God to His people.

This is therefore a great song of God as Shepherd. The aspects of the shepherd nature dealt with are those of His guidance and care and protection. The Shepherd of glory, Who by the shining of His face reveals the way, and by the stirring up of His might saves from danger, is appealed to. Then the figure is changed, and God is the Husbandman. His vine, which He planted and which flourished so perfectly has become a prey to the ravages of wild beasts and fire. Suddenly the figure ceases, and its meaning is revealed in the words,

"Let Thy hand be upon the man of Thy right hand,
Upon the son of man whom Thou madest strong for Thyself."

The burden of the psalm is expressed in the thrice repeated prayer (vers. 3, 7, 19). The suffering of the people is due to their own sin in turning away from God as Shepherd, Husbandman, and King. Their restoration can only come as He turns them back to Himself. Notice the ascent in these verses in the names which the singer uses for God. "God," "God of hosts," "Jehovah God of hosts."

PSALM 81

God the Strength of the Loyal

SING aloud unto God our strength:
Make a joyful noise unto the God of Jacob.

2 Raise a song, and bring hither the timbrel,
The pleasant harp with the psaltery.

3 Blow the trumpet at the new moon,
At the full moon, on our feast-day.

4 For it is a statute for Israel,
An ordinance of the God of Jacob.

5 He appointed it in Joseph for a
testimony,
When he went out over the land
of Egypt,
Where I heard a language that I
knew not.
6 I removed his shoulder from the
burden:
His hands were freed from the
basket.
7 Thou calledst in trouble, and I
delivered thee;
I answered thee in the secret
place of thunder;
I proved thee at the waters of
Meribah.
8 Hear, O my people, and I will
testify unto thee:
O Israel, if thou wouldest
hearken unto me!
9 There shall no strange god be in
thee;
Neither shalt thou worship any
foreign god.
10 I am Jehovah thy God,
Who brought thee up out of the
land of Egypt:

Open thy mouth wide, and I will
fill it.
11 But my people hearkened not
to my voice;
And Israel would none of me.
12 So I let them go after the stub-
bornness of their heart,
That they might walk in their
own counsels.
13 Oh that my people would
hearken unto me,
That Israel would walk in my
ways!
14 I would soon subdue their enemies,
And turn my hand against their
adversaries.
15 The haters of Jehovah should
submit themselves unto him:
But their time should endure for
ever.
16 He would feed them also with
the finest of the wheat;
And with honey out of the rock
would I satisfy thee.

This is a psalm for the Feast of Trumpets. In the calendar
of the Hebrews this feast prepared the way for the Day of
Atonement and the Feast of Tabernacles. The first day of the
seventh month was the Feast of Trumpets. The tenth day of
the seventh month was Atonement. The fifteenth day of the
seventh month was Tabernacles (Lev. xxiii).

The psalm opens with a call to the Feast of Trumpets, and
a declaration of its Divine appointment (vers. 1–5). Then the
singer expresses the attitude of God to His people, and the
song proceeds as in the words of Jehovah (vers. 6–10). First
He tells of His deliverance of them from bondage, and His
answer to them at Sinai (vers. 6, 7). Then He reminds them
of the terms of the covenant with them. He would speak and

they should hearken. They were to have no God but Himself, and He would be to them Jehovah God. They were to open the mouth and He would fill it (vers. 8–10). They failed in refusing to hearken and obey, and therefore He abandoned them to their choice (vers. 11, 12). Finally He expresses His desire that they should return, and declares His ability still to deliver them (vers. 13–16). It is still the same burden of the faithfulness of God, and the unfaithfulness of His people. Panic and defeat on the part of the people of God are always due to their departure from Him. The enemies who overcome us are without strength in the conflict against Him. When they overcome us it is because we have departed from Him.

PSALM 82

God the Judge of the Judges

GOD standeth in the congregation of God;
He judgeth among the gods.
2 How long will ye judge unjustly,
And respect the persons of the
wicked?
3 Judge the poor and fatherless:
Do justice to the afflicted and
destitute.
4 Rescue the poor and needy:
Deliver them out of the hand of
the wicked.
5 They know not, neither do they
understand;

They walk to and fro in darkness:
All the foundations of the earth
are shaken.
6 I said, Ye are gods,
And all of you sons of the Most
High.
7 Nevertheless ye shall die like
men,
And fall like one of the princes.
8 Arise, O God, judge the earth;
For thou shalt inherit all the nations.

This psalm is a cry for justice, born of a sense of the mal-administration of those in authority. It first announces the fact that God is the supreme Judge. This is a recognition of the perfect equity of the standard of justice. The judges in mind have erred in that they have shown respect for the persons of the wicked, and thus departed from that strict justice which ever characterizes the dealings of the God to Whom they are all responsible.

The singer then sets forth what are the essential functions of the judges. They are specially to care for all those who are in circumstances of difficulty and danger. This had not been done, for such people were without knowledge or guidance. The judges have had the name of authority, and its position, but through their failure they are to be degraded.

The song ends with an appeal to God to arise and judge the earth. This is ever the cry of the man of faith when he stands in the presence of the wrongs and oppressions obtaining among the poor and afflicted. There is nothing the world needs to-day more than the administration of strict and impartial justice, and there is no greater comfort to the heart than the conviction that the prayer of the psalmist, multiplied ten thousand fold in the passing centuries by all who have been and still are, conscious of prevailing injustice, will yet be answered. God's day of judgment will be a day of mercy in the largest sense.

PSALM 83

God Vindicated as Most High

O GOD, keep not thou silence: Hold not thy peace, and be not still, O God.

2 For, lo, thine enemies make a tumult; And they that hate thee have lifted up the head.

3 They take crafty counsel against thy people. And consult together against thy hidden ones.

4 They have said, Come, and let us cut them off from being a nation; That the name of Israel may be no more in remembrance.

5 For they have consulted together with one consent; Against thee do they make a covenant:

6 The tents of Edom and the Ishmaelites; Moab, and the Hagarenes;

7 Gebal, and Ammon, and Amalek; Philistia with the inhabitants of Tyre:

8 Assyria also is joined with them; They have helped the children of Lot.

9 Do thou unto them as unto Midian,
As to Sisera, as to Jabin, at the river Kishon;
10 Who perished at En-dor,
Who became as dung for the earth.
11 Make their nobles like Oreb and Zeeb;
Yea, all their princes like Zebah and Zalmunna;
12 Who said, Let us take to ourselves in possession
The habitations of God.
13 O my God, make them like the whirling dust;
As stubble before the wind.
14 As the fire that burneth the forest.

And as the flame that setteth the mountains on fire,
15 So pursue them with thy tempest,
And terrify them with thy storm.
16 Fill their faces with confusion,
That they may seek thy name, O Jehovah.
17 Let them be put to shame and dismayed for ever;
Yea, let them be confounded and perish;
18 That they may know that thou alone, whose name is Jehovah,
Art the Most High over all the earth.

The psalmist has a vision of the confederacy of all the enemies of the people of God. This he describes as to its process, it constitution, and its purpose. They have taken counsel together with the avowed purpose of the annihilation of the very name of Israel. The combining peoples are named, and the first part of the psalm ends (vers. 1–8).

The song then becomes a prayer definitely for the destruction of this confederacy, and the confusion of its purpose. Past victories are referred to, and in a strong and overwhelming sense of peril the cry for the Divine activity is poured forth. Here again, as constantly, this attitude of the singer must be accounted for according to his own declaration. In describing the confederacy he declared,

"For they have consulted together with one consent;
Against Thee do they make a covenant."

At the close of the prayer he says,

"That they may know that Thou alone, Whose name is Jehovah
Art the Most High over all the earth."

These singers of the ancient people were all inspired supremely with a passion for the honour of God. With them, as with the prophets, selfish motives were unknown. Selfishness sings no songs, and sees no visions. On the other hand, a passion for the glory of God is capable of great sternness, as well as of great tenderness.

PSALM 84

God the Strength of the Pilgrim

HOW amiable are thy tabernacles,
O Jehovah of hosts!

2 My soul longeth, yea, even fainteth for the courts of Jehovah;
My heart and my flesh cry out unto the living God.

3 Yea, the sparrow hath found her a house,
And the swallow a nest for herself, where she may lay her young,
Even thine altars, O Jehovah of hosts,
My King, and my God.

4 Blessed are they that dwell in thy house:
They will be still praising thee.

5 Blessed is the man whose strength is in thee;
In whose heart are the highways to Zion.

6 Passing through the valley of Weeping they make it a place of springs;
Yea, the early rain covereth it with blessings.

7 They go from strength to strength;
Every one of them appeareth before God in Zion.

8 O Jehovah God of hosts, hear my prayer;
Give ear, O God of Jacob.

9 Behold, O God our shield,
And look upon the face of thine anointed.

10 For a day in thy courts is better than a thousand.
I had rather be a doorkeeper in the house of my God,
Than to dwell in the tents of wickedness.

11 For Jehovah God is a sun and a shield:
Jehovah will give grace and glory;
No good thing will he withhold from them that walk uprightly.

12 O Jehovah of hosts,
Blessed is the man that trusteth in thee.

This is a pilgrim psalm. It falls into three strophes divided by Selahs. The first describes the pilgrim's hope (vers. 1–4);

the second, the pilgrim's experience (vers. 5–8); the third, pilgrim's prayer (vers. 9–12).

The hope of the pilgrim is centred in the dwelling-place of God. The earthly temple suggests the heavenly home. It is a place of rest and of worship. The light of it shines upon the pathway, and is the inspiration of the pilgrimage.

The experience of the pilgrim is then described. Faith has an anchorage; it is found in God when the heart is set upon the consummation. Faith has an activity; it passes through dry valleys, and fills them with springs of refreshment. Faith has an assurance; it goes from strength to strength, confident of finally appearing before God.

The pilgrim finally pours out his prayer, and it is full of praise and confidence. Its desire is for the vision of God, which by comparison is infinitely to be preferred, even though it be the distant view of a doorkeeper, to all the world has to offer. The lessons of the psalm for all the pilgrims of hope are first, that the heart should be set upon the upper things; secondly, that faith may dig wells in driest places and find the living Water; and finally, that pilgrimage develops strength, rather than produces weakness, as these conditions are fulfilled.

PSALM 85

Jehovah the Restorer of the Wanderer

JEHOVAH, thou hast been favorable unto thy land;
Thou hast brought back the captivity of Jacob.

2 Thou hast forgiven the iniquity of thy people;
Thou hast covered all their sin.

3 Thou hast taken away all thy wrath;
Thou hast turned *thyself* from the fierceness of thine anger.

4 Turn us, O God of our salvation,
And cause thine indignation toward us to cease.

5 Wilt thou be angry with us for ever?
Wilt thou draw out thine anger to all generations?

6 Wilt thou not quicken us again,
That thy people may rejoice in thee?

7 Show us thy lovingkindness, O
   Jehovah,
And grant us thy salvation.
8 I will hear what God Jehovah
   will speak;
For he will speak peace unto his
   people, and to his saints:
But let them not turn again to
   folly.
9 Surely his salvation is nigh
   them that fear him,
That glory may dwell in our
   land.
10 Mercy and truth are met together;

Righteousness and peace have
   kissed each other.
11 Truth springeth out of the
   earth;
And righteousness hath looked
   down from heaven.
12 Yea, Jehovah will give that
   which is good;
And our land shall yield its increase.
13 Righteousness shall go before
   him,
And shall make his footsteps a
   way *to walk in.*

This psalm would seem to have been written in a day when some Divine deliverance had been wrought for the people of God. Yet the singer is conscious that in the heart of the people there remain dispositions not in harmony with the will of God; and therefore, there abides with them a deadness and a lack of joy. And yet further he is confident that God, Jehovah, has purposes of the highest and best for His own; and moreover, that He will accomplish these purposes.

These three matters are evident in the threefold movement of thanksgiving offered (vers. 1–3), of petition presented (vers. 4–7), and of confidence affirmed (vers. 8–13). In the thanksgiving the relation between captivity and sin is remembered, and the ending of the first by the putting away of the second is declared. Yet the imperfection of their loyalty creates the long discipline of sorrow and shame, and the prayer is that God will turn the people to Himself. And this is surely His will, for when he pauses to hear what Jehovah will say, he hears tender and gracious words which tell of salvation, first in the spiritual realm, and then in the material. In this psalm which breathes the spirit of the tender compassion of God, the name Jehovah is the predominant one.

PSALM 86

The Lord the Mighty Helper of the Needy

BOW down thine ear,
O Jehovah, and answer me;
For I am poor and needy.

2 Preserve my soul; for I am godly:
O thou my God, save thy servant that trusteth in thee.

3 Be merciful unto me, O Lord;
For unto thee do I cry all the day long.

4 Rejoice the soul of thy servant;
For unto thee, O Lord, do I lift up my soul.

5 For thou, Lord, art good, and ready to forgive,
And abundant in lovingkindness unto all them that call upon thee.

6 Give ear, O Jehovah, unto my prayer:
And hearken unto the voice of my supplications.

7 In the day of my trouble I will call upon thee;
For thou wilt answer me.

8 There is none like unto thee among the gods, O Lord;
Neither *are there any works* like unto thy works.

9 All nations whom thou hast made shall come and worship before thee, O Lord;
And they shall glorify thy name.

10 For thou art great, and doest wondrous things:

Thou art God alone.

11 Teach me thy way, O Jehovah;
I will walk in thy truth:
Unite my heart to fear thy name.

12 I will praise thee, O Lord my God, with my whole heart;
And I will glorify thy name for evermore.

13 For great is thy lovingkindness toward me;
And thou has delivered my soul from the lowest Sheol.

14 O God, the proud are risen up against me,
And a company of violent men have sought after my soul,
And have not set thee before them.

15 But thou, O Lord, art a God merciful and gracious,
Slow to anger, and abundant in lovingkindness and truth.

16 Oh turn unto me, and have mercy upon me;
Give thy strength unto thy servant,
And save the son of thy handmaid.

17 Show me a token for good,
That they who hate me may see it, and be put to shame,
Because thou, Jehovah, hast helped me, and comforted me.

This psalm is peculiar in many ways. Its first peculiarity is that the name of God which dominates is Adonahy, or Lord, which indicates absolute Lordship, and by the use of which the singer shows his sense of submission and loyalty. The name Jehovah is used four times, thus revealing the singer's sense of God as Helper; and the name God five times, thus revealing his consciousness of the Divine might. The supreme sense however, is that of the Divine authority.

The next matter of special note is that while the psalm is a beautiful and consecutive song, it is largely composed of quotations from other psalms, thus revealing the singer's familiarity with them. The references in the Revised Version will enable the reader to trace these quotations.

Finally, the psalm is unique in its method of urging a petition upon the ground of some known fact. This is clearly seen if the use of the word "for" is noticed (vers. 1–5, 7, 10, 13). In the first four verses the facts are those which indicate his attitude toward God. In the last four the facts are those revealing God's attitude toward him. The revelation for us is that of true approach to God in times of need. This must be based upon our relation of absolute submission to Him. It must be expressed in harmony with spiritual desires as expressed by the fellowship of the faithful. It must be urged in consecration and courage.

PSALM 87

Jehovah, His City and His People

HIS foundation is in the holy mountains.
2 Jehovah loveth the gates of Zion
More than all the dwellings of Jacob.
3 Glorious things are spoken of thee,
O city of God.
4 I will make mention of Rahab and Babylon as among them that know me:
Behold, Philistia, and Tyre, with Ethiopia:
This one was born there.
5 Yea, of Zion it shall be said, This one and that one was born in her;
And the Most High himself will establish her.
6 Jehovah will count, when he writeth up the peoples,
This one was born there.
7 They that sing as well as they that dance *shall say*,
All my fountains are in thee.

This is a prophecy. The singer is looking on. The order of the earthly realization of the Kingdom of God is seen as established. First, the city is contemplated at the centre of everything, with Jehovah as its God. Then the peoples of the earth are seen in their true relation to that city.

It is a most remarkable utterance. Though brief, it is as comprehensive and full of beauty as any of the inspired predictions. Without specific statement, the sovereignty of God is taken for granted. There is no argument given for this. It is a fact beyond dispute and needing no proof. Thus God has the city of His chosen people as the centre and foundation of His administration. His love is set upon the city, and her fame is wide-spread; glorious things are spoken of her. The outcome is seen in the effect produced upon the surrounding peoples. Her ancient enemies are finally to be born, that is, realize their true life, through this governing city of God.

This is the highest function of the chosen people according to the purpose of God. Under His government they are to bring the other nations to Him, so that they also shall find their highest in His Kingdom. This is not a story of Israel conquering by force of arms, but of that higher victory not yet won, when by manifestation and administration of the Divine government, the peoples shall dance and sing in the finding of their fountains and fulness in God.

PSALM 88

Jehovah the Only Hope of the Sorrowing

O JEHOVAH, the God of my salvation,
I have cried day and night before thee.
2 Let my prayer enter into thy presence;
Incline thine ear unto my cry.
3 For my soul is full of troubles,
And my life draweth nigh unto Sheol.
4 I am reckoned with them that go down into the pit;
I am as a man that hath no help,
5 Cast off among the dead,

Like the slain that lie in the grave,
Whom thou rememberest no more,
And they are cut off from thy hand.

6 Thou hast laid me in the lowest pit,
In dark places, in the deeps.

7 Thy wrath lieth hard upon me,
And thou hast afflicted me with all thy waves.

8 Thou hast put mine acquaintance far from me;
Thou has made me an abomination unto them:
I am shut up, and I cannot come forth.

9 Mine eye wasteth away by reason of affliction:
I have called daily upon thee, O Jehovah;
I have spread forth my hands unto thee.

10 Wilt thou show wonders to the dead?
Shall they that are deceased arise and praise thee?

11 Shall thy lovingkindness be declared in the grave?
Or thy faithfulness in Destruction?

12 Shall thy wonders be known in the dark?
And thy righteousness in the land of forgetfulness?

13 But unto thee, O Jehovah, have I cried;
And in the morning shall my prayer come before thee.

14 Jehovah, why castest thou off my soul?
Why hidest thou thy face from me?

15 I am afflicted and ready to die from my youth up:
While I suffer thy terrors I am distracted.

16 Thy fierce wrath is gone over me;
Thy terrors have cut me off.

17 They came round about me like water all the day long;
They compassed me about together.

18 Lover and friend hast thou put far from me,
And mine acquaintance into darkness.

This is a song sobbing with sadness from beginning to end. It seems to have no gleam of light or of hope. Commencing with an appeal to Jehovah to hear, it proceeds to describe the terrible sorrows through which the singer is passing. He is whelmed with trouble, and nigh unto death. Moreover he is alone; his acquaintances are put away from him. Death is a terrible outlook, for the singer sees no light in it. Therein God Himself will be unknown, and unable to succour.

Again the song sings in yet profounder notes of sadness, which are like the breaking of great waves over the soul; which seem as though they must silence it utterly. The last declaration is a most terrible one of utter loneliness, "lover and friend" are put away from him, and the final word is "darkness." One cannot help the consciousness that this psalm was a foreshadowing of sorrow which, being national, yet only reached its fulfilment of realization in the Messiah. The note of present value however, is that while, as we said at the beginning, there seems to be no light, there is light everywhere. The singer is in great sorrow, but he comes to Jehovah. He is afraid of going into death because there Jehovah cannot help him; but he has come there, and therefore still cries out for God. While the sense of God abides, darkness has not triumphed.

PSALM 89

Jehovah the God of Discipline

I WILL sing of the lovingkindness of Jehovah for ever:
  With my mouth will I make known thy faithfulness to all generations.
2 For I have said, Mercy shall be built up for ever;
  Thy faithfulness wilt thou establish in the very heavens.
3 I have made a covenant with my chosen,
  I have sworn unto David my servant:
4 Thy seed will I establish for ever,
  And built up thy throne to all generations.
5 And the heavens shall praise thy wonders, O Jehovah;
  Thy faithfulness also in the assembly of the holy ones.
6 For who in the skies can be compared unto Jehovah?

Who among the sons of the mighty is like unto Jehovah,
7 A God very terrible in the council of the holy ones,
  And to be feared above all them that are round about him?
8 O Jehovah God of hosts,
  Who is a mighty one, like unto thee, O Jehovah?
  And thy faithfulness is round about thee.
9 Thou rulest the pride of the sea:
  When the waves thereof arise, thou stillest them.
10 Thou hast broken Rahab in pieces, as one that is slain;
  Thou hast scattered thine enemies with the arm of thy strength.
11 The heavens are thine, the earth also is thine:
  The world and the fulness thereof, thou has founded them.

12 The north and the south, thou
hast created them:
Tabor and Hermon rejoice in
thy name.

13 Thou hast a mighty arm;
Strong is thy hand, and high is
thy right hand.

14 Righteousness and justice are
the foundation of thy throne:
Lovingkindness and truth go before thy face.

15 Blessed is the people that know
the joyful sound:
They walk, O Jehovah, in the
light of thy countenance.

16 In thy name do they rejoice all
the day;
And in thy righteousness are
they exalted.

17 For thou art the glory of their
strength;
And in thy favor our horn shall
be exalted.

18 For our shield belongeth unto
Jehovah;
And our king to the Holy One
of Israel.

19 Then thou spakest in vision to
thy saints,
And saidst, I have laid help
upon one that is mighty;
I have exalted one chosen out
of the people.

20 I have found David my servant;
With my holy oil have I
anointed him:

21 With whom my hand shall be
established:
Mine arm also shall strengthen
him.

22 The enemy shall not exact from
him,
Nor the son of wickedness, afflict him.

23 And I will beat down his adversaries before him,
And smite them that hate him.

24 But my faithfulness and my
lovingkindness shall be with
him;
And in my name shall his horn
be exalted.

25 I will set his hand also on the
sea,
And his right hand on the rivers.

26 He shall cry unto me,
Thou art my Father,
My God, and the rock of my
salvation.

27 I also will make him *my* first-
born,
The highest of the kings of the
earth.

28 My lovingkindness will I keep
for him for evermore;
And my covenant shall stand
fast with him.

29 His seed also will I make to endure for ever,
And his throne as the days of
heaven.

30 If his children forsake my law,
And walk not in mine ordinances;

31 If they break my statutes,
And keep not my command-
ments;

32 Then will I visit their transgression with the rod,
And their iniquity with stripes.

33 But my lovingkindness will I
not utterly take from him,
Nor suffer my faithfulness to
fail.

34 My covenant will I not break,
Nor alter the thing that is gone
out of my lips.

35 Once have I sworn by my holiness:

I will not lie unto David:

36 His seed shall endure for ever,
And his throne as the sun before
me.

37 It shall be established for ever
as the moon,
And *as* the faithful witness in
the sky.

38 But thou hast cast off and rejected,
Thou hast been wroth with
thine anointed.

39 Thou hast abhorred the covenant of thy servant:
Thou hast profaned his crown
by casting it to the ground.

40 Thou hast broken down all his
hedges;
Thou hast brought his strong-
holds to ruin.

41 All that pass by the way rob
him:
He is become a reproach to his
neighbors.

42 Thou has exalted the right hand
of his adversaries;
Thou hast made all his enemies
to rejoice.

43 Yea, thou turnest back the edge
of his sword,
And hast not made him to stand
in the battle.

44 Thou hast made his brightness
to cease,
And cast his throne down to the
ground.

45 The days of his youth hast thou
shortened:
Thou hast covered him with
shame.

46 How long, O Jehovah? wilt thou
hide thyself for ever?
How long shall thy wrath burn
like fire?

47 Oh remember how short my
time is:
For what vanity hast thou
created all the children of
men!

48 What man is he that shall live
and not see death,
That shall deliver his soul from
the power of Sheol?

49 Lord, where are thy former
lovingkindnesses,
Which thou swarest unto David
in thy faithfulness?

50 Remember, Lord, the reproach
of thy servants;
How I do bear in my bosom *the
reproach of* all the mighty
peoples,

51 Wherewith thine enemies have
reproached, O Jehovah,
Wherewith they have re-
proached the footsteps of
thine anointed.

52 Blessed be Jehovah for evermore.
Amen, and Amen.

Taken as a whole, this song is one of the finest in the collection as a revelation of how the man of faith is compelled to
view circumstances of calamity. In a poem of great beauty he
first sets forth the praises of God (vers. 1–37). Then he sur-
veys the present condition of His people, and so creates a contrast (vers. 38-52). No present defeat can dim the glory of

past history as it reveals the facts of the Divine majesty. Yet these past facts and confidences may be the reason of present enquiry and approach to God.

In the first part, which is a song of praise, the singer tells of the covenant made with David, and then breaks out into adoration. The heavens and the angels witness to His greatness (vers. 5–7). The earth and men also. All nature, the sea and the mountains, the north and the south, are conscious of His power. In His government the foundations are unshakable, and the method full of tenderness (vers. 8–14).

It follows naturally that the people who are peculiarly His own are indeed blessed (vers. 15–18). This is not theory only; it is experience. For them Jehovah had found a king, and had made him and the people under him invincible in the days of their obedience. Such facts issue in confidence that the future must be one of victory and blessing.

"But," and the word suggests a change, and a great change it is. Instead of the glowing picture of the former verses is a dark one of present experience. The people are scattered, their defences broken down, their enemies triumphant, and their king is robbed of glory, and covered with shame (vers. 38–45).

Yet most carefully notice that all this is spoken of as the work of Jehovah. The key phrase to this portion is "Thou hast." The mighty One Who had found the king and blessed the nation is the One Who has broken the nation and cast out the king. Upon the basis of that conviction the final prayer rises, "How long, Jehovah." This is the true attitude of the interceding soul in the day of calamity. First, a sense of the greatness and goodness of God, as revealed in the first part of the song. Then the conviction that this same One is visiting the people in discipline. To know the faithfulness of God is to know that when He afflicts there is meaning of mercy in it. When that is recognized, prayer for deliverance is proper, for it must inevitably be accompanied by a turning back to Jehovah from those things which have been the reason of His punishments.

The psalm ends with the doxology which closes the book, and expresses the worship of Jehovah as the essential Helper of His people.

BOOK IV.

PSALMS 90–106

BOOK IV. PSALMS 90–106

DOXOLOGY

"Blessed be the Lord, the God of Israel,
From everlasting even to everlasting,
And let all the people say, Amen,
Praise ye the Lord."—Ps. 106–48.

A. THE TITLE.	B. THE RELATION.	C. THE QUALITY.	D. THE QUANTITY.	E. THE EXTENT.
"Jehovah." The essential Helper. (See first Doxology.)	"The God of Israel."	"Blessed." "Hallelujah."	"From everlasting to everlasting."	"And let all the people say, Amen."

The Divine Name.

The dominant name in this book is again "Jehovah." It occurs more than once in every psalm, and in two as many as 11 times.

The name "God" is absent altogether from five, and occurs only 27 times, 9 of them being singular (El), and 18 plural (Elohim).

The general title "Lord" (Adonahy) only occurs twice.

"Jah" is found 7 times.

The Dominant Thought.

In this book the worship of Jehovah is rendered by all people. They are songs of His government and administration, for which the heart is lifted in adoration.

ANALYSIS

A. THE PRINCIPLES. 90-92	B. THE PRACTICE. 93-100	C. THE PRAISE. 101-106

I. The age-abiding Fact. Man's Failure. — 90	I. The enthroned King. 93 to 96
	  i. The Fact. — 93
	  ii. The Courage of Faith. — 94
	  iii. The Caution of Faith. — 95
	  iv. Worship. — 96
		I. The Attitude of Praise. Submission. — 101

II. The unshaken One. Man's Hope. — 91	II. The Activity of the King. 97 to 100
	  i. His Judgments. — 97
	  ii. Worship. — 98
	  iii. His Reign. — 99
	  iv. Worship. — 100
		II. The Benefits. 102 to 106
		  i. The age-abiding God. — 102
		  ii. The loving Father. — 103
		  iii. The Creator and Sustainer. — 104
		  iv. The true and Mighty One. — 105
		  v. The faithful and patient One. — 106

III. The new Realization. Man's Restoration. — 92		

PSALM 90

Jehovah the Eternal Refuge of Man

LORD, thou hast been our dwelling-place
In all generations.

2 Before the mountains were brought forth,
Or ever thou hadst formed the earth and the world,
Even from everlasting to everlasting, thou art God.

3 Thou turnest man to destruction,
And sayest, Return ye children of men.

4 For a thousand years in thy sight
Are but as yesterday when it is past,
And as a watch in the night.

5 Thou carriest them away as with a flood; they are as a sleep:
In the morning they are like grass which groweth up.

6 In the morning it flourisheth, and groweth up;
In the evening it is cut down, and withereth.

7 For we are consumed in thine anger,
And in thy wrath are we troubled.

8 Thou hast set our iniquities before thee,
Our secret sins in the light of thy countenance.

9 For all our days are passed away in thy wrath:

We bring our years to an end as a sigh.

10 The days of our years are threescore years and ten,
Or even by reason of strength fourscore years;
Yet is their pride but labor and sorrow;
For it is soon gone, and we fly away.

11 Who knoweth the power of thine anger,
And thy wrath according to the fear that is due unto thee?

12 So teach us to number our days,
That we may get us a heart of wisdom.

13 Return, O Jehovah; how long?
And let it repent thee concerning thy servants.

14 Oh satisfy us in the morning with thy lovingkindness,
That we may rejoice and be glad all our days.

15 Make us glad according to the days wherein thou hast afflicted us,
And the years wherein we have seen evil.

16 Let thy work appear unto thy servants
And thy glory upon their children.

17 And let the favor of the Lord our God be upon us;
And establish thou the work of our hands upon us;
Yea, the work of our hands establish thou it.

The main purpose of this psalm is revealed in the prayer with which it concludes (vers. 13–17). This prayer is prefaced by a meditation on the frailty of man (vers. 3–12), in the light of the eternity of God (vers. 1, 2). By this backward method of analysis we gain a conception of the general scheme of the psalm which now enables us to take the three movements in their orderly sequence.

The eternity of God is described in three stages. First, as measured by the history of His people, He has ever been their dwelling-place. Secondly, as measured by creation, He was before all. Finally, whether the mind travel backward or forward to the vanishing point, He is still God. In this light man is seen in the frailty of his being. To God a thousand years are comparatively nothing, and in every millennium men appear and pass in a sequence as orderly as that of the grass, but in a life as transitory. This frailty is the more feeble because man is a sinner; and therefore out of harmony with God. Yet this very eternity of God is the hope of man in his frailty and sin, and the heart is lifted to Jehovah in a prayer that the mornings, the days, the years of brief life may all be set in true relation to Him. Satisfaction, gladness, success in work must all come from the right relation of man in his frailty to the eternal Lord.

PSALM 91

Jehovah the Sanctuary of the Soul

HE that dwelleth in the secret place of the Most High
Shall abide under the shadows of the Almighty.
2 I will say of Jehovah, He is my refuge and my fortress;
My God, in whom I trust.
3 For he will deliver thee from the snare of the fowler,
And from the deadly pestilence.

4 He will cover thee with his pinions,
And under his wings shalt thou take refuge:
His truth is a shield and a buckler.
5 Thou shalt not be afraid for the terror by night,
Nor for the arrow that flieth by day;

6 For the pestilence that walketh
   in darkness,
   Nor for the destruction that
   wasteth at noonday.
7 A thousand shall fall at thy side,
   And ten thousand at thy right
   hand;
   But it shall not come nigh thee.
8 Only with thine eyes shalt thou
   behold,
   And see the reward of the
   wicked.
9 For thou, O Jehovah, art my
   refuge!
   Thou hast made the Most High
   thy habitation;
10 There shall no evil befall thee,
   Neither shall any plague come
   nigh thy tent.
11 For he will give his angels
   charge over thee,
   To keep thee in all thy ways.

12 They shall bear thee up in their
   hands,
   Lest thou dash thy foot against
   a stone.
13 Thou shalt tread upon the lion
   and adder:
   The young lion and the serpent
   shalt thou trample under
   foot.
14 Because he hath set his love
   upon me, therefore will I deliver him:
   I will set him on high, because
   he hath known my name.
15 He shall call upon me, and I will
   answer him;
   I will be with him in trouble:
   I will deliver him, and honor
   him.
16 With long life will I satisfy him,
   And show him my salvation.

This psalm is one of the greatest possessions of the saints. It is a great song of the safety of such as put their trust in Jehovah, and contains the Divine assurance of such faith as fruitful. Very little of exposition is necessary. There is a change in the use of pronouns from first to second person twice over, and from third to first at the beginning, and from second to third at the close; which, although it has created some sense of difficulty, is yet a key to the psalm for purposes of analysis.

Let us set out the scheme of the psalm round these changes, leaving its familiar words to speak for themselves.

Ver. 1.   The statement of truth.
Ver. 2.   Personal affirmation of realization.
Vers. 3–8.   The address of the singer, either to his own soul, or to some other person, or to the nation, in which he affirms the convictions resulting from personal realization of the truth.

Ver. 9a.	Repetition of personal realization.
Vers. 9b–13.	Same as verses 3–8.
Vers. 14, 15.	Conclusion of psalm, in which the singer with holy boldness expresses as in the words of Jehovah, the safety of the trusting soul, and thus gives the testimony of God as well as that of man to the truth.

PSALM 92

Jehovah Praised for His Righteous Dealing

IT is a good thing to give thanks unto Jehovah,
And to sing praises unto thy name, O Most High;

2 To show forth thy lovingkindness in the morning,
And thy faithfulness every night,

3 With an instrument of ten strings, and with the psaltery;
With a solemn sound upon the harp.

4 For thou, Jehovah, hast made me glad through thy work:
I will triumph in the works of thy hands.

5 How great are thy works, O Jehovah!
Thy thoughts are very deep.

6 A brutish man knoweth not;
Neither doth a fool understand this:

7 When the wicked spring as the grass,
And when all the workers of iniquity do flourish;
It is that they shall be destroyed for ever.

8 But thou, O Jehovah, art on high for evermore.

9 For, lo, thine enemies, O Jehovah,
For, lo, thine enemies shall perish;
All the workers of iniquity shall be scattered.

10 But my horn hast thou exalted like *the horn of* the wild-ox:
I am anointed with fresh oil.

11 Mine eye also hath seen *my desire* on mine enemies,
Mine ears have heard *my desire* of the evil-doers that rise up against me.

12 The righteous shall flourish like the palm-tree:
He shall grow like a cedar in Lebanon.

13 They are planted in the house of Jehovah;
They shall flourish in the courts of our God.

14 They shall still bring forth fruit in old age;
They shall be full of sap and green:

15 To show that Jehovah is upright;
He is my rock, and there is no unrighteousness in him.

This is a song of praise. The seemliness of praise is first declared (vers. 1–3); and then reasons for it are given (vers. 4–15). Praise is good as the first exercise of the day and also as the last. *Lovingkindness* in the morning, the sense of all the provision made for us as we face the responsibilities and conflicts of the day. *Faithfulness* at night, the conviction that Jehovah has been true to His covenant, through all the hours of need.

The song proceeds to rejoice first in that general and wholly beneficent government of God, whereby the wicked are dealt with in judgment. That is a weak and perilous tenderness which permits evil to continue its work of destruction. That is a strong and tender pity which without relenting, smites evil, and destroys it.

The song ends with a gracious description of the growth and perennial freshness of the righteous. Such, planted in the courts of God will flourish and grow, and yet know no senility —age with all its wealth of experience and fruitage, but with no failing or weakness.

PSALM 93

Jehovah the King. The Fact

JEHOVAH reigneth; he is clothed with majesty;
Jehovah is clothed with strength; he hath girded himself therewith:
The world also is established, that it cannot be moved.
2 Thy throne is established of old: Thou art from everlasting.
3 The floods have lifted up, O Jehovah,
The floods have lifted up their voice;
The floods lift up their waves.
4 Above the voices of many waters, The mighty breakers of the sea, Jehovah on high is mighty.
5 Thy testimonies are very sure: Holiness becometh thy house, O Jehovah, for evermore.

There is a great majesty about this song. It celebrates Jehovah's assumption of the throne and government. The form in which the preliminary statements are made conveys the impression, not so much of the eternal sovereignty of the King, as that He has taken up His position, and acted upon it. The result is that the stability of all things is assured. This assumption of authority is but the enforcement of a perpetual fact, for

> "Thy throne is established of old;
> Thou art from everlasting."

Moreover, this assumption has not been without opposition, and the figure of the storm-tossed sea is made use of to indicate the strength of this opposition, "The floods have lifted up against him."

All this has been of no avail. The King is high above, and therefore Lord of them. This psalm was written in all likelihood after some deliverance Jehovah wrought for His people, but through the open window the singer, consciously or unconsciously, saw the far distant light of another day in which the Kingdom of God will be set up in His might, and the song of an established order shall be the anthem of His praise.

PSALM 94

Jehovah the King. Faith's Affirmation

O JEHOVAH, thou God to whom vengeance belongeth,
Thou God to whom vengeance belongeth, shine forth.
2 Lift up thyself, thou judge of the earth:
Render to the proud *their* desert.
3 Jehovah, how long shall the wicked,
How long shall the wicked triumph?
4 They prate, they speak arrogantly:
All the workers of the iniquity boast themselves.
5 They break in pieces thy people, O Jehovah,
And afflict thy heritage.
6 They slay the widow and the sojourner,
And murder the fatherless.
7 And they say, Jehovah will not see,
Neither will the God of Jacob consider.
8 Consider, ye brutish among the people;

And ye fools, when will ye be wise?

9 He that planted the ear, shall he not hear?
He that formed the eye, shall he not see?

10 He that chastiseth the nations, shall not he correct,
Even he that teacheth man knowledge?

11 Jehovah knoweth the thoughts of man,
That they are vanity.

12 Blessed is the man whom thou chastenest, O Jehovah,
And teachest out of thy law;

13 That thou mayest give him rest from the days of adversity,
Until the pit be digged for the wicked.

14 For Jehovah will not cast off his people,
Neither will he forsake his inheritance.

15 For judgment shall return unto righteousness;
And all the upright in heart shall follow it.

16 Who will rise up for me against the evil-doers?

Who will stand up for me against the workers of iniquity?

17 Unless Jehovah had been my help,
My soul had soon dwelt in silence.

18 When I said, My foot slippeth;
Thy lovingkindness, O Jehovah, held me up.

19 In the multitude of my thoughts within me
Thy comforts delight my soul.

20 Shall the throne of wickedness have fellowship with thee,
Which frameth mischief by statute?

21 They gather themselves together against the soul of the righteous,
And condemn the innocent blood.

22 But Jehovah hath been my high tower,
And my God the rock of my refuge.

23 And he hath brought upon them their own iniquity,
And will cut them off in their own wickedness;
Jehovah our God will cut them off.

The placing of this song immediately after the one which sets forth the fact of the enthronement of Jehovah is remarkable. It creates a contrast, while it suggests a continuity of ideas. The contrast is seen in the fact that while the previous psalm celebrates the victory of Jehovah over all opposition, this one is an appeal to Him out of circumstances in which His enemies seem to triumph. The continuity of ideas is however, equally apparent. To whom should His own turn in times of such distress, save to the One Who sits high above the force and fury of the flood?

The psalm has three main movements. First, an appeal to Jehovah the Mighty, in the presence of the triumph of the wicked (vers. 1–7). This is followed by an address to such as are doubting because of apparent inactivity of God. They are reminded that God hears, sees, and must act (vers. 8–11). Finally, the song again becomes a prayer in which faith makes its great affirmations. The period of waiting is one of blessed chastening. Jehovah cannot ultimately cast off His people. Past experience testifies to this. The wrong of those apparently victorious enemies makes it impossible to believe that they can have fellowship with God. Therefore, the final words tell of the psalmist's confidence.

PSALM 95

Jehovah the King. A Warning

OH come, let us sing unto Jehovah;
 Let us make a joyful noise to the rock of our salvation.
2 Let us come before his presence with thanksgiving;
 Let us make a joyful noise unto him with psalms.
3 For Jehovah is a great God,
 And a great King above all gods.
4 In his hand are the deep places of the earth;
 The heights of the mountains are his also.
5 The sea is his, and he made it;
 And his hands formed the dry land.
6 Oh come, let us worship and bow down;
 Let us kneel before Jehovah our Maker:

7 For he is our God,
 And we are the people of his pasture, and the sheep of his hand.
 To-day, oh that ye would hear his voice!
8 Harden not your heart, as at Meribah,
 As in the day of Massah in the wilderness;
9 When your fathers tempted me,
 Proved me, and saw my work.
10 Forty years long was I grieved with *that* generation,
 And said, It is a people that do err in their heart,
 And they have not known my ways:
11 Wherefore I sware in my wrath,
 That they should not enter into my rest.

We pause here to note a connection between a group of psalms, viz., xciii–c. These eight constitute the songs of the King, arranged in conformity with the needs of the people. The first (xciii) affirms His enthronement and government. The next (xciv) expresses the hope of His people even in the midst of circumstances of trial. Then follow six, dealing with the fact of His Kingship in varied ways.

The present one declares His supremacy, and utters a note of warning against that which must inevitably hinder His people from realizing the Rest of His reign. Calling first for praise to the King, the singer celebrates His supremacy. He is above all other authority, and is the God of all nature. He is, moreover, the God of His people; and therefore they should worship in submission and reverence before Him (vers. 1–7a). Then the warning note follows reminding them of the sins of their fathers which, as to their cause, consisted in failure of faith, which expressed itself in refusal to bow in submission to His will. That sin excluded them from rest, and the children are warned to profit by the ancient story. Such a King demands loyalty, and it must be more than that of a song; it must express itself in submission to His government.

PSALM 96

Jehovah the King. Worship

OH sing unto Jehovah a new song:
Sing unto Jehovah, all the earth.
2 Sing unto Jehovah, bless his name;
Show forth his salvation from day to day.
3 Declare his glory among the nations,
His marvellous works among all the peoples.

4 For great is Jehovah, and greatly to be praised:
He is to be feared above all gods.
5 For all the gods of the peoples are idols;
But Jehovah made the heavens.
6 Honor and majesty are before him:
Strength and beauty are in his sanctuary.

7 Ascribe unto Jehovah, ye kindreds of the peoples,
Ascribe unto Jehovah glory and
strength.
8 Ascribe unto Jehovah the glory
due unto his name:
Bring an offering, and come into
his courts.
9 Oh worship Jehovah in holy
array:
Tremble before him, all the
earth.
10 Say among the nations, Jehovah
reigneth:
The world also is established
that it cannot be moved:

He will judge the peoples with
equity.
11 Let the heavens be glad, and
let the earth rejoice;
Let the sea roar, and the fulness
thereof;
12 Let the field exult, and all that
is therein;
Then shall all the trees of the
wood sing for joy
13 Before Jehovah; for he cometh,
For he cometh to judge the
earth:
He will judge the world with
righteousness,
And the peoples with his truth.

There is a beauty about this song which irresistibly appeals
to the submissive soul. The previous warning must be heeded
in order to sing it. When the personal life is loyal to His
throne, the song of God's wide and beneficent dominion thrills
with exultation.

It moves out in widening circles. The first is that of His
own people, and sets forth His supremacy over all the gods of
the peoples. They are "things of nought"; He is the Creator,
and all things high and beautiful are His (vers. 1–6). The
second calls upon the nations to recognize His Kingship, and
to give Him His due, submitting themselves also in worship
and reverence (vers. 7–9). The third sweeps the whole earth
into its circumference, and rejoices in the equity of His reign.

No study of the devotional literature of these people is
possible without an ever-recurring consciousness of this far-
reaching purpose of God. If the song of the Lord begin in the
heart it always grows into the chorus in which others are
included in its music. To know the gracious glory of His reign
in personal life, is to reveal it to those beyond, and to desire
its victories in the uttermost reaches.

PSALM 97

Jehovah the King. His Judgments

JEHOVAH reigneth; let the earth rejoice;
Let the multitude of the isles be glad.

2 Clouds and darkness are round about him:
Righteousness and justice are the foundation of his throne.

3 A fire goeth before him,
And burneth up his adversaries round about.

4 His lightnings lightened the world:
The earth saw, and trembled.

5 The mountains melted like wax at the presence of Jehovah,
At the presence of the Lord of the whole earth.

6 The heavens declare his righteousness,
And all the peoples have seen his glory.

7 Let all them be put to shame that serve graven images,
That boast themselves of idols:
Worship him, all ye gods.

8 Zion heard and was glad,
And the daughters of Judah rejoiced,
Because of thy judgments, O Jehovah.

9 For thou, Jehovah, art most high above all the earth:
Thou art exalted far above all gods.

10 O ye that love Jehovah, hate evil:
He preserveth the souls of his saints;
He delivereth them out of the hand of the wicked.

11 Light is sown for the righteous,
And gladness for the upright in heart.

12 Be glad in Jehovah, ye righteous;
And give thanks to his holy memorial *name*.

The reign of Jehovah, while wholly beneficent in purpose and in ultimate issue, is yet full of terror and of judgment in its process toward the issue. This is also cause for rejoicing.

The method of God's judgments is described. They are mysterious, "Clouds and darkness are round about Him." They are founded upon strictest justice, "Righteousness and judgment are the foundation of His throne." They are forceful, "A fire goeth before Him."

The effects of His judgments are declared. His adversaries are destroyed, His glory is revealed, His people are filled with joy. The vision of the certainty, method, and victory of the judgments of the King gives rise to a sense of their underlying reason. He is the Holy One, and all wickedness is hateful to Him because of the harm it works among His people, for the fierceness of God's holiness is ever His love. Therefore let His saints learn the lesson and "hate evil." The promise to those who obey is very full of beauty. "Light is sown . . . and gladness." It is a figure of the dawn, shedding its light everywhere. To hate evil is to walk in light. To walk in light is to be able to discover the true pathway leading toward the desired consummation. To walk in that pathway is to have gladness in the heart indeed.

PSALM 98

Jehovah the King. Worship

OH sing unto Jehovah a new song;
For he hath done marvellous things:
His right hand, and his holy arm, hath wrought salvation for him.

2 Jehovah hath made known his salvation:
His righteousness hath he openly showed in the sight of the nations.

3 He hath remembered his lovingkindness and his faithfulness toward the house of Israel:
All the ends of the earth have seen the salvation of our God.

4 Make a joyful noise unto Jehovah, all the earth:
Break forth and sing for joy, yea, sing praises.

5 Sing praises unto Jehovah with the harp;
With the harp and the voice of melody.

6 With trumpets and sound of cornet
Make a joyful noise before the King, Jehovah.

7 Let the sea roar, and the fulness thereof;
The world, and they that dwell therein;

8 Let the floods clap their hands;
Let the hills sing for joy together

9 Before Jehovah; for he cometh to judge the earth:
He will judge the world with righteousness,
And the peoples with equity.

Another song of worship on the pattern of psalm xcvi. It opens and closes in the same way. A new song and its ultimate reason, the judging of the earth by Jehovah with righteousness and with truth. Here also the circles widen. Beginning with

Israel (vers. 1–3), the whole earth is included (vers. 4–6); and finally all nature (vers. 7, 8).

As the singer rejoices over the salvation of God manifested on behalf of Israel, he emphasizes the fact that it has been wrought by Jehovah alone. *"His* right hand, and *His* holy arm"; these were the only instruments available for, or capable of working deliverance. In proportion as the vision is filled with the glory of the Lord, the heart is filled with gladness, and the lips with song. This is as true to-day as ever. It sometimes seems as though all singing were out of place save as faith keeps its eye fixed on the occupied throne of Jehovah. The days are dark and mysterious as ever, and the outlook as full of gloom. Yes "He hath done marvellous things," and "He cometh to judge." This vision of God in the past and the future creates the song of the present.

PSALM 99

Jehovah the King. His Reign

JEHOVAH reigneth; let the peoples tremble:
He sitteth *above* the cherubim;
let the earth be moved.
2 Jehovah is great in Zion;
And he is high above all the peoples.
3 Let them praise thy great and terrible name:
Holy is he.

4 The king's strength also loveth justice;
Thou dost establish equity;
Thou executest justice and righteousness in Jacob.
5 Exalt ye Jehovah our God,
And worship at his foot-stool:
Holy is he.

6 Moses and Aaron among his priests,
And Samuel among them that call upon his name;
They called upon Jehovah, and he answered them.
7 He spake unto them in the pillar of cloud:
They kept his testimonies,
And the statute that he gave them.
8 Thou answeredst them, O Jehovah our God:
Thou wast a God that forgavest them,
Though thou tookest vengeance of their doings.
9 Exalt ye Jehovah our God,
And worship at his holy hill;
For Jehovah our God is holy.

This is a song of the Kingdom of Jehovah as founded upon and administered in holiness. There are three distinct parts, each ending with practically the same refrain. The first acclaims the King as enthroned (vers. 1–3). The second affirms the absolute integrity of His administration (vers. 4, 5). The third declares the constant and faithful guidance of His own representatives (vers. 6–9).

In each there is a call to the attitude of response to the fact declared. The enthroned King is to be praised. The governing King is to be exalted and worshipped in submission at His footstool. The guiding King is to be exalted and worshipped in fellowship in His holy hill. Finally, in each case, the underlying reason of the King's position and activity, and also therefore, of the response, is that of His holiness. The throne is established in holiness. The guidance is motived in holiness.

In the fuller light of the Christian revelation we see the threefold fact in the life of God suggested. The Father enthroned; the Son administering His Kingdom; the Spirit interpreting His will through leaders and circumstances, through pity and through punishment.

PSALM 100

Jehovah the King. Worship

MAKE a joyful noise unto Jehovah, all ye lands.

2 Serve Jehovah with gladness:
Come before his presence with singing.

3 Know ye that Jehovah, he is God:
It is he that hath made us, and we are his;
We are his people, and the sheep of his pasture.

4 Enter into his gates with thanksgiving,
And into his courts with praise:
Give thanks unto him, and bless his name.

5 For Jehovah is good; his lovingkindness *endureth* for ever,
And his faithfulness unto all generations.

This is the last song of the series, and forms a fitting conclusion to the movement which commenced in psalm xciii. There the Divine assumption of the throne and government was the subject. Here it is that of the benefits resulting to the whole earth. All lands are called upon to sing the song of His reign. The strength of their song is to be their service rendered with gladness. Israel is viewed as the witness to the Divine power and goodness. The peoples are supposed to see the position of the chosen people in all its desirableness, and they are reminded that their well-being is the result of the government of God.

Then the great invitation is given to the outlying people to enter His gates, to yield to Him, and share in His benefits. This is the true position and witness of God's chosen people according to His purpose for them, and through them, for others. It is a glimpse of a glory not realized by the ancient people. They never learned how to invite the outsider into the place of privilege. Because of their failure to do this, Israel as an earthly people is scattered and peeled. The Church, the spiritual Israel, fulfills, or ought to fulfill this function.

PSALM 101

Jehovah Recognized in Public and Private Life

I WILL sing of lovingkindness and justice:
Unto thee, O Jehovah, will I sing praises.

2 I will behave myself wisely in a perfect way:
Oh when wilt thou come unto me?
I will walk within my house with a perfect heart.

3 I will set no base thing before mine eyes:

I hate the work of them that turn aside;
It shall not cleave unto me.

4 A perverse heart shall depart from me:
I will know no evil thing.

5 Whoso privily slandereth his neighbor, him will I destroy:
Him that hath a high look and a proud heart will I not suffer.

6 Mine eyes shall be upon the faithful of the land, that they may dwell with me:

He that walketh in a perfect way, he shall minister unto me.
7 He that worketh deceit shall not dwell within my house:
He that speaketh falsehood shall not be established before mine eyes.

8 Morning by morning will I destroy all the wicked of the land;
To cut off all the workers of iniquity from the city of Jehovah.

A fine sense of the fitness of things is exhibited by the editor of the psalter in placing this psalm here. Following immediately upon the songs of the enthroned Jehovah, in which there has been perpetually recurrent the recognition of the holiness of His reign, it describes the true attitude of the earthly ruler who recognizes the sovereignty of God, and how that ought to affect his own life and rule. It is a clear testimony moreover, to the fact that private and public life are very closely allied.

It has two movements. The key note of the first is "within my house" (ver. 2). That of the second is "the city of God." Between these there is the closest relation. No man is able to make the city in which he dwells anything like the city of God who does not know how to behave himself in his own house. This is the true order also. The first thing for every public man to do who would serve his city for God, is to see to it that his private life is ordered aright before Him. The private life which answers the enthroned Jehovah is described first (vers. 1–4). It is a life cautious and watchful, refusing to countenance anything contrary to the holiness of Jehovah. The public life is one which respects the same holiness in all matters of administration. Evil workers are to be destroyed, and the counsellors of the ruler are to be sought among the faithful of the land.

PSALM 102

Jehovah the Eternal God

HEAR my prayer, O Jehovah,
And let my cry come unto
thee.
2 Hide not thy face from me in
the day of my distress:
Incline thine ear unto me;
In the day when I call answer
me speedily.
3 For my days consume away
like smoke,
And my bones are burned as a
firebrand.
4 My heart is smitten like grass,
and withered;
For I forget to eat my bread.
5 By reason of the voice of my
groaning
My bones cleave to my flesh.
6 I am like a pelican of the wilderness;
I am become as an owl of the
waste places.
7 I watch, and am become like a
sparrow
That is alone upon the house-
top.
8 Mine enemies reproach me all
the day;
They that are mad against me
do curse by me.
9 For I have eaten ashes like
bread,
And mingled my drink with
weeping,
10 Because of thine indignation and
thy wrath:
For thou hast taken me up, and
cast me away.
11 My days are like a shadow that
declineth;
And I am withered like grass.

12 But thou, O Jehovah, wilt abide
for ever;
And thy memorial *name* unto
all generations.
13 Thou wilt arise, and have mercy
upon Zion;
For it is time to have pity upon
her,
Yea, the set time is come.
14 For thy servants take pleasure
in her stones,
And have pity upon her dust.
15 So the nations shall fear the
name of Jehovah,
And all the kings of the earth
thy glory.
16 For Jehovah hath built up
Zion;
He hath appeared in his glory;
17 He hath regarded the prayer of
the destitute,
And hath not despised their
prayer.
18 This shall be written for the
generation to come;
And a people which shall be
created shall praise Jehovah.
19 For he hath looked down from
the height of his sanctuary;
From heaven did Jehovah behold the earth;
20 To hear the sighing of the prisoner;
To loose those that are appointed to death;
21 That men may declare the name
of Jehovah in Zion,
And his praise in Jerusalem;
22 When the peoples are gathered
together,

And the kingdoms, to serve Jehovah.

23 He weakened my strength in the way;
He shortened my days.

24 I said, O my God, take me not away in the midst of my days:
Thy years are throughout all generations.

25 Of old didst thou lay the foundation of the earth;
And the heavens are the work of thy hands.

26 They shall perish, but thou shalt endure;
Yea, all of them shall wax old like a garment;
As a vesture shalt thou change them, and they shall be changed:

27 But thou art the same,
And thy years shall have no end.

28 The children of thy servants shall continue,
And their seed shall be established before thee.

This is a song of faith triumphing over affliction. Beginning with a prayer for deliverance, and a statement of the circumstances of suffering in which he then was, together with a recognition of those sufferings as the chastisements of Jehovah (vers. 1–11), it rises to a great song of hope in the consciousness of the eternity of God, and the consequent conviction of the restoration of His own people to favour and blessing (vers. 12–22). Finally it returns to his own suffering, yet recognizes that suffering again, as part of the Divine process, and gains confidence in setting that also in the light of the eternity of God (vers. 23–28).

While there are great beauties in the details of the song, it is this general atmosphere which creates its greatest value for us. There is nothing more calculated to strengthen the heart in suffering, or inspire the spirit with courage in days of danger and difficulty, than the sense of the eternity of God. In it is to be found the certainty that the purpose defeated to-day will yet be completed. In the vision of the eternity of God there is revealed the continuity of humanity, and a great sense of the solidarity of the race is created. Let us set our limitations always in the light of His limitlessness.

PSALM 103

Jehovah the Loving Father

BLESS Jehovah, O my soul;
And all that is within me,
bless his holy name.
2 Bless Jehovah, O my soul,
And forget not all his benefits:
3 Who forgiveth all thine iniquities;
Who healeth all thy diseases;
4 Who redeemeth thy life from
destruction;
Who crowneth thee with lovingkindness and tender mercies;
5 Who satisfieth thy desire with
good things,
So that thy youth is renewed
like the eagle.
6 Jehovah executeth righteous
acts,
And judgments for all that are
oppressed.
7 He made known his ways unto
Moses,
His doings unto the children of
Israel.
8 Jehovah is merciful and gracious,
Slow to anger, and abundant in
lovingkindness.
9 He will not always chide;
Neither will he keep *his anger*
for ever.
10 He hath not dealt with us after
our sins,
Nor rewarded us after our iniquities.
11 For as the heavens are high
above the earth,
So great is his lovingkindness
toward them that fear him.
12 As far as the east is from the
west,

So far hath he removed our
transgressions from us.
13 Like as a father pitieth his children,
So Jehovah pitieth them that
fear him.
14 For he knoweth our frame;
He remembereth that we are
dust.
15 As for man, his days are as
grass;
As a flower of the field, so he
flourisheth.
16 For the wind passeth over it,
and it is gone;
And the place thereof shall
know it no more.
17 But the lovingkindness of Jehovah is from everlasting to
everlasting upon them that
fear him,
And his righteousness unto children's children;
18 To such as keep his covenant,
And to those that remember his
precepts to do them.
19 Jehovah hath established his
throne in the heavens;
And his kingdom ruleth over all.
20 Bless Jehovah, ye his angels,
That are mighty in strength,
that fulfil his word,
Hearkening unto the voice of
his word.
21 Bless Jehovah, all ye his hosts,
Ye ministers of his, that do his
pleasure.
22 Bless Jehovah, all ye his works,
In all places of his dominion:
Bless Jehovah, O my soul.

It seems almost a work of supererogation to write anything about this psalm. It is perhaps the most perfect song of pure praise to be found in the Bible. It has become the common inheritance of all who through suffering and deliverance have learned the goodness of Jehovah. Through centuries it has been sung by glad hearts, and to-day is as fresh and full of beauty as ever. It is praise intensive and extensive.

As to its intensity, notice how the entire personality of the singer is recognized. The spirit of the man speaks. He addresses his soul, or mind, and calls it to praise first for spiritual benefits, and then for physical. And again notice how in the sweep of the song, things so small as the frame of the physical and its constituent dust are recognized, while yet the immeasurable reaches of east and west are included.

The extensive mercy of Jehovah, as evident in the same system, is seen in other psalms, but perhaps never so majestically as here. It begins with individual consciousness (vers. 1–5); proceeds in recognition of national blessings (vers. 6–18); and ends with the inclusion of all the angels, and hosts, and works in the vast dominion of Jehovah. The "my" of personal experience merges into the "our" of social fellowship, and thus culminates in the "all" of universal consciousness. Yet all ends with the personal word, and the perfect music of the psalm is revealed in the fact that it opens and closes on the same note.

PSALM 104

Jehovah the Creator and Sustainer

BLESS Jehovah, O my soul.
O Jehovah my God, thou art
very great;
Thou art clothed with honor
and majesty:
2 Who coverest thyself with light
as with a garment;
Who stretchest out the heavens
like a curtain;

3 Who layeth the beams of his
chambers in the waters;
Who maketh the clouds his
chariot;
Who walketh upon the wings of
the wind;
4 Who maketh winds his messengers;
Flames of fire his ministers;

5 Who laid the foundations of the
earth,
That it should not be moved
for ever.
6 Thou coveredst it with the deep
as with a vesture;
The waters stood above the
mountains.
7 At thy rebuke they fled;
At the voice of thy thunder they
hasted away
8 (The mountains rose, the valleys sank down)
Unto the place which thou hadst
founded for them.
9 Thou hast set a bound that they
may not pass over;
That they turn not again to
cover the earth.
10 He sendeth forth springs into
the valleys;
They run among the mountains;
11 They give drink to every beast
of the field;
The wild asses quench their
thirst.
12 By them the birds of the heavens
have their habitation;
They sing among the branches.
13 He watereth the mountains
from his chambers:
The earth is filled with the fruit
of thy works.
14 He causeth the grass to grow
for the cattle,
And herb for the service of
man;
That he may bring forth food
out of the earth,
15 And wine that maketh glad the
heart of man,
And oil to make his face to
shine,
And bread that strengtheneth
man's heart.

16 The trees of Jehovah are filled
with moisture,
The cedars of Lebanon, which
he hath planted;
17 Where the birds make their
nests:
As for the stork, the fir-trees
are her house.
18 The high mountains are for the
wild goats;
The rocks are a refuge for the
conies.
19 He appointed the moon for seasons:
The sun knoweth his going
down.
20 Thou makest darkness, and it is
night,
Wherein all the beasts of the
forest creep forth.
21 The young lions roar after their
prey,
And seek their food from God.
22 The sun ariseth, they get them
away,
And lay them down in their
dens.
23 Man goeth forth unto his work
And to his labor until the evening.
24 O Jehovah, how manifold are
thy works!
In wisdom hast thou made them
all:
The earth is full of thy riches.
25 Yonder is the sea, great and
wide,
Wherein are things creeping innumerable,
Both small and great beasts.
26 There go the ships;
There is leviathan, whom **thou**
hast formed to play therein.
27 These wait all for thee,

That thou mayest give them their food in due season.

28 Thou givest unto them, they gather;
Thou openest thy hand, they are satisfied with good.

29 Thou hidest thy face, they are troubled;
Thou takest away their breath, they die,
And return to their dust.

30 Thou sendest forth thy Spirit, they are created;
And thou renewest the face of the ground.

31 Let the glory of Jehovah endure for ever;
Let Jehovah rejoice in his works:

32 Who looketh on the earth, and it trembleth;
He toucheth the mountains, and they smoke.

33 I will sing unto Jehovah as long as I live:
I will sing praise to my God while I have any being.

34 Let my meditation be sweet unto him:
I will rejoice in Jehovah.

35 Let sinners be consumed out of the earth,
And let the wicked be no more.
Bless Jehovah, O my soul.
Praise ye Jehovah.

Again we have a great song of praise commencing and closing with the same note of personal praise. While in the former the dominant note is that of the mercy of Jehovah, here it is that of His majesty. The former is the song of love to Love. This is a song of loyalty to Royalty.

The psalm opens with a declaration of the essential greatness of God, and then proceeds in poetic language to describe the manifestations of His greatness in creation. All through, beneficent purpose is recognized. The springs among the valleys are for the quenching of the thirst of birds and beasts. Grass and herbs are for service, and so on throughout.

Then in a burst of praise the singer recognizes the dependence of all upon Jehovah. The hiding of His face is trouble, and if He withdraw breath, death ensues. Finally, he cries out for the continuity of the realization of Divine purpose everywhere, in order that Jehovah may rejoice in His works. To this end he declares he will make the contribution of his personal worship. The conception is full of beauty. The widespread revelation of the power and glory of God makes its appeal to the individual responsibility of the one man.

PSALM 105

Jehovah the True and Mighty One

OH give thanks unto Jehovah,
call upon his name;
Make known among the peoples
his doings.

2 Sing unto him, sing praises unto
him;
Talk ye of all his marvellous
works.

3 Glory ye in his holy name:
Let the heart of them rejoice
that seek Jehovah.

4 Seek ye Jehovah and his
strength;
Seek his face evermore.

5 Remember his marvellous works
that he hath done,
His wonders, and the judgments
of his mouth,

6 O ye seed of Abraham his servant,
Ye children of Jacob, his chosen
ones.

7 He is Jehovah our God:
His judgments are in all the
earth.

8 He hath remembered his covenant for ever,
The word which he commanded
to a thousand generations,

9 *The covenant* which he made
with Abraham,
And his oath unto Isaac,

10 And confirmed the same unto
Jacob for a statute,
To Israel for an everlasting
covenant,

11 Saying, Unto thee will I give
the land of Canaan,
The lot of your inheritance;

12 When they were but a few men
in number,

Yea, very few, and sojourners
in it.

13 And they went about from nation to nation,
From one kingdom to another
people.

14 He suffered no man to do them
wrong;
Yea, he reproved kings for their
sakes,

15 *Saying*, Touch not mine
anointed ones,
And do my prophets no harm.

16 And he called for a famine upon
the land;
He brake the whole staff of
bread.

17 He sent a man before them;
Joseph was sold for a servant:

18 His feet they hurt with fetters:
He was laid in *chains of* iron,

19 Until the time that his word
came to pass,
The word of Jehovah tried him.

20 The king sent and loosed him;
Even the ruler of peoples, and
let them go free.

21 He made him lord of his house,
And ruler of all his substance;

22 To bind his princes at his pleasure,
And teach his elders wisdom.

23 Israel also came into Egypt;
And Jacob sojourned in the land
of Ham.

24 And he increased his people
greatly,
And made them stronger than
their adversaries.

25 He turned their heart to hate
his people,

To deal subtly with his servants.

26 He sent Moses his servant,
And .Aaron whom he had chosen.

27 They set among them his signs,
And wonders in the land of Ham.

28 He sent darkness, and made it dark;
And they rebelled not against his words.

29 He turned their waters into blood,
And slew their fish.

30 Their land swarmed with frogs
In the chambers of their kings.

31 He spake, and there came swarms of flies,
And lice in all their borders.

32 He gave them hail for rain,
And flaming fire in their land.

33 He smote their vines also and their fig-trees,
And brake the trees of their borders.

34 He spake, and the locust came,
And the grasshopper, and that without number,

35 And did eat up every herb in their land,
And did eat up the fruit of their ground.

36 He smote also all the first-born in their land,
The chief of all their strength.

37 And he brought them forth with silver and gold;
And there was not one feeble person among his tribes.

38 Egypt was glad when they departed;
For the fear of them had fallen upon them.

39 He spread a cloud for a covering,
And fire to give light in the night.

40 They asked, and he brought quails,
And satisfied them with the bread of heaven.

41 He opened the rock, and waters gushed out;
They ran in the dry places like a river.

42 For he remembered his holy word,
And Abraham his servant.

43 And he brought forth his people with joy,
And his chosen with singing.

44 And he gave them the lands of the nations;
And they took the labor of the peoples in possession:

45 That they might keep his statutes,
And observe his laws.
Praise ye Jehovah.

This and the following psalm are companions. They reveal the two sides of the relation between God and His people during a long period. This one sings the song of His faithfulness and power; while the next tells the sad story of repeated failure and rebellion on the part of His people.

In singing His praise the psalmist opens with an appeal

which recognizes the responsibility of those who have been
recipients of blessing. The words, "Make known His doings
among the peoples" reveal this. The leaders and singers of
these people repeated this message of responsibility with almost monotonous reiteration, and yet it was not obeyed. In
order that the doings of God may be proclaimed, he calls upon
men to "remember," and he proceeds to trace the Divine hand
in their history. First, he goes back to the ancient covenant,
and sings of how God cared for them while they were few in
number in the land, rebuking kings for their sakes.

Then follows a recognition of the government of God as
overruling even what appeared so disastrous a matter as the
famine. Through that, Joseph was given his opportunity, and
the people were brought into Egypt, for the time being a place
of quietness and increase.

The master word in the psalm is the pronoun "He." In
constant repetition it shows the one thought uppermost in the
mind of the singer. It is that of the perpetual activity of God
in all those experiences through which His people have passed.
Verse 25 commences with a statement which is almost startling—"He turned their heart to hate His people." Yet this
is a recognition of the fact that circumstances which appeared
to be most disastrous, were nevertheless all under His government. It was through the oppression of the Egyptians that
Israel passed through a baptism of suffering which toughened
the fibre of the national life, and prepared for all that lay
ahead.

Then the singer passes in review God's wonderful deliverance of them from Egypt, until in a graphic sentence he writes,
"Egypt was glad when they departed." Finally the song
speaks of the bringing of them into possession of the land. It
is a noble song of the might of God, and of His fidelity to His
people. With unswerving loyalty to His covenant, in spite of
all difficulties, and by means of suffering as well as joy, He

moved in their history ever onward. Such a song is prophecy, in its function of interpreting history, and revealing the orderliness in the economy of God, of days and events which seem to be the most calamitous.

PSALM 106

Jehovah the Faithful and Patient One

PRAISE ye Jehovah.
Oh give thanks unto Jehovah; for he is good;
For his lovingkindness *endureth* for ever.

2 Who can utter the mighty acts of Jehovah,
Or show forth all his praise?

3 Blessed are they that keep justice,
And he that doeth righteousness at all times.

4 Remember me, O Jehovah, with the favor that thou bearest unto thy people;
Oh visit me with thy salvation,

5 That I may see the prosperity of thy chosen,
That I may rejoice in the gladness of thy nation,
That I may glory with thine inheritance.

6 We have sinned with our fathers,
We have committed iniquity, we have done wickedly.

7 Our fathers understood not thy wonders in Egypt;
They remembered not the multitude of thy lovingkindnesses,
But were rebellious at the sea, even at the Red Sea.

8 Nevertheless he saved them for his name's sake,

That he might make his mighty power to be known.

9 He rebuked the Red Sea also, and it was dried up:
So he led them through the depths, as through a wilderness.

10 And he saved them from the hand of him that hated them,
And redeemed them from the hand of the enemy.

11 And the waters covered their adversaries;
There was not one of them left.

12 Then believed they his words;
They sang his praise.

13 They soon forgat his works;
They waited not for his counsel,

14 But lusted exceedingly in the wilderness,
And tempted God in the desert.

15 And he gave them their request,
But sent leanness into their soul.

16 They envied Moses also in the camp,
And Aaron the saint of Jehovah.

17 The earth opened and swallowed up Dathan,
And covered the company of Abiram

18 And a fire was kindled in their company;
The flame burned up the wicked.

19 They made a calf in Horeb,

And worshipped a molten image.
20 Thus they changed their glory
    For the likeness of an ox that
    eateth grass.
21 They forgat God their Saviour,
    Who had done great things in
    Egypt,
22 Wondrous works in the land of
    Ham,
    And terrible things by the Red
    Sea.
23 Therefore he said that he would
    destroy them,
    Had not Moses his chosen stood
    before him in the breach,
    To turn away his wrath, lest he
    should destroy *them.*
24 Yea, they despised the pleasant
    land,
    They believed not his word,
25 But murmured in their tents,
    And hearkened not unto the
    voice of Jehovah.
26 Therefore he sware unto them,
    That he would overthrow them
    in the wilderness,
27 And that he would overthrow
    their seed among the nations,
    And scatter them in the lands.
28 They joined themselves also
    unto Baal-peor,
    And ate the sacrifices of the
    dead.
29 Thus they provoked him to
    anger with their doings;
    And the plague brake in upon
    them.
30 Then stood up Phinehas, and
    executed judgment;
    And so the plague was stayed.
31 And that was reckoned unto
    him for righteousness,
    Unto all generations for ever-
    more.

32 They angered him also at the
    waters of Meribah,
    So that it went ill with Moses
    for their sakes;
33 Because they were rebellious
    against his spirit,
    And he spake unadvisedly with
    his lips.
34 They did not destroy the peo-
    ples,
    As Jehovah commanded them,
35 But mingled themselves with
    the nations,
    And learned their works,
36 And served their idols,
    Which became a snare unto
    them.
37 Yea, they sacrificed their sons
    and their daughters unto
    demons,
38 And shed innocent blood,
    Even the blood of their sons and
    of their daughters,
    Whom they sacrificed unto the
    idols of Canaan;
    And the land was polluted with
    blood.
39 Thus were they defiled with
    their works,
    And played the harlot in their
    doings.
40 Therefore was the wrath of Je-
    hovah kindled against his
    people,
    And he abhorred this inherit-
    ance.
41 And he gave them into the hand
    of the nations;
    And they that hated them ruled
    over them.
42 Their enemies also oppressed
    them,
    And they were brought into
    subjection under their hand.

43 Many times did he deliver
    them;
But they were rebellious in their
    counsel,
And were brought low in their
    iniquity.
44 Nevertheless he regarded their
    distress,
When he heard their cry:
45 And he remembered for them
    his covenant,
And repented according to the
    multitude of his lovingkind-
    nesses.
46 He made them also to be pitied
Of all those that carried them
    captive.
47 Save us, O Jehovah our God,
And gather us from among the
    nations,
To give thanks unto thy holy
    name,
And to triumph in thy praise.

48 Blessed be Jehovah, the God of
    Israel,
From everlasting even to ever-
    lasting.
And let all the people say,
    Amen.
Praise ye Jehovah.

The previous psalm called the people to talk of the "marvel-lous works" of Jehovah. This one calls to praise, and the reason is that "His mercy endureth for ever." This fact is then illustrated by a declaration of how the people of God have persistently sinned against Him, and how He has patiently borne with them, restoring them constantly to Himself.

The first section (vers. 1–31) deals with the history of the people from Egypt, and in the wilderness. The description of what happened immediately after the crossing of the Red Sea is graphic:—

"Then believed they His words;
    They sang His praise.
    They soon forgot His works;
    They waited not for His counsel."

That is the explanation of all the story. In the hour of deliverance faith aided by sight is strong, and it is easy to sing. But directly strain and stress return, the past of God's might is forgotten, and His counsel is not sought. And so the story runs on through Dathan and Abiram, by way of Horeb and to Baal Peor. Over against all the unutterable folly of the people, the faithfulness and matchless patience of Jehovah is seen.

Continuing the same sad story, the psalmist then turned to the unfaithfulness of the people in the land (vers. 32–48). This he begins by referring to Moses' exclusion. This reference seems to be a remarkable recognition of the strength of the man. The fair deduction from the setting of the story seems to be that if he had entered with them, some of the things might have been different.

The story of their failure in the land is tragic, but there is evident a recognition on the part of the singer of a poetic justice in their calamity. Moses was excluded because of his failure to represent God to His people, but that failure was provoked by their sin; and they, passing into the land without him, were from the beginning in greater or less degree corrupted. Their initial sin was that of disobedience, either on the ground of pity, or for purpose of compromise. The result was that they descended to all the abominations of which the peoples were guilty. Very beautiful is the revelation of God which occurs in the statement. "He made them also to be pitied of all those that carried them captives." While their persistent and terrible sin made His wrath burn and His judgment inevitable, yet the love of His heart never ceased toward the people of His choice.

BOOK V.

PSALMS 107–150

BOOK V. PSALMS 107–150

DOXOLOGY

"Praise ye the Lord. Praise God in His sanctuary. Praise Him in the firmament of His power.
Praise Him for His mighty acts: Praise Him according to His excellent greatness.
Praise Him with the sound of the trumpet: Praise Him with the psaltery and harp.
Praise Him with the timbrel and dance: Praise Him with stringed instruments and the pipe.
Praise Him upon the loud cymbals: Praise Him upon the high sounding cymbals.
Let everything that hath breath praise the Lord. Praise ye the Lord." Ps. 150.

A. THE TITLE.	B. THE QUALITY.	C. THE PLACE.	D. THE REASON.	E. THE MEASURE.	F. THE MEANS.	G. THE CONDITIONS.
In this Doxology, which occupies the whole psalm, the name of God only appears: 1. As "Jah" in the perfect note of Praise, "Hallelujah" twice repeated. "Jah" being in such case a contraction of "Jehovah." 2. As "God" in the singular form "El," which is always significant of His might.	"Praise Him."	"In" "Sanctuary" Centre. "Firmament." Circumference.	"For" "His mighty Acts."	"According to" "His excellent greatness."	"With" "Instruments of Music."	"Everything that hath breath."

The Divine Name.

Again in the final book "Jehovah" is the predominant name. It occurs in every psalm but 2, in some of them many times—236 in all.

The name "God" is absent from 22 of these psalms. It occurs 40 times, 10 in the singular, and 30 in the plural.

The general title "Lord" (Adonahy) is found 12 times, "Jah" 32 times.

The Dominant Thought.

In this book, as an examination of the doxology will show, the worship of Jehovah is consummated. It rises in volume and beauty until in the closing words of the doxology ultimate purpose is declared. "Let everything that hath breath praise the Lord. Hallelujah."

Still the songs are those arising out of various experiences. A large section is devoted to Songs of Ascent, which are those of the pilgrims as they gathered by many ways and along different paths to the place of the Divine glory.

ANALYSIS

A. SONGS OF THE HOPE. 107 to 112	B. SONGS OF THE PROCESS. 113 to 118	C. SONGS OF THE REVEALED WILL. 119
I. The Hope. 107 to 109	**I. Jehovah's Activity.** 113 to 114	Aleph. 1 to 8 The perfect Law.
i. Assurance of Faith. 107	i. His Humility. 113	Beth. 9 to 16 The Way of Cleansing.
ii. Fixity of Faith. 108	ii. His Accomplishment. 114	Gimel. 17 to 24 The Fountain of Joy. Daleth. 25 to 32 The Strength of Trial.
iii. Triumph of Faith. 109		He. 33 to 40 The Medium of Guidance. Vau. 41 to 48 The Inspiration of Testimony.
II. The Reason. 110 to 112	**II. Jehovah's Servant.** 115 to 116	Zain. 49 to 56 The Comfort of Sorrow.
i. The coming One. 110	i. The Passion. The Glory of His Name. 115	Cheth. 57 to 64 The Medium of Fellowship. Teth. 65 to 72 The Key of Affliction.
ii. The Greatness and Grace of Jehovah. 111	ii. The Experience. Darkness and Deliverance. 116	Jod. 73 to 80 The Depths of Desire. Caph. 81 to 88 The Confidence of Darkness.
iii. The Blessedness of the trusting Man. 112		Lamed. 89 to 96 The Foundation of Faith. Mem. 97 to 104 The Delight of Life.
	III. Jehovah's Praise. 117-118	Nun. 105 to 112 The Light of Pilgrimage. Samech. 113 to 120 The Line of Rectitude.
	i. The Call of the ideal Servant. 117	Ain. 121 to 128 The Hope of Distress. Pe. 129 to 136 The Light of Life.
	ii. The Song of the Redeemed. 118	Tzade. 137 to 144 The Knowledge of God. Koph. 145 to 152 The Inspiration of Devotion.
		Resh. 153 to 160 The Principle of Life. Shin. 161 to 168 The true Wealth.
		Tau. 169 to 176 The Perfect Law.

ANALYSIS

PSALM 107

Jehovah the Redeemer

OH give thanks unto Jehovah;
for he is good;
For his lovingkindness *endureth*
for ever.

2 Let the redeemed of Jehovah
say *so*,
Whom he hath redeemed from
the hand of the adversary,

3 And gathered out of the lands,
From the east and from the
west,
From the north and from the
south.

4 They wandered in the wilderness in a desert way;
They found no city of habitation.

5 Hungry and thirsty,
Their soul fainted in them.

6 Then they cried unto Jehovah
in their trouble,
And he delivered them out of
their distresses,

7 He led them also by a straight
way,
That they might go to a city of
habitation.

8 Oh that men would praise Jehovah for his lovingkindness,
And for his wonderful works to
the children of men!

9 For he satisfieth the longing
soul,
And the hungry soul he filleth
with good.

10 Such as sat in darkness and in
the shadow of death,
Being bound in affliction and
iron,

11 Because they rebelled against
the words of God,
And contemned the counsel of
the Most High:

12 Therefore he brought down
their heart with labor;
They fell down, and there was
none to help.

13 Then they cried unto Jehovah
in their trouble,
And he saved them out of their
distresses.

14 He brought them out of darkness and the shadow of death,
And brake their bonds in
sunder.

15 Oh that men would praise Jehovah for his lovingkindness,
And for his wondeful works to
the children of men!

16 For he hath broken the gates of
brass,
And cut the bars of iron in
sunder.

17 Fools because of their transgression,
And because of their iniquities,
are afflicted.

18 Their soul abhorreth all man-
ner of food;
And they draw near unto the
gates of death.

19 Then they cry unto Jehovah in
their trouble,
And he saveth them out of their
distresses.

20 He sendeth his word, and healeth them,
And delivereth *them* from their
destructions.

21 Oh that men would praise Jehovah for his lovingkindness,
And for his wonderful works to
the children of men!

22 And let them offer the sacrifices
of thanksgiving,
And declare his works with singing.

23 They that go down to the sea
in ships,
That do business in great
waters;

24 These see the works of Jehovah,
And his wonders in the deep.

25 For he commandeth, and raiseth
the stormy wind,
Which lifteth up the waves
thereof.

26 They mount up to the heavens,
they go down again to the
depths:
Their soul melteth away because
of trouble.

27 They reel to and fro, and stag-
ger like a drunken man,
And are at their wits' end.

28 Then they cry unto Jehovah in
their trouble,
And he bringeth them out of
their distresses.

29 He maketh the storm a calm,
So that the waves thereof are
still.

30 Then are they glad because they
are quiet;
So he bringeth them unto their
desired haven.

31 Oh that men would praise Jehovah for his lovingkindness,
And for his wonderful works to
the children of men!

32 Let them exalt him also in the
assembly of the people,
And praise him in the seat of
the elders.

33 He turneth rivers into a wilderness,
And watersprings into a thirsty
ground;

34 A fruitful land into a salt desert,
For the wickedness of them that
dwell therein.

35 He turneth a wilderness into a
pool of water,
And a dry land into watersprings.

36 And there he maketh the hungry
to dwell,
That they may prepare a city
of habitation,

37 And sow fields, and plant vine-
yards,
And get them fruits of increase.

38 He blesseth them also, so that
they are multiplied greatly;
And he suffereth not their cattle
to decrease.

39 Again, they are diminished and
bowed down
Through oppression, trouble,
and sorrow.

40 He poureth contempt upon
princes,
And causeth them to wander in
the waste, where there is no
way.

41 Yet setteth he the needy on
high from affliction,
And maketh *him* families like
a flock.

42 The upright shall see it, and be
glad;
And all iniquity shall stop her
mouth.

43 Whoso is wise will give heed to
these things;
And they will consider the lovingkindnesses of Jehovah.

We now begin the fifth and last book of the Psalter. In this book the music is richest and fullest. It begins in this psalm on the fundamental notes, and rises through major and minor, by the way of the songs of ascents, to the final measures of perfect praise contained in the doxology.

The first thirty-two verses contain a wonderful story of redemption, using that word in its sense of deliverance from positions and circumstances of peril. In a prologue the theme of the songs is stated. A people redeemed and gathered by Jehovah is called upon to declare the fact.

Then follow four strophes in which the redemption is illustrated in four ways. Each of these ends with the same appeal for praise, varied by description suitable to the previous illustration. The first illustration is that of homelessness. The second is that of bondage. The third if that of affliction. The last is that of a storm. The homeless, Jehovah led to a city of habitation; the enslaved, He led into liberty; the afflicted, He healed; the storm-tossed, He led to calm and a haven. All through, the connection between sorrow and sin is clearly seen. The method of Jehovah is described as that of dealing with sin in order to the healing of sorrow. Such deliverances demand worship, and the song is a psalm of praise interspersed with sighings after more perfect praise.

At verse 33 the psalm changes its tone, and becomes meditative. With the facts of Divine deliverances still in mind, the underlying principles of Divine activity are stated. Things which appear contradictory are seen to be evidences of consistency. Jehovah turns fruitful places into a wilderness; He turns the wilderness into a fruitful place. His activities are destructive and constructive. He blesses and multiplies a people. Again they are abased and afflicted. He is the Author of good as prosperity, and evil as adversity. He dethrones the high, and exalts the lowly. Everything results from the attitude of the men with whom He deals. Upright men are made to rejoice. Men of iniquity are silenced.

The concluding words draw attention to the importance of understanding these matters. The wise will give heed to them. The mercies of Jehovah are to be considered. This means much more than they are to be remembered. The Authorized "understand," and the Revised "consider" are both partial interpretations of the Hebrew word. It very literally means to distinguish. That is to say, God's "mercies" or "lovingkindnesses" are to be considered in their method and meaning, that they may be understood and not misinterpreted. They are not capricious, but proceed ever in harmony with fixed principles.

PSALM 108

Jehovah the Anchorage of Hope

MY heart is fixed, O God;
I will sing, yea, I will sing
praises, even with my glory.

2 Awake, psaltery and harp:
I myself will awake right early.

3 I will give thanks unto thee, O
Jehovah, among the peoples;
And I will sing praises unto thee
among the nations.

4 For thy lovingkindness is great
above the heavens;
And thy truth *reacheth* unto the
skies.

5 Be thou exalted, O God, above
the heavens,
And thy glory above all the
earth.

6 That thy beloved may be delivered,
Save with thy right hand, and
answer us.

7 God hath spoken in his holiness: I will exult;
I will divide Shechem, and mete
out the valley of Succoth.

8 Gilead is mine; Manasseh is
mine;
Ephraim also is the defence of
my head;
Judah is my sceptre.

9 Moab is my washpot;
Upon Edom will I cast my
shoe;
Over Philistia will I shout.

10 Who will bring me into the
fortified city?
Who hath led me unto Edom?

11 Hast not thou cast us off, O
God?
And thou goest not forth, O
God, with our hosts.

12 Give us help against the adversary;
For vain is the help of man.

13 Through God we shall do valiantly:
For he is it that will tread down
our adversaries.

This psalm is composed of two quotations from former songs. The first part (vers. 1–5) is taken from psalm lvii, of which the theme is "God the Refuge in calamity" (vers. 7–11). The second part is found in psalm lx, of which the theme is "God the Hope of His people" (vers. 5–12). That with which this psalm opens was the culmination of the earlier psalm, in which, out of calamity, the singer finds refuge in fixity of heart in God. Here in this book of perfected praise it is the opening declaration in a song of triumph over circumstances of difficulty and danger.

The latter part of this psalm was also the close of psalm lx, and there, was preceded by a detailed description of affliction. The point of interest then in this song is that of the attitude of mind indicated by this selection. The circumstances of the writer would seem to be very similar to those obtaining in the earlier psalms. They are only hinted at in passing. The soul's fixity of heart enables the singer to rejoice from beginning to end. Relation to God affects all the relationships. To be homed in His will, and submissive to His throne, is to be triumphant under all circumstances. Triumph in the very hour of defeat is the finest, but it is only possible when the heart is fixed in God.

PSALM 109

Jehovah the Vindicator of the Persecuted

HOLD not thy peace, O God of my praise;
2 For the mouth of the wicked and the mouth of deceit have they opened against me:
They have spoken unto me with a lying tongue.
3 They have compassed me about also with words of hatred,
And fought against me without a cause.

4 For my love they are my adversaries:
But I *give myself unto* prayer.
5 And they have rewarded me evil for good,
And hatred for my love.
6 Set thou a wicked man over him;
And let an adversary stand at his right hand.
7 When he is judged, let him come forth guilty;

And let his prayer be turned
into sin.

8 Let his days be few;
And let another take his office.

9 Let his children be fatherless,
And his wife a widow.

10 Let his children be vagabonds,
and beg;
And let them seek *their bread*
out of their desolate places.

11 Let the extortioner catch all
that he hath;
And let strangers make spoil of
his labor.

12 Let there be none to extend
kindness unto him;
Neither let there be any to have
pity on his fatherless children.

13 Let his posterity be cut off;
In the generation following let
their name be blotted out.

14 Let the iniquity of his fathers
be remembered with Jehovah;
And let not the sin of his mother
be blotted out.

15 Let them be before Jehovah
continually,
That he may cut off the memory
of them from the earth;

16 Because he remembered not to
show kindness,
But persecuted the poor and
needy man,
And the broken in heart, to slay
them.

17 Yea, he loved cursing, and it
came unto him;
And he delighted not in blessing,
and it was far from him.

18 He clothed himself also with
cursing as with his garment,
And it came into his inward
parts like water,
And like oil into his bones.

19 Let it be unto him as the rai-
ment wherewith he covereth
himself,
And for the girdle wherewith he
is girded continually.

20 This is the reward of mine adversaries from Jehovah,
And of them that speak evil
against my soul.

21 But deal thou with me, O Jehovah the Lord, for thy name's
sake:
Because thy lovingkindness is
good, deliver thou me;

22 For I am poor and needy,
And my heart is wounded within
me;

22 For I am poor and needy,
And my heart is wounded
within me.

23 I am gone like the shadow when
it declineth:
I am tossed up and down as the
locust.

24 My knees are weak through
fasting;

25 I am become also a reproach
unto them:
When they see me, they shake
their head.

26 Help me, O Jehovah my God;
Oh save me according to thy
lovingkindness:

27 That they may know that this is
thy hand;
That thou, Jehovah, hast done
it.

28 Let them curse, but bless thou:
When they arise, they shall be
put to shame,
But thy servant shall rejoice.

29 Let mine adversaries be clothed
with dishonor,
And let them cover themselves
with their own shame as with
a robe.

30 I will give great thanks unto Jehovah with my mouth;
Yea, I will praise him among
the multitude.

31 For he will stand at the right
hand of the needy,
To save him from them that
judge his soul.

This is a psalm full of interest. The singer is in a place of terrible suffering due to the implacable hostility of his foes. The passage containing the imprecations (vers. 6–19) contains the singer's quotation of what his enemies say about him, rather than what he says about them. In a translation published by the Jewish Publication Society of America, that fact is clearly shown. They render vers. 5 and 20 thus:—

"They repay me evil for good,
And hatred for my love (saying)——"
"This it is which mine enemies seek to obtain of the Lord,
And those that speak evil against my life."

This is extremely probable in view of the fact that the opening complaint is, "The mouth of the wicked and the mouth of deceit have they opened against me." The singer complains, "For my love they are my adversaries" (which the translation already referred to gives as, "In return for my love they persecute me.")

Taking this view of the psalm it is a sob, which is also a song. The circumstances are terrible. Perhaps there is nothing harder to bear than accusations which are untrue, and these were terrible things which they said, and horrible things they desired for him. But the heart pours out its complaint to God, and ends with a note of praise.

PSALM 110

Jehovah and His Messiah

JEHOVAH saith unto my lord,
Sit thou at my right hand,
Until I make thine enemies thy
footstool.

2 Jehovah will send forth the rod
of thy strength out of Zion:
Rule thou in the midst of thine
enemies.

3 Thy people offer themselves willingly
In the day of thy power, in holy array:
Out of the womb of the morning
Thou hast the dew of thy youth.
4 Jehovah hath sworn, and will not repent:
Thou art a priest for ever
After the order of Melchizedek.
5 The Lord at thy right hand

Will strike through kings in the day of his wrath.
6 He will judge among the nations.
He will fill *the places* with dead bodies;
He will strike through the head in many countries.
7 He will drink of the brook in the way:
Therefore will he lift up the head.

This psalm is purely Messianic, and was always considered to be so. When Jesus quoted it in His conversation with the rulers, it is perfectly evident that they looked upon it in that light. It is equally certain that He made use of it in that sense. While we believe the authorship of many of these psalms to be uncertain, we claim that the words of Jesus put the question of authorship in this case beyond dispute. Then the beauty of the song is seen in all its fulness. David the king, sings of Another as Lord, and therefore superior to himself.

In the first half of the song (vers. 1–4) he sings of the relation of the coming King to Jehovah. The second half (vers. 5–7) tells of the might and victory of the appointed King. This division is clearly marked by the names of the psalm. "Jehovah said unto Adonahy," "Jehovah shall send forth," "Jehovah hath sworn, and will not repent," "Adonahy at Thy right hand." Both these names or titles are used often of God. Here Jehovah is used of God, and Adonahy of the coming King. This King is appointed by Jehovah. He is strengthened by Jehovah. He is a King to Whom His people will gather in loyalty, and with the perpetual freshness of youth. He is moreover, by the will of Jehovah, to be Priest as well as King. In the might of this Divine appointment He is to go forth to conquest. The fulfilment of its every word is realized in Christ.

PSALM 111

Jehovah the Great and Gracious

PRAISE ye Jehovah.
I will give thanks unto Jehovah with my whole heart,
In the council of the upright, and in the congregation.

2 The works of Jehovah are great,
Sought out of all them that have pleasure therein.

3 His work is honor and majesty;
And his righteousness endureth for ever.

4 He hath made his wonderful works to be remembered:
Jehovah is gracious and merciful.

5 He hath given food unto them that fear him:
He will ever be mindful of his covenant.

6 He hath showed his people the power of his works,

In giving them the heritage of the nations.

7 The works of his hands are truth and justice;
All his precepts are sure.

8 They are established for ever and ever;
They are done in truth and uprightness.

9 He hath sent redemption unto his people;
He hath commanded his covenant for ever:
Holy and reverend is his name.

10 The fear of Jehovah is the beginning of wisdom;
A good understanding have all they that do *his commandments*:
His praise endureth for ever.

This psalm is closely connected with the one which follows it. In this the subject is the greatness and graciousness of Jehovah. In the Hebrew there are ten verses, the first eight having two lines in each, and the last two three lines in each. That makes a total of twenty-two lines. The first letters of these lines constitute the alphabet. Thus it is a song of praise constructed as an alphabetical acrostic.

Another division is that of taking the first seven lines which tell of His greatness; the next twelve which proclaim His graciousness; and the last three which declare the wisdom of such as fear Him and act accordingly. This last division prepares the way for the next psalm. The greatness of Jehovah is manifest in His works, the supreme characteristics of which are honour, majesty, and righteousness. The graciousness is evident in all His dealings with His people. These are characterized by compassion and constancy; by uprightness and redemption. In view of such greatness and graciousness, how true it is that to fear Him is wisdom, and to do His will is evidence of good understanding.

PSALM 112

Jehovah the Blessedness of the Trusting

PRAISE ye Jehovah.
Blessed is the man that feareth Jehovah,
That delighteth greatly in his commandments.

2 His seed shall be mighty upon earth:
The generation of the upright shall be blessed.

3 Wealth and riches are in his house;
And his righteousness endureth for ever.

4 Unto the upright there ariseth light in the darkness:
He is gracious, and merciful, and righteous.

5 Well is it with the man that dealeth graciously and lendeth;
He shall maintain his cause in judgment.

6 For he shall never be moved;
The righteous shall be had in everlasting remembrance.

7 He shall not be afraid of evil tidings:
His heart is fixed, trusting in Jehovah.

8 His heart is established, he shall not be afraid,
Until he see *his desire* upon his adversaries.

9 He hath dispersed, he hath given to the needy;
His righteousness endureth for ever:
His horn shall be exalted with honor.

10 The wicked shall see it, and be grieved;
He shall gnash with his teeth, and melt away:
The desire of the wicked shall perish.

This song follows immediately upon the last as to meaning. While that has set forth the praises of Jehovah as great and gracious, this declares the blessedness of the man who lives in true relation with Jehovah. The connection is clearly seen in the relation of the closing verse of the former to the opening verse of this. "The fear of Jehovah is the beginning of wisdom." "Blessed is the man that feareth Jehovah." The remarkable thing about this psalm is the way in which, in describing the blessed condition of the man who fears Jehovah, it makes use of words which the previous psalm made use of in describing Jehovah. Of Jehovah the psalmist said, "His righteousness endureth for ever." Of the man who fears he says, "His righteousness endureth for ever." Jehovah is declared to be "gracious and full of compassion." So also is the upright man.

The relation of these psalms sets forth truth which is of perpetual application. A man becomes like his God. When a man's God is blessed, the man is blessed also. To have a great God is to become a great man. True wisdom consists in the maintenance of right relationships with the one God. True happiness consists in becoming like Him Who is at once great and gracious.

PSALM 113

Jehovah the High and Lowly

PRAISE ye Jehovah.
Praise, O ye servants of Jehovah,
Praise the name of Jehovah.
2 Blessed be the name of Jehovah
From this time forth and for evermore.
3 From the rising of the sun unto the going down of the same
Jehovah's name is to be praised.
4 Jehovah is high above all nations,
And his glory above the heavens.
5 Who is like unto Jehovah our God,
That hath his seat on high,

6 That humbleth himself to behold
The things that are in heaven and in the earth?
7 He raiseth up the poor out of the dust,
And lifteth up the needy from the dunghill;
8 That he may set him with princes.
Even with the princes of his people.
9 He maketh the barren woman to keep house,
And to be a joyful mother of children.
Praise ye Jehovah.

This is the first of six psalms which constitute the Hallel or Hymn of Praise, which the Hebrews sang at Passover, Pentecost, and the Feast of Tabernacles. This group is necessarily of special interest to us because in all probability, these psalms were sung by our Lord and His disciples on that dark night in which He was betrayed. While we shall read them and think of them as the songs of the ancient people, we cannot help thinking of them as uttered by that Voice which was and is the perfect music.

The first psalm celebrates the name of Jehovah on two accounts. He is high, yet He is lowly; above the nations and above the heavens, yet humbling Himself to behold the heavens and the earth. This is a startling way of stating the fact. The thing which exalts man, the contemplation and consideration of creation and its glories, humbles God, so far is He above creation in the awful majesty of His essential life. Yet how He humbles Himself! Think of these words passing the lips of Him Who "humbled Himself," and became "obedient unto death." Then notice the evidences of God's humility and height. He stoops to lift, for He raiseth the poor, lifteth up the needy, and turns barrenness into the joy of motherhood. Again, think how amid the deepening shadows the Incarnate Word sang with a little band of men of the purpose of His humbling, and try and imagine the joy set before Him, and so approach to an understanding of how He endured.

PSALM 114

God the Mighty Presence Leading His People's Exodus

WHEN Israel went forth out of Egypt,
The house of Jacob from a people of strange language;

2 Judah became his sanctuary, Israel his dominion.

3 The sea saw it, and fled; The Jordan was driven back.

4 The mountains skipped like rams, The little hills like lamps.

5 What aileth thee, O thou sea, that thou fleest?

Thou Jordan, that thou turnest back?

6 Ye mountains, that ye skip like rams; Ye little hills, like lambs?

7 Tremble, thou earth, at the presence of the Lord, At the presence of the God of Jacob,

8 Who turned the rock into a pool of water, The flint into a fountain of waters.

This is the second psalm in the Hallel. The first set forth the might and mercy of Jehovah. This is pre-eminently a song of His might, and so the name of God is used. If however it sings of His might, it sings of it as manifested in mercy. It is the song of the Exodus, and is full of beauty.

The first movement declares that the people passing out of Egypt, did so as the result of the presence of God. Among them was His sanctuary, and they were His dominion. Nature recognized His presence and obeyed His will. The sea fled, Jordan was driven back, mountains and little hills were moved. The singer asks the reason of this commotion, and without waiting for answer charges the earth to tremble at His presence.

Notice that this song includes the whole deliverance, the going out under Moses through the sea, and the going in under Joshua through Jordan. Again we imagine the great Leader about to accomplish His Exodus singing these words. Ere long all Nature would be convulsed as He passed out, and in breaking the way through for the oncoming hosts. It is possible in imagination to hear the thrill of triumph as the stately words so full of spiritual significance, sounded forth in that upper room.

PSALM 115

Jehovah and the Glory of His Name

NOT unto us, O Jehovah, not unto us,
But unto thy name give glory,
For thy lovingkindness, and for thy truth's sake.

2 Wherefore should the nations say,
Where is now their God?

3 But our God is in the heavens:
He hath done whatsoever he pleased.

4 Their idols are silver and gold,
The work of men's hands.

5 They have mouths, but they speak not;
Eyes have they, but they see not;

6 They have ears, but they hear not;
Noses have they, but they smell not;

7 They have hands, but they handle not;

Feet have they, but they walk
not;
Neither speak they through
their throat.
8 They that make them shall be
like unto them;
Yea, every one that trusted in
them.
9 O Israel, trust thou in Jehovah:
He is their help and their shield.
10 O house of Aaron, trust ye in
Jehovah:
He is their help and their shield.
11 Ye that fear Jehovah, trust in
Jehovah:
He is their help and their shield.
12 Jehovah hath been mindful of
us; he will bless *us*:
He will bless the house of Israel;

He will bless the house of Aaron.
13 He will bless them that fear Jehovah,
Both small and great.
14 Jehovah increase you more and
more,
You and your children.
15 Blessed are ye of Jehovah,
Who made heaven and earth.
16 The heavens are the heavens of
Jehovah;
But the earth hath he given to
the children of men.
17 The dead praise not Jehovah,
Neither any that go down into
silence;
18 But we will bless Jehovah
From this time forth and for
evermore.
Praise ye Jehovah.

This third psalm in the Hallel is born of passion for the
glory of the name of Jehovah. That is its opening note, and
all that follows must be explained thereby. The singer's distress is heard in the cry:—

"Wherefore should the nations say,
Where is now their God?"

Not first for the welfare of the people does he care, but for the
vindication of his God. This is a deep note, and all too rare in
our music. We are ever in danger of putting the welfare of
man before the glory of God.

The song having uttered its keynote proceeds in a passage
of fine scorn for idols and idol worshippers. These idols have
form without power, appearance without life, and the effect
of worshipping them is that the worshippers become insensate
as they are.

Following this there is a fine appeal to the people of God to
trust in Him, with a confident assurance that He will help.
There then pass before the mind of the singer the heavens,

God's own habitation; the earth, entrusted to men; and Sheol, the place of silence. All ends with a declaration that sounds the note of triumph even over death, for the praise of His people is to continue for evermore. And again the thought reverts to the upper room, and the Singer Whose deepest passion was ever the will of God and the glory of His name; to the One Who was soon going into the silence where no note of praise would be heard; and yet to the One Who would turn the silence into song for evermore.

PSALM 116

Jehovah the Deliverer from Death

I LOVE Jehovah, because he heareth
My voice and my supplications.

2 Because he hath inclined his ear unto me,
Therefore will I call *upon him* as long as I live.

3 The cords of death compassed me,
And the pains of Sheol gat hold upon me:
I found trouble and sorrow.

4 Then called I upon the name of Jehovah:
O Jehovah, I beseech thee, deliver my soul.

5 Gracious is Jehovah, and righteous;
Yea, our God is merciful.

6 Jehovah preserveth the simple:
I was brought low, and he saved me.

7 Return unto thy rest, O my soul;
For Jehovah hath dealth bountifully with thee.

8 For thou hast delivered my soul from death,

Mine eyes from tears.
And my feet from falling.

9 I will walk before Jehovah
In the land of the living.

10 I believe, for I will speak:
I was greatly afflicted:

11 I said in my haste,
All men are liars.

12 What shall I render unto Jehovah
For all his benefits toward me?

13 I will take the cup of salvation,
And call upon the name of Jehovah.

14 I will pay my vows unto Jehovah,
Yea, in the presence of all his people.

15 Precious in the sight of Jehovah
Is the death of his saints.

16 O Jehovah, truly I am thy servant:
I am thy servant, the son of thy handmaid:
Thou hast loosed my bonds.

17 I will offer to thee the sacrifice of thanksgiving,

And will call upon the name of Jehovah.

18 I will pay my vows unto Jehovah,
Yea, in the presence of all his people,

19 In the courts of Jehovah's house,
In the midst of thee, O Jerusalem.
Praise ye Jehovah.

This is the fourth song of the Hallel. In it the note of triumph over death, with which the last one closed, is elaborated. The singer had evidently been in some grave peril in which he had practically despaired of life. From the peril he has been delivered by Jehovah, and now he sings His praise. It has two movements. The first tells of his love, and declares its reason and its issue (vers. 1–9). The second tells of his resulting faith, breaks forth into new exultation, and affirms his determination to praise (vers. 10–19).

His love is the outcome of Jehovah's love manifested on his behalf when in the very bonds of death he cried to Him. The issue is that he will walk before Jehovah. His faith thus confirmed, he breaks into new song, and dedicates himself afresh to the high service of thanksgiving.

Whatever the local circumstances which give rise to this song, it is evident that all its rich meaning was fulfilled, when in the midst of that little company of perplexed souls, the shadows of the One Death already on Him, Jesus sang this song of prophetic triumph over the sharpness of the hour of passion to which He was passing. He has made it over to all His own as their triumph song over death.

PSALM 117

Jehovah the Centre of Earth's Worship

OH praise Jehovah, all ye nations;
Laud him, all ye peoples.
2 For his lovingkindness is great toward us;

And the truth of Jehovah *endureth* for ever.
Praise ye Jehovah.

The fifth song of the Hallel is the shortest in the Psalter. In it in a very deep sense, is fulfilled the saying so common that "Brevity is the soul of wit." It lives indeed with the wisdom of perfect realization. It is the pure song of the people of Jehovah. It is the song of Israel, the ideal servant of Jehovah.

It is addressed to all peoples. They are called upon to praise and laud Jehovah because of the greatness of His grace toward His own, and because His truth endureth for ever. In the long processes of the centuries Israel never fully realized this ideal. At last the purpose was consummated in a Person. All the ancient prophecies found in Him their potential fulfilment. In that upper room the song was a solo as to actual experience. By the union of grace and truth, in and through Jesus, the call to praise went out to all nations and peoples. Those who joined Him in the song that night were made able to sing in following days with meaning and with force; and that is the song with which the Church has gone forth ever since to woo and win the peoples to Jehovah. Ere the work of Jesus be finally completed, the Israel of God herself will sing that song perfectly, and the nations and peoples will respond.

PSALM 118

Jehovah and His Enduring Mercy

OH give thanks unto Jehovah; for he is good;
For his lovingkindness *endureth* for ever.

2 Let Israel now say,
That his lovingkindness *endureth* for ever.

3 Let the house of Aaron now say,
That his lovingkindness *endureth* for ever.

4 Let them now that fear Jehovah say,
That his lovingkindness *endureth* for ever.

5 Out of my distress I called upon Jehovah:
Jehovah answered me *and set me* in a large place.

6 Jehovah is on my side; I will not fear:
What can man do unto me?

7 Jehovah is on my side among them that help me:
Therefore shall I see *my desire* upon them that hate me.

8 It is better to take refuge in Jehovah
Than to put confidence in man.
9 It is better to take refuge in Jehovah
Than to put confidence in princes.
10 All nations compassed me about:
In the name of Jehovah I will cut them off.
11 They compassed me about; yea, they compassed me about:
In the name of Jehovah I will cut them off.
12 They compassed me about like bees; they are quenched as the fire of thorns:
In the name of Jehovah I will cut them off.
13 Thou didst thrust sore at me that I might fall;
But Jehovah helped me.
14 Jehovah is my strength and song;
And he is become my salvation.
15 The voice of rejoicing and salvation is in the tents of the righteous:
The right hand of Jehovah doeth valiantly.
16 The right hand of Jehovah is exalted:
The right hand of Jehovah doeth valiantly.
17 I shall not die, but live,
And declare the works of Jehovah.
18 Jehovah hath chastened me sore;
But he hath not given me over unto death.

19 Open to me the gates of righteousness:
I will enter into them, I will give thanks unto Jehovah.
20 This is the gate of Jehovah;
The righteous shall enter into it.
21 I will give thanks unto thee; for thou hast answered me,
And art become my salvation.
22 The stone which the builders rejected
Is become the head of the corner.
23 This is Jehovah's doing;
It is marvellous in our eyes.
24 This is the day which Jehovah hath made;
We will rejoice and be glad in it.
25 Save now, we beseech thee, O Jehovah:
O Jehovah, we beseech thee, send now prosperity.
26 Blessed be he that cometh in the name of Jehovah:
We have blessed you out of the house of Jehovah.
27 Jehovah is God, and he hath given us light:
Bind the sacrifice with cords, even unto the horns of the altar.
28 Thou art my God, and I will give thanks unto thee:
Thou art my God, I will exalt thee.
29 Oh give thanks unto Jehovah; for he is good;
For his lovingkindness *endureth* for ever.

This is the sixth and last of the psalms of the Hallel. It is the song of perfect victory, and was undoubtedly arranged to

be sung by a triumphal procession as it made its way to the
Temple for thanksgiving and worship. It is almost impossible
however to trace its divisions in that way. As to its subject-
matter it may be thus divided:—

> Introduction. The Call to Praise (vers. 1–4).
> The threefold Song of Israel, of Aaron, of the People
> (vers. 5–27).
> Conclusion (vers. 28, 29).

The call is to praise specifically for Jehovah's enduring
mercy. It is addressed to Israel as the ideal servant; to the
house of Aaron as the priesthood; to all that fear the Lord.
To this call Israel personified first replies in a song which sets
forth the story of distress and deliverance which had characterized the history of the long years (vers. 5–18). Then Aaron
as the priest, who had the right to enter through all the gates,
takes up the song, and challenges them to admit him, rejoicing in Jehovah's exaltation of him (vers. 19–22). Then the
people sing of the marvel of the Lord's doings, and devote
themselves to Him (vers. 23–27). Finally the psalmist strikes
the note of personal thanksgiving, ending with a call to praise.
This is pre-eminently the triumph song of the Christ, He the
ideal Servant, He the perfect Priest, He the Leader of the
people. How much all these words meant to Him as He sang
them on that night in the upper room.

PSALM 119

The Perfection of the Revealed Will

א ALEPH.

BLESSED are they that are perfect in the way,
Who walk in the law of Jehovah.
2 Blessed are they that keep his
testimonies,
That seek him with the whole
heart.
3 Yea, they do no unrighteousness;
They walk in his ways.
4 Thou hast commanded *us* thy
precepts,

That we should observe them diligently.

5 Oh that my ways were established
To observe thy statutes!

6 Then shall I not be put to shame,

When I have respect unto all thy commandments.

7 I will give thanks unto thee with uprightness of heart,
When I learn thy righteous judgments.

8 I will observe thy statutes:
Oh forsake me not utterly.

ALEPH. 1–8. *The perfect Law*

This first division sets forth the perfection of God's law by declaring the blessedness of such as observe it, and expressing the desire of the psalmist for perfect conformity thereto. The revelation of the will of God is described in this division by seven different words. If we notice them now we shall be able to understand them as they recur in subsequent divisions.

"The law" indicates the whole method of guidance and direction. "His testimonies" refers to special and direct revelations of His will. "His ways" indicates the pathway of His appointment. "Thy precepts" is a poetical expression indicating definte injunctions. "Thy statutes" refers to the written words of law. "Thy commandments" is the phrase which describes positive and particular orders of God. "Thy judgments" refers to the decisions of God in places of doubt or perplexity. In the use of these varied phrases, and others yet to follow, there is revealed the perfection of the will of God in its methods as well as in its intention. In every possible way needed by man, God reveals His will to meet the need. Human responsibility is marked by the words "walk," "keep," "observe," "respect," "learn." Such obedience to such a will must indeed issue in blessedness.

ב BETH.

9 Wherewith shall a young man cleanse his way?
By taking heed *thereto* according to thy word.

10 With my whole heart have I

sought thee:
Oh let me not wander from thy commandments.

11 Thy word have I laid up in my heart,
That I might not sin against

thee.

12 Blessed art thou, O Jehovah:
Teach me thy statutes.
13 With my lips have I declared
All the ordinances of thy mouth.
14 I have rejoiced in the way of
thy testimonies,

As much as in all riches.
15 I will meditate on thy precepts,
And have respect unto thy
ways.
16 I will delight myself in thy statutes:
I will not forget thy word.

BETH. 9–16. *The Way of Cleansing*

The cry of the young man is heard and answered. The deepest and highest aspiration of the soul of youth is that for purity. The thought is not that of cleansing from contracted defilement, but rather that of keeping clean as in the presence of the possibility of such defilement. The answer is clear and concise. The path of purity is that of caution conditioned by the Word of God. This caution is further manifested in the distrust of self, and earnest seeking to be kept in the way of God's commandments.

The closing words breathe the spirit of intense devotion to that will in its varied aspects or methods. Three new descriptions are introduced in this division. "Thy word" in verses 9 and 16, is the most inclusive term of all, as descriptive of the entire method of the Divine manifestation to man. "Thy word" in verse 11 is a poetical word literally meaning "sayings," but standing for the same idea, as the former word. "Thy ways" is also a poetical term having the same value as the word translated "thy ways" in verse 3. In these first two divisions all the descriptions are found. They will recur often through the remaining divisions, but always with the same significance.

ɔ GIMEL.

17 Deal bountifully with thy servant, that I may live;
So will I observe thy word.
18 Open thou mine eyes, that I
may behold

Wondrous things out of thy law.
19 I am a sojourner in the earth:
Hide not thy commandments
from me.
20 My soul breaketh for the longing

That it hath unto thine ordinances at all times.

21 Thou hast rebuked the proud that are cursed,
That do wander from thy commandments.

22 Take away from me reproach and contempt;

For I have kept thy testimonies.

23 Princes also sat and talked against me;
But thy servant did meditate on thy statutes.

24 Thy testimonies also are my delight
And my counsellors.

GIMEL. 17–24. *The Fountain of Joy.*

The fitness of this title may not be at first manifest. There seems to be a note of sorrow and of strong desire running through all the prayer. Yet a careful examination will show that all this is in the doing of the will of God.

The opening verse reveals his conception of the delight there is in the doing of the will of God. Life he desires and asks, but not in order that he may please himself, but in order that he may keep His word. The earth is meaningless save as he is able to discover the law of God. That is the secret key to all its treasures. The singer is in circumstances of suffering, for the proud and the princes are against him. He rises superior to these sorrowful circumstances by keeping the testimonies, meditating on the statutes, and so finding delight therein. Thus this division reminds us that peace and joy are never created by prosperous circumstances, neither can they be destroyed by circumstances of difficulty. The soul desiring, discovering, doing the will of God, is the soul finding true delight in life.

ר DALETH.

25 My soul cleaveth unto the dust:
Quicken thou me according to thy word.

26 I declared my ways, and thou answeredst me:
Teach me thy statutes.

27 Make me to understand the way of thy precepts:

So shall I meditate on thy wondrous works.

28 My soul melteth for heaviness:
Strengthen thou me according unto thy word.

29 Remove from me the way of falsehood;
And grant me thy law graciously.

30 I have chosen the way of faithfulness:
Thine ordinances have I set *before me.*
31 I cleave unto thy testimonies:

O Jehovah, put me not to
shame.
32 I will run the way of thy commandments,
When thou shalt enlarge my
heart.

DALETH. 25–32. *The Strength of Trial*

In this division we have a new revelation of the perfection
of the Divine will. As to circumstances this is wholly a sob.
Two sentences are pregnant with pain—"My soul cleaveth
unto the dust," "My soul melteth for heaviness." The singer
is bowed down, overwhelmed. He sorely needs succour and
strength. How does he seek it? Not by asking for pity, but
by a determined application to the law of his God. Carefully
notice the earnestness of his desire for a quickening according
to the word, which is the revealed will of God. We are not
usually accustomed to turn to law for comfort, and therein
lies our mistake. The truest comforters are the statutes, the
precepts, the judgments, the testimonies, the commandments
of God. To find these, and to obey them is to pursue a pathway which leads ever toward light and liberty. There can be
no circumstances of trial out of which the will of God has
made no way of deliverance. To find that way is the highest
wisdom. His sternest requirements are His tenderest methods.
In the dark days let us "understand" and "choose" and "cleave
unto" the will of God.

ה HE.

33 Teach me, O Jehovah, the way
of thy statutes;
And I shall keep it unto the end.
34 Give me understanding, and I
shall keep thy law;
Yea, I shall observe it with my
whole heart.
35 Make me to go in the path of
thy commandments;
For therein do I delight.

36 Incline my heart unto thy testimonies,
And not to covetousness.
37 Turn away mine eyes from be-
holding vanity,
And quicken me in thy ways.
38 Confirm unto thy servant thy
word,
Which *is in order* unto the fear
of thee.
39 Turn away my reproach where-

of I am afraid;
For thine ordinances are good.
40 Behold, I have longed after thy

precepts:
Quicken me in thy righteousness.

He. 33–40. *The Medium of Guidance*

The general desire expressed in this division is that for guidance. It is not an appeal for direction in some special case of difficulty, but rather for the clear manifestation of the meaning of the will of God. How often to-day the question is asked as to how we may know what the will of God is. This would seem to be the thought in the mind of the psalmist here. Every sentence breathes conviction of the perfection of the Divine will as revealed. The only fear of his heart is that he may not understand the revelation. This fear drives him to prayer that he may understand.

Notice the advance of the petitions themselves. "Teach me," "give me understanding," "make me to go," "incline my heart." Then two perils are recognized. The first is that of the allurements which may hinder the singleness of his devotion, and he prays, "Turn away my reproach." Thus taken as a whole we have a valuable teaching that when we fear that we may not know the meaning of God's will, we had better turn to Himself for clear guidance and safe keeping.

ꝩ VAV.

41 Let thy lovingkindnesses also come unto me, O Jehovah,
Even thy salvation, according to thy word.
42 So shall I have an answer for him that reproacheth me;
For I trust in thy word.
43 And take not the word of truth utterly out of my mouth;
For I have hoped in thine ordinances.
44 So shall I observe thy law continually

For ever and ever.
45 And I shall walk at liberty;
For I have sought thy precepts.
46 I will also speak of thy testimonies before kings,
And shall not be put to shame.
47 And I will delight myself in thy commandments,
Which I have loved.
48 I will lift up my hands also unto thy commandments, which I have loved;
And I will meditate on thy statutes.

Vau. 41–48. *The Inspiration of Testimony*

In this section the psalmist recognizes his responsibility as a witness. He desires to have an answer to the man who reproaches him. He desires to be able to speak of the testimonies of Jehovah before kings without being ashamed. He recognizes that such power consists in true familiarity with the law of his God.

This is all expressed in the first place in a prayer in general terms (vers. 41, 42). He desires the mercies of Jehovah, but very carefully notice that he says "according to Thy word"; that is to say he recognizes that the mercies of the Lord, even His salvation, result from His will.

This general prayer then passes into a more particular description, which reveals the accuracy of this view. It is in the word of truth abiding with him, and in the judgments of God that he hopes; and consequently it is for these things that he prays. If the prayer is answered he will be able to bear testimony. Notice the progress he suggests; "So shall I observe Thy law . . . I will walk at liberty . . . I will also speak." The issue of this will be the delight of his own soul, and continued devotion to the law of his God. Thus the inspiration of testimony for God is created in His will known, obeyed, proved.

       ז ZAYIN.

49 Remember the word unto thy servant,
    Because thou hast made me to hope.

50 This is my comfort in my affliction;
    For thy word hath quickened me.

51 The proud have had me greatly in derision:
    Yet have I not swerved from thy law.

52 I have remembered thine ordinances of old, O Jehovah,
    And have comforted myself.

53 Hot indignation hath taken hold upon me,
    Because of the wicked that forsake thy law.

54 Thy statutes have been my songs
    In the house of my pilgrimage.

55 I have remembered thy name, O Jehovah, in the night,
    And have observed thy law.

56 This I have had,
    Because I have kept thy precepts.

ZAIN. 49–56. *The Comfort of Sorrow*

In a previous division the revealed will of God as the strength of trial was dealt with (Daleth 25–32). Therein it will be remembered that he prayed, "Quicken Thou me according to Thy word." In this division he sings of the comfort which fills his soul because he has been quickened by that word.

The experience of this comfort is described. It would seem as though this section expressed the feelings of one in the midst of affliction. It does not sing the song of deliverance therefrom. The word is distinctly, "This is my comfort in my affliction." Quickened by the word of his God he has a three-fold consciousness. The first phase is that of loyalty in the presence of reproach. Though he has been held in derision, he has not swerved from the law. The second is that of hot indignation. He has seen others foresaking the law of God, and there has been born within him this sense of anger. The third phase is that of songs. Very beautiful are the words, "Thy statutes have been my songs." He is not referring to songs of sentiment. The statutes are the songs. He has heard the music of the Divine severity. In loyalty to the will of God he has discovered its poetry. He closes by declaring:—

> "This I have had,
> Because I kept Thy precepts,"

which is his final affirmation that his comfort in the midst of trial and affliction has been the outcome of the fact of his abiding in the will of God. If the marginal reading here:—

> "This I have had,
> That I have kept Thy precepts,"

is to be accepted, then the psalmist puts the keeping of the precepts of God as a rare possession, notwithstanding all the limitation of his life of affliction. There is no comfort equal

to that of the certainty of the soul obedient to the revealed
Will of God. Such an one is ever able to sing:—

> "Ill that He blesses is our good,
>   And unblest good is ill;
> And all is right that seems most wrong,
>   If it be His sweet will."

ח HHETH.

57 Jehovah is my portion:
I have said that I would observe
thy words.

58 I entreated thy favor with my
whole heart:
Be merciful unto me according
to thy word.

59 I thought on my ways,
And turned my feet unto thy
testimonies.

60 I made haste, and delayed not,
To observe thy commandments.

61 The cords of the wicked have
wrapped me round;
But I have not forgotten thy
law.

62 At midnight I will rise to give
thanks unto thee
Because of thy righteous ordinances.

63 I am a companion of all them
that fear thee,
And of them that observe thy
precepts.

64 The earth, O Jehovah, is full of
thy lovingkindness:
Teach me thy statutes.

CHETH. 57–64. *The Medium of Fellowship*

The first words tell the whole burden of this section, "Jehovah is my portion." This opening is singularly fitting if the
marginal reading of the last verse of the previous division be
accepted. In that case the psalmist, having made his boast
supremely in the fact that he has kept the precepts of God,
immediately declares that the outcome of that is that Jehovah
Himself is his possession, and this would indeed seem to be so
from the fact that having affirmed Jehovah to be his portion,
he links the affirmation with the declaration, "I have said that
I would observe Thy words."

Thus, loyalty to the will of God is not only comfort in
sorrow, it is the medium of fellowship. One is almost of necessity reminded of the words of Jesus; "He that hath My commandments, and keepeth them, he it is that loveth Me; and

he that loveth Me shall be loved of My Father, and I will love him, and will manifest Myself unto him."

He then explains the whole process in his own experience. This process is clearly seen if we take the simple declarations of the next few verses: "I entreated Thy favour ... I thought on my ways ... I turned my feet ... I made haste ... I have not forgotten ... I will rise to give thanks." There is first of all the desire for the favour of Jehovah. Then follows thought upon the ways, and the turning of the feet unto the testimonies of God. This is done with consecration, without delay. This is done in spite of opposition, and finally this issues in the singing of praise at midnight, that is, at the very centre of darkness. The cause of the song is again the righteous judgments of God. This fellowship with God means fellowship with all such as fear Him, so that indeed the loyal soul is brought into the richest of companionships. The consequent consciousness is that the earth is seen to be full of the mercy of Jehovah. The division ends with the brief prayer, "Teach me Thy statutes."

ט TETH.

65 Thou hast dealt well with thy servant,
O Jehovah, according unto thy word.
66 Teach me good judgment and knowledge;
For I have believed in thy commandments.
67 Before I was afflicted I went astray;
But now I observe thy word.
68 Thou art good, and doest good;
Teach me thy statutes.
69 The proud have forged a lie against me:
With my whole heart will I keep thy precepts.
70 Their heart is as fat as grease;
But I delight in thy law.
71 It is good for me that I have been afflicted;
That I may learn thy statutes.
72 The law of thy mouth is better unto me
Than thousands of gold and silver.

TETH. 65–72. *The Key of Affliction*

Again there is an advance of thought manifest in this division. The soul who has entered into fellowship with God through loyalty to His will is now able to make the affirmation, "Thou hast dealt well with Thy servant." All the after part of the division shows that that statement refers to the very affliction which the singer has experienced.

This affliction is described in verses 69 and 70. Yet be it noted that when mentioning this, he sets it in the light of his loyalty to the will of God. A specific trouble is that men have forged a lie against him, and he makes this the occasion for declaring his whole-hearted obedience. These people are incapable of spiritual illumination. The words, "Their heart is as fat as grease," indicate sensuality; but he dwells in the light of Jehovah.

Having confirmed his conviction that God has dealt well with him, he explains it. Before he was afflicted he went astray. Therefore it is indeed good to have been afflicted. The decision at which he arrives after the process is that the law of the mouth of Jehovah is better than all material wealth. Affliction to the trusting and obedient soul is invariably beneficent. The rebellious are broken and embittered by it. The obedient are healed and ennobled.

י YODH.

73 Thy hands have made me and fashioned me:
Give me understanding, that I may learn thy commandments.

74 They that fear thee shall see me and be glad,
Because I have hoped in thy word.

75 I know, O Jehovah, that thy judgments are righteous,
And that in faithfulness thou hast afflicted me.

76 Let, I pray thee, thy lovingkindness be for my comfort,
According to thy word unto thy servant.

77 Let thy tender mercies come onto me, that I may live;
For thy law is my delight.

78 Let the proud be put to shame; for they have overthrown me wrongfully:
But I will meditate on thy precepts.

79 Let those that fear thee turn unto me;
And they shall know thy testimonies.

80 Let my heart be perfect in thy statutes,
That I be not put to shame.

Jod. 73–80. *The Depths of Desire*

The great petition of this section is, "Give me understanding that I may learn Thy commandments." This is introduced by the psalmist's recognition of the fact that he is the workmanship of God. "Thy hands have made me and fashioned me." This is a very profound word, and one we all do well to learn. One of the deepest reasons for the abandonment of the life to the government of God is the fact that He Who has made and fashioned, knows perfectly what are the laws, obedience to which will ensure the final realization of all highest purposes.

And yet the psalmist has a wider vision than that of mere personal perfecting. He desires understanding in order that through his own realization of the will of God others may see and profit. The rest of this section expresses this aspiration in greater detail. Affirmation is evidence that the judgments of Jehovah are righteous, and that affliction is part of His faithfulness. He makes his requests. There are five distinct petitions in the last five verses, each one of which opens in our translation with the word "Let." The first is for comfort, but it is to be "according to Thy word." The second is for tender mercies, but these are in order that he may live, and the reason urged is that "Thy law is my delight." The third is for vindication that "the proud may be ashamed." The fourth is for the power of witness, in order that he may strengthen the faith of others. The last is for perfection, but it is that he may be "perfect in Thy statutes."

כ KAPH.

81 My soul fainteth for thy salvation;
   But I hope in thy word.
82 Mine eyes fail for thy word,
   While I say, When wilt thou comfort me?
83 For I am become like a wineskin in the smoke;
   Yet do I not forget thy statutes.
84 How many are the days of thy servant?
   When wilt thou execute judgment on them that persecute me?
85 The proud have digged pits for me,

Who are not according to thy law.

86 All thy commandments are faithful;
They persecute me wrongfully; help thou me.

87 They had almost consumed me upon earth;
But I forsook not thy precepts.

88 Quicken me after thy lovingkindness;
So shall I observe the testimony of thy mouth.

CAPH. 81–88. *The Confidence of Darkness*

This division is again a sob. The circumstances are all of darkness, and the most terrible consciousness is that of the apparent abandonment of the trusting soul by God Himself. His "soul fainteth for salvation." His "eyes fail for Thy word." He is like a bottle in the smoke, that is, a wine-skin shrivelling, tending to destruction.

To this there is to be added the persecution of foes. Men have digged pits for him, have persecuted him wrongfully, have almost consumed him. Yet all through notice carefully the gleams of light: "I hope ... I do not forget ... Thy commandments are faithful ... I forsook not thy precepts." Thus in the very darkest hour, when God appears to be inactive as a helper, and the activities of foes seem to be successful, the trusting soul clings to the will of God. The whole ends with the prayer, "Quicken me," and the heart affirms even here its unshaken confidence in the Divine lovingkindness. Moreover, the reason for the prayer is that there may be continued loyalty to the will of God. It is almost certain that this division could never have been written save by one who had entered into the experiences described in the former parts of this wonderful song.

ל LAMEDH.

89 For ever, O Jehovah,
Thy word is settled in heaven.

90 Thy faithfulness is unto all generations:
Thou hast established the earth, and it abideth.

91 They abide this day according to thine ordinances;
For all things are thy servants.

92 Unless thy law had been my delight,
I should then have perished in mine affliction.

93 I will never forget thy precepts:
   For with them thou hast quickened me.
94 I am thine, save me;
   For I have sought thy precepts.
95 The wicked have waited for me,
   to destroy me;

But I will consider thy testimonies.
96 I have seen an end of all perfection;
But thy commandment is exceeding broad.

LAMED. 89–96. *The Foundation of Faith*

In the previous division we have had a most remarkable manifestation of faith triumphing over circumstances of the greatest darkness and difficulty. Now the song proceeds to reveal to us the foundation of such faith. The opening affirmation (vers. 89–91) declares the consciousness which created the strength of the soul in the day of darkness. The word of Jehovah is settled. His faithfulness is continuous through the generations. The evidences of these things are to be found in all Nature. All things serve Jehovah.

He then distinctly affirms how it came about that in the midst of darkness he was still able to trust.

"Unless Thy law had been my delight,
   I should then have perished in mine affliction,"

and affirms his new determination, "I will never forget Thy precepts"; and the reason for this determination is that the prayer he offered in the midst of the darkness has been answered, "With them Thou hast quickened me." Upon the basis therefore of victory won, he prays again, for he is evidently still in a place of trial.

The division ends with this wonderful word:—

"I have seen an end of all perfection;
   But Thy commandment is exceeding broad."

That is to say he has considered all the perfections of things other than Jehovah Himself, that is, of created things; and he has discovered their limits; but the heart is firm and steady because he has found that stretching out beyond them, and

enwrapping them all is the commandment of God. This is but
another way of saying that the whole universe is conditioned
within the spacious will of God.

נ MEM.

97 Oh how love I thy law!
   It is my meditation all the day.
98 Thy commandments make me
   wiser than mine enemies;
   For they are ever with me.
99 I have more understanding than
   all my teachers;
   For thy testimonies are my
   meditation.
100 I understand more than the
   aged,
   Because I have kept thy precepts.

101 I have refrained my feet from
   every evil way,
   That I might observe thy word.
102 I have not turned aside from
   thine ordinances;
   For thou hast taught me.
103 How sweet are thy words unto
   my taste!
   Yea, sweeter than honey to my
   mouth!
104 Through thy precepts I get
   understanding:
   Therefore I hate every false
   way.

MEM. 97–104. *The Delight of Life*

This is a pure song of praise. It contains no single petition,
but is just one glad outpouring of the heart. It commences
with an outburst:—

"Oh, how love I Thy law!
It is my meditation all the day."

The connection of this with what has immediately preceded
must not be forgotten; the trusting soul in the midst of the
darkness; the reason of this trust in the absolute certainty of
the Divine authority and government. And now the song that
tells of the heart's gladness. It is not a song of thankfulness
for pity or for deliverance. It is a song of delight in law. After
the opening exclamation the psalmist speaks of the advantage
of his experience when homed in the will of God.

This he sets forth in a threefold comparison. He is wiser
than his enemies. He has more understanding than his teachers. He understands better than the aged. That is to say that
the men who plot and plan against him are foolish in comparison with him, because the commandments of God are ever

with him. There are no contingencies for which provision is not made in the law of his God. He has more understanding than his teachers, that is to say that in his personal relation to the testimonies of God he is independent of human interpretation. He understands more than the aged, that is, the direct keeping of the Divine precepts is of more value than the advice of others, even though they have had long experience. He then describes the habit of his life, which has become the occasion of his song (vers. 101, 102) and ends with another declaration of the delight of his heart.

נ NUN.

105 Thy word is a lamp unto my feet,
And light unto my path.
106 I have sworn, and have confirmed it,
That I will observe thy righteous ordinances.
107 I am afflicted very much:
Quicken me, O Jehovah, according unto thy word.
108 Accept, I beseech thee, the freewill-offerings of my mouth, O Jehovah,
And teach me thine ordinances.

109 My soul is continually in my hand;
Yet do I not forget thy law.
110 The wicked have laid a snare for me;
Yet have I not gone astray from thy precepts.
111 Thy testimonies have I taken as a heritage for ever;
For they are the rejoicing of my heart.
112 I have inclined my heart to perform thy statutes
For ever, even unto the end.

NUN. 105–112. *The Light of Pilgrimage*

Again the division opens with an affirmation. It is one in which the psalmist is thinking of himself as a pilgrim passing through a world of darkness in which it would be easy for him to miss his way. On such a pilgrimage the revealed will of his God is a lamp and a light. Thus he recognizes at once the sacredness of the actual commandment, and the value of the spiritual illumination which shines through it.

He next makes his attestation. His attitude is that of one who has sworn to observe the righteous judgments of God; and moreover, it is that of one who has confirmed his decision.

Experience has vindicated his choice. The darkness of circumstances, which was evidently the background of the opening affirmation, is then referred to in detail. He is afflicted very much. His life is in his hand. He walks amid sinners. Because of his confidence in the illumination of his life by the will of God, he prays for quickening and for teaching, and declares his continued loyalty.

The whole movement ends with a declaration which must be read in the light of the opening affirmation, and the following experience and need. It is that of complete abandonment to the will of God, His testimonies being taken as a heritage; and the heart of the trusting soul being bent toward the statutes for ever, even unto the end.

ᴅ SAMEKH.

113 I hate them that are of a double mind;
But thy law do I love.
114 Thou art my hiding-place and my shield:
I hope in thy word.
115 Depart from me, ye evil-doers,
That I may keep the commandments of my God.
116 Uphold me according unto thy word, that I may live;
And let me not be ashamed of my hope.
117 Hold thou me up, and I shall be safe,
And shall have respect unto thy statutes continually.
118 Thou hast set at nought all them that err from thy statutes;
For their deceit is falsehood.
119 Thou puttest away all the wicked of the earth like dross:
Therefore I love thy testimonies.
120 My flesh trembleth for fear of thee;
And I am afraid of thy judgments.

SAMECH. 113–120. *The Line of Rectitude*

All through this division of the psalm it is evident that the singer is contemplating the course and curse of wickedness. He first declares his hatred for such as are of a double mind, that is, those who are not loyal, the undecided, such as lack singleness of purpose. Later, he calls upon all evildoers to depart from him. Finally, he declares that God sets at naught and causes to cease all such evil men. In the presence of the double-minded he affirms his own loyalty to the law, and his consequent confidence in God. He declares that his reason for calling upon evil-doers to leave him is that he may keep the commandments of God. In view of God's judgments of the wicked, he is filled with trembling. This is the utterance of a quick and sensitive conscience.

It is good to have such exercise of fear in the presence of the holiness of God, and in view of the certainty of His judgments against evil men. This very trembling is evidence of his profound conviction of the perfection of the Divine will; and over against the fear, the hope of the heart is declared to be in the word of God.

ע AYIN.

121 I have done justice and righteousness:
Leave me not to mine oppressors.
122 Be surety for thy servant for good:
Let not the proud oppress me.
123 Mine eyes fail for thy salvation,
And for thy righteous word.
124 Deal with thy servant according unto thy lovingkindness,
And teach me thy statutes.

125 I am thy servant; give me understanding,
That I may know thy testimonies.
126 It is time for Jehovah to work;
For they have made void thy law.
127 Therefore I love thy commandments
Above gold, yea, above fine gold.
128 Therefore I esteem all *thy* precepts concerning all *things* to be right;
And I hate every false way.

Ain. 121–128. *The Hope of Distress*

The circumstances of distress manifest here are those of a man true to God in the midst of those who seem to be in power, notwithstanding the fact that they make void the law of Jehovah. There is manifest in the movement the victory of faith.

The song opens with a note of despondency. He is in the hands of oppressors, who are actively oppressing. His eyes fail for salvation, that is, it seems as though it would not come.

This sense of his distress expresses itself next in prayer. That prayer is the supreme evidence of faith. He asks for the mercy of teaching and understanding. There is no question of the rectitude of the Divine method. What is needful for him is that he should understand. Yet his passion for the law of his God is such that in view of the way in which men are making it void, he declares his conviction that it is time for Jehovah to work.

Then everything ends with a declaration of certainty that the precepts of Jehovah are right. The three movements are full of suggestion for all the men of faith. They are (i) a test of faith, (ii) an activity of faith, (iii) a victory of faith. Such a song is only possible to a man who can honestly make the opening declaration, "I have done judgment and justice."

 פ PE.

129 Thy testimonies are wonderful;
Therefore doth my soul keep them.

130 The opening of thy words giveth light;
It giveth understanding unto the simple.

131 I opened wide my mouth, and panted;
For I longed for thy commandments.

132 Turn thee unto me, and have mercy upon me,
As thou usest to do unto those that love thy name.

133 Establish my footsteps in thy word;
And let not any iniquity have dominion over me.

134 Redeem me from the oppression of man:
So will I observe thy precepts.

135 Make thy face to shine upon thy servant;
And teach me thy statutes.

136 Streams of water run down mine eyes,
Because they observe not thy law.

Pe. 129–136. *The Light of Life*

In a previous division he has declared that the will of God is light upon the pathway of the pilgrim (*Nun.* 105–112). In this one the thought is deeper. It is that of the illumination of the inner life of the soul rather than that of the external pathway.

He first declares his conviction of the wonder of the testimonies of Jehovah. The word "wonderful" is equivalent to our use of the word miraculous. These testimonies are supernatural, superhuman. These words received, and then opened, that is, having their meaning unfolded, give light. In intense language he describes his desire for them, and urges his plea as something which he has a right to claim, for the words, "as Thou usest to do" mean, according to Thy accustomed method. His petition is based upon his desire for freedom from the foe within, his own iniquity; and the hindrance without, the oppression of man. The light of the opened words of God is indeed the shining of the face of God, and for this he prays. As in previous divisions we have seen his anger with the wickedness of those who make void the law of God, here we see his pity for them in the rivers of his tears. These two things are not contradictory. Both are the common experience of obedient souls, and both were supremely manifest in Jesus when He wept over the city whose doom He uttered.

צ TSADHE.

137 Righteousness art thou, O Jehovah,
And upright are thy judgments.
138 Thou hast commanded thy testimonies in righteousness
And very faithfulness.
139 My zeal hath consumed me,
Because mine adversaries have forgotten thy words.
140 Thy word is very pure;
Therefore thy servant loveth it.

141 I am small and despised;
Yet do I not forget thy precepts.
142 Thy righteousness is an everlasting righteousness,
And thy law is truth.
143 Trouble and anguish have taken hold on me;
Yet thy commandments are my delight.
144 Thy testimonies are righteous for ever:
Give me understanding and I shall live.

TZADE. 137–144. *The Knowledge of God*

In this division the psalmist reveals his conception of Jehovah. It is a consciousness of the character of God resulting from his acquaintance with His law, and his experience of its perfections.

He first makes his affirmation (vers. 137, 138); and then describes the experiences through which he has come to this decision (vers. 139–144); ending with a prayer for still further understanding. The affirmation is of the essential rightness of Jehovah in character and in government. The proof is reflexive. The God Who is right must govern righteously. The God Who governs righteously must be righteous. When consumed with zeal for the honour of the words of Jehovah, that inclusive word or will has been tried, and therefore he loves it. Despised by men, he has remembered the precepts of Jehovah, and has been conscious of their abiding nature and essential truth. In the midst of trouble and anguish he has found delight in the commandments. He cries for understanding that he may live. Jehovah is ever known through obedience, and in such obedience the heart finds rest and life. There is a very close connection between this division and its closing prayer, and the words of Jesus concerning His Father, "Whom to know is life eternal."

ק QOPH.

145 I have called with my whole heart; answer me, O Jehovah:
I will keep thy statutes.
146 I have called unto thee; save me,
And I shall observe thy testimonies.
147 I anticipated the dawning of the morning, and cried:
I hoped in thy words.
148 Mine eyes anticipated the night-watches,
That I might meditate on thy word.
149 Hear my voice according unto thy lovingkindness:
Quicken me, O Jehovah, according to thine ordinances.
150 They draw nigh that follow after wickedness;
They are far from thy law.
151 Thou art nigh, O Jehovah;
And all thy commandments are truth.
152 Of old have I known from thy testimonies,
That thou hast founded them for ever.

KOPH. 145–152. *The Inspiration of Devotion*

This division opens with memories of how in times past he had cried to Jehovah, and what he had said. In each case the words, "I have called," indicate the habit of the past, rather than refer to any one particular occasion. This habit of the past was never a careless or indifferent one. He had prevented the dawning of the morning and the night watches; that is, in his eagerness of devotion he had anticipated all set times and seasons.

Then suddenly the song becomes a prayer of present need. It is also an old prayer, "Quicken me." Immediately the song merges into a great affirmation of faith. Of his enemies he says, "They draw nigh." Of Jehovah he says, "Thou art nigh." The last statement harmonizes with, and explains the beginning of the division, "Of old I have known." Thus the inspiration of present devotion to the will of God is the experience won out of past devotion, wherein the faithfulness of Jehovah has been proved. In the dark days it is good to strengthen the heart by remembering. It is good moreover, to remember that all present fidelity is lighting a candle for some dark night yet to be.

ר RESH.

153 Consider mine affliction, and deliver me;
For I do not forget thy law.
154 Plead thou my cause and redeem me:
Quicken me according to thy word.
155 Salvation is far from the wicked;
For they seek not thy statutes.
156 Great are thy tender mercies, O Jehovah:
Quicken me according to thine ordinances.

157 Many are my persecutors and mine adversaries;
Yet have I not swerved from thy testimonies.
158 I beheld the treacherous, and was grieved,
Because they observe not thy word.
159 Consider how I love thy precepts:
Quicken me, O Jehovah, according to thy lovingkindness.
160 The sum of thy word is truth;
And every one of thy righteous ordinances *endureth* for ever.

RESH. 153–160. *The Principle of Life*

This is again a song of the will of God, sung amid circumstances of great affliction. The surroundings are evident in the use of the possessive pronouns of the first person—"mine afflictions"; "my cause" (as of a suit at law); "my persecutors"; "mine adversaries." The consciousness of need is revealed in the thrice repeated, "Quicken me." He feels the weakening of his very life under the pressure of circumstances.

The confidence of his soul is seen in his use of the possessive pronoun in the second person, "Thy law," "Thy word," "Thy statutes," "Thy tender mercies," "Thy judgments," "Thy testimonies," "Thy precepts," "Thy lovingkindness," "Thy righteous ordinances." It is this supreme consciousness of the breadth and beneficence of the will of God which turns even a song of sorrow into a prayer of faith. Weakened is he, but he knows there is quickening for him within the provision of Jehovah's will. The principle of life is declared in the appeal made in each case as he asks for quickening, "according to Thy word," "according to Thine ordinances," "according to Thy lovingkindness." The first is inclusive, the second tells the method, the third reveals the underlying impulse.

ש SHIN.

161 Princes have persecuted me without a cause;
But my heart standeth in awe of thy words.
162 I rejoice at thy word,
As one that findeth great spoil.
163 I hate and abhor falsehood;
But thy law do I love.
164 Seven times a day do I praise thee,
Because of thy righteous ordinances.

165 Great peace have they that love thy law;
And they have no occasion of stumbling.
166 I have hoped for thy salvation, O Jehovah,
And have done thy commandments.
167 My soul hath observed thy testimonies;
And I love them exceedingly.
168 I have observed thy precepts and thy testimonies;

SHIN. 161–168. *The true Wealth*

This division is remarkable in that it is one of the only two which contain no petition (the other was Mem. 97–104). That fact is the more remarkable because its opening sentence shows that the singer is still conscious of the circumstances of trial out of the midst of which the song of the last division was uttered.

This is a pure psalm of thanksgiving, and the opening declaration creates a background which throws up all the rainbow tints of gladness into brighter relief. The first note of the praise is one of awe. That is always so when joy is deep and profound. Merriment without foundation in reverence is always hollow and transient. When awe fills the soul, rejoicing immediately follows.

Again a note is struck which is unknown in the laughter of frivolity. "I hate and abhor falsehood" is the prelude to all the gladness which follows. Then the song runs on in full measure, and speaks of praise, and peace, and triumph over all stones of stumbling. Yet all the wealth which makes the heart glad is the relation of the singer's life to the judgments, the law, the testimonies, the precepts, which had ever kept the heart firm and steady in the midst of circumstances of trial. The greatest possession any life can hold is that of being able to sing, "All my ways are before Thee."

ת TAV.

For all my ways are before thee.

169 Let my cry come near before thee, O Jehovah:
Give me understanding according to thy word.

170 Let my supplication come before thee:
Deliver me according to thy word.

171 Let my lips utter praise;
For thou teachest me thy statutes.

172 Let my tongue sing of thy word;

For all thy commandments are righteousness.

173 Let thy hand be ready to help me;
For I have chosen thy precepts.

174 I have longed for thy salvation, O Jehovah;
And thy law is my delight.

175 Let my soul live, and it shall praise thee;
And let thine ordinances help me.

176 I have gone astray like a lost sheep; seek thy servant;
For I do not forget thy commandments.

TAU. 169–176. *The Perfect Law*

The great psalm closes with a division which sets forth anew the singer's consciousness of the perfections of the law of Jehovah. Unlike the last division this one is a series of petitions. They all breathe the same spirit of earnest desire to know and do the will of God. It is a most human cry, and appeals irresistibly to all such as are following hard after God, and desiring to walk in the way of His commandments, because from first to last it breathes a twofold consciousness common to all such.

The consciousness of need is revealed in each successive petition. Yet the song is never a wail of despair, because side by side with the sense of need, there is evident throughout a profound conviction of the sufficiency of the will of God. The final declaration, "I have gone astray like a lost sheep," has caused some difficulty. It may be that the psalmist is simply describing his circumstances of trial and affliction. It is far more likely that it is a confession of his sense of failure. The more perfectly acquainted a soul is with the good and acceptable and perfect will of God the more acute is the sense of personal unworthiness. Yet the final word is not that of confession of failure. It is rather the affirmation of loyalty of intention and purpose. "I do not forget Thy commandments." Happy indeed is the soul who wills to do the will of God!

PSALM 120

Jehovah the Hope of the Pilgrim

IN my distress I cried unto Jehovah,
And he answered me.
2 Deliver my soul, O Jehovah, from lying lips.
And from a deceitful tongue.
3 What shall be given unto thee, and what shall be done more unto thee,

Thou deceitful tongue?
4 Sharp arrows of the mighty,
With coals of juniper.
5 Woe is me, that I sojourn in Meshech,
That I dwell among the tents of Kedar!
6 My soul hath long had her dwelling

With him that hateth peace. | But when I speak, they are for
7 I am *for* peace: | war.

The next fifteen psalms appear to have formed a book of themselves bearing that title, The Songs of Ascents. That collection is incorporated by the editor at this point, not without purpose.

The title appearing at the head of each has been variously translated, "A Song of Degrees," "A Song of Ascents," "A Song for the Goings Up." In the Hebrew translation to which we have already referred, it appears as "A song of the ascents," and in the title index in each case the psalm is called "Pilgrim's Song."

The meaning of this title has been variously interpreted also. Without referring to the different suggestions made, we shall consider them as songs of which those pilgrims who went up to Jerusalem to worship, made use.

The placing of the collection immediately after the great psalm dealing with the perfection of the will of God is significant. Those who know that Will, turn their faces toward the temple of worship. These songs of desire and hope and approach, are fitted for their use as they go up to worship.

The first of these songs is wholly a cry of the soul acquainted with the perfection of the will of God. The first declaration is one of experience gained. He looks back and remembers how he has been heard and answered. His present circumstances are those of absence from the house of his God. He is dwelling among a people whose motives and activities are contrary to his deepest convictions and desires. Mesech and the tents of Kedar figuratively describe the distance of his abode from the home and centre of peace. He is surrounded by lying and deceitful people, such as hate peace, and are all for war. His heart turns toward Jehovah and the dwelling of His glory, the holy house of worship. He cries to Jehovah for deliverance, and in the midst of these circumstances of adversity declares his confidence that the judgments of God will operate against the evildoers.

Taken as the first of these songs of ascents the psalm reveals that keen dual consciousness of the atmosphere of ungodliness, and the experience of Jehovah which creates the desire for worship. How well we all know it. The stress and strain of living in the midst of ungodly surroundings creates a longing for the sacred place, and the ascent into the house of God.

PSALM 121

Jehovah the Help of the Pilgrim

I WILL lift up mine eyes unto the mountains:
From whence shall my help come?
2 My help *cometh* from Jehovah,
Who made heaven and earth.

3 He will not suffer thy foot to be moved:
He that keepeth thee will not slumber.
4 Behold he that keepeth Israel
Will neither slumber nor sleep.

5 Jehovah is thy keeper:
Jehovah is thy shade upon thy right hand.
6 The sun shall not smite thee by day,
Nor the moon by night.
7 Jehovah will keep thee from all evil;
He will keep thy soul.
8 Jehovah will keep thy going out and thy coming in
From this time forth and for evermore.

This song, so full of beauty, marks another stage in the approach of the worshipper, in that it sets forth his assurance of the present help of Jehovah. The singer is still far away from the appointed place of worship, lifting his eyes toward the distant mountains. He is not far away from Jehovah however. In His keeping, even though far away from the centre of external worship, the pilgrim realizes his safety. He lifts his longing eyes towards the mountains of Zion where stands the house of his God, and asks "From whence shall my help come?" Not from those mountains, precious as they are, but from Jehovah, Who is with him even in the valley of distance.

He then addresses his heart in words of comfort and assurance. Jehovah keeps His children safe, never slumbering or sleeping in the faithfulness of His tender vigil. The stately sentences which describe the keeping care of Jehovah need no exposition. They are the common language of all who know Jehovah. These two psalms, revealing as they do the consciousness of the difficulty of the circumstances of exile, and the heart's confidence in Jehovah prepare for the outburst of the next song as the day dawns for approach to the place of worship.

PSALM 122

Jehovah the Glory of the Pilgrim

I WAS glad when they said unto me,
Let us go unto the house of Jehovah.
2 Our feet are standing
Within thy gates, O Jerusalem,
3 Jerusalem, that art builded
As a city that is compact together;
4 Wither the tribes go up, even the tribes of Jehovah,
For an ordinance for Israel,
To give thanks unto the name of Jehovah.
5 For there are set thrones for judgment,
The thrones of the house of David.
6 Pray for the peace of Jerusalem:
They shall prosper that love thee.
7 Peace be within thy walls,
And prosperity within thy palaces.
8 For my brethren and companions' sakes,
I will now say, Peace be within thee.
9 For the sake of the house of Jehovah our God
I will seek thy God.

This is the song of the pilgrims in anticipation of Jerusalem, and the house of worship. It sets forth the glory of the stablished and compacted city where the tribes gather to give thanks to Jehovah. Yet through it all it is evident that the glory of city and temple consists in the fact that they are the city and house of Jehovah. It is not a song of buildings, or of material magnificence. It is rather the song of assembly, of testimony, of judgment, of peace, of prosperity.

These all issue from the supreme fact of Jehovah's presence. To Him the tribes are gathered. Their testimony is of His name. The judgment, peace and prosperity are all the outcome of Jehovah's relation to His people. The tenses of the song have caused some bewilderment as they seem to indicate the presence of the worshippers in the city, while yet they suggest the attitude of absence. The affirmation, "Our feet are standing within thy gates," is that of the confidence of faith. It is the claim of citizenship even though the citizen has not yet actually reached the city. The call has come to ascend to the house of the Lord; and with songs of praise and prayers for the city, the pilgrim prepares to respond, while the hope becomes a present consciousness of the joy of assembly.

PSALM 123

Jehovah the Helper of the Pilgrim

UNTO thee do I lift up mine eyes,
O thou that sittest in the heavens.
2 Behold, as the eyes of servants *look* unto the hand of their master,
As the eyes of a maid unto the hand of her mistress;
So our eyes *look* unto Jehovah our God,

Until he have mercy upon us.
3 Have mercy upon us, O Jehovah, have mercy upon us;
For we are exceedingly filled with contempt.
4 Our soul is exceedingly filled With the scoffing of those that are at ease,
And with the contempt of the proud.

The Singer, now within the City and the Temple, lifts his eyes to Jehovah. The atmosphere of this song is that of those who were in circumstances very far from the ideal celebrated in the previous Psalm. Their experience was not that of peace and prosperity, but that of turmoil and adversity. Nevertheless, because of their spiritual apprehension of the ideal, they were able thus to lift up their eyes to God, and wait His deliverance.

The nature of that waiting is beautifully set forth in the

figure employed, that of servants and handmaidens. These look to the hands of their master and mistress and has a three-fold significance. The first is that of dependence. The second is that of submission. The third is that of discipline. Here, then, is the true way of looking for help from Jehovah. When the eyes lifted to Him are those of such as fulfil these conditions, the help sought is ever found, the mercy of Jehovah is ever active towards them.

PSALM 124

Jehovah the Deliverer of the Pilgrim

IF it had not been Jehovah who was on our side,
Let Israel now say,

2 If it had not been Jehovah who was on our side,
When men rose up against us;

3 Then they had swallowed us up alive,
When their wrath was kindled against us:

4 Then the waters had overwhelmed us,
The stream had gone over our soul;

5 Then the proud waters had gone over our soul.

6 Blessed be Jehovah,
Who hath not given us as a prey to their teeth.

7 Our soul is escaped as a bird out of the snare of the fowlers:
The snare is broken, and we are escaped.

8 Our help is in the name of Jehovah,
Who made heaven and earth.

The journey from the place of exile to the city and temple of Jehovah has now commenced. The heart of the song is in the words, "Our soul is escaped as a bird out of the snare of the fowlers." Escape brings a sense of the dangers left behind; and therefore, a keen appreciation of the fact that Jehovah has been acting as Deliverer. "If it had not been the Lord!" What a tone of joy is in that sigh. We often speak of a sigh of relief, and here is one indeed. The thunder of the threatening flood is heard behind. It was a strong tide against which these pilgrims could have had no might. Oh, if Jehovah had not helped, how great would have been the calamity! But He has helped, and the sigh which trembles with the consciousness of past peril merges into the glad song, "Blessed be Jehovah."

This first experience of escape is ever one of great delight. There stretches before the pilgrim a long road yet, and there will be much searching of heart before the final rest is won; but "The snare is broken and we are escaped" is a song full of rapture, and one which prepares the heart for all that waits for it upon the way.

PSALM 125

Jehovah the Protector of the Pilgrim

THEY that trust in Jehovah
Are as mount Zion, which cannot be moved, but abideth for ever.
2 As the mountains are round about Jerusalem,
So Jehovah is round about his people
From this time forth and for evermore.
3 For the sceptre of wickedness shall not rest upon the lot of the righteous;
That the righteous put not forth their hands unto iniquity.
4 Do good, O Jehovah, unto those that are good,
And to them that are upright in their hearts.
5 But as for such as turn aside unto their crooked ways,
Jehovah will lead them forth with the workers of iniquity.
Peace be upon Israel.

The pilgrims catch the first glimpse of the city toward which their faces are set. The journey is not ended, but from some vantage ground there in the distance is seen the home of the heart. It is founded upon rock, and stands out in all the majesty and strength of its assured position. Round about it are the mountains, guarding it against its foes. Over it is the throne of God, ensuring a government which gives the righteous their opportunity. It is an ideal picture, but a true one as to Divine intention.

Yet it is not of the material fact that the pilgrims sing. All that is but a symbol of the safety and protection and government of the trusting people. Jehovah is their rock foundation, their encompassing protection, their enthroned King. In Him is all their strength and confidence, and on the pathway, with the city seen afar, of Him they sing.

The song merges into a prayer that He will exercise on their behalf all that guidance and deliverance in which they make their boast. As in the previous song they looked back to that from which they had escaped, in this they look forward to that to which they go; and in each case their song is of Jehovah. This is true retrospect and prospect, and both minister to the strength of pilgrimage.

PSALM 126

Jehovah the Restorer of the Pilgrim

WHEN Jehovah brought back those that returned to Zion, We were like unto them that dream.

2 Then was our mouth filled with laughter,
And our tongue with singing:
Then said they among the nations,
Jehovah hath done great things for them.

3 Jehovah hath done great things for us,

Whereof we are glad.

4 Turn again our captivity, O Jehovah,
As the streams in the South.

5 They that sow in tears shall reap in joy.

6 He that goeth forth and weepeth, bearing seed for sowing,
Shall doubtless come again with joy, bringing his sheaves *with him*.

The general movement of these songs of Ascents is preserved in this case by the marginal reading of the first verse, better than by the text as it stands in the R.V. "When Jehovah brought back those that returned to Zion." The pilgrims have looked back and praised Jehovah for escape. They have looked on, and praised Him for their hope and present sense of security. Now they break forth into an expression of their glad experience.

It is all so wonderful this restoration by Jehovah, that it is hardly believable, it is as though they dreamed. Laughter and singing are the only fitting expressions of their rejoicing hearts. Even the nations are compelled to recognize the doings of Jehovah on their behalf. Yet in the consciousness of the wonders wrought by Jehovah is created a keen sense of their own imperfection. The deliverance is not yet complete, and the prayer is offered, "Turn again our captivity," or as Dr. Kirkpatrick translates, "Restore our fortunes." The restoration already in progress is the inspiration of the prayer for its fulfilment. The song ends with a declaration of confidence that the sorrowful experiences of the past must issue in the realization of all that they so earnestly desire.

PSALM 127

Jehovah the Home-maker of the Pilgrim

EXCEPT Jehovah build the house,
They labor in vain that build it:
Except Jehovah keep the city,
The watchman waketh but in vain.
2 It is vain for you to rise up early,
To take rest late,
To eat the bread of toil;
For so he giveth unto his beloved sleep.

3 Lo, children are a heritage of Jehovah;
And the fruit of the womb of *his* reward.
4 As arrows in the hand of a mighty man,
So are the children of youth.
5 Happy is the man that hath his quiver full of them:
They shall not be put to shame,
When they speak with their enemies in the gate.

The thought of the pilgrim centres upon the city toward which his face is turned as the place of home. The strength of the Hebrew people in the past, and all that remains of it to-day, largely results from the keen sense which they ever cherished of the importance of the home and the family. The house, the city, labour, are all important to the conserving of the strength of the family. Towards these the pilgrims look but as they hope, they recognize that, as in the settlement which will make these possible Jehovah is the one Worker, so in these also He is the one and only Strength of His people. He must build the house and guard the city. He must be the Partner in toil, giving to His beloved even when they rest in sleep, after toil is over.

That last is a thought full of comfort to the toiler. Jehovah is never weary, and carries on the enterprise while His trusting child gains new strength in sleep. Children, the glory of the house, are His gift, and they become the support and defence of their parents. Thus the pilgrims look forward to the rest which follows exile, in the city of God; and recognize that this also in all its details, will result from His power and working.

PSALM 128

Jehovah the Home-Keeper of the Pilgrim

BLESSED is every one that feareth Jehovah,
That walketh in his ways.
2 For thou shalt eat the labor of thy hands:
Happy shalt thou be, and it shall be well with thee.
3 Thy wife shall be as a fruitful vine,
In the innermost parts of thy house;

Thy children like olive plants,
Round about thy table.
4 Behold, thus shall the man be blessed
That feareth Jehovah.
5 Jehovah bless thee out of Zion:
And see thou the good of Jerusalem all the days of thy life.
6 Yea, see thou thy children's children.
Peace be upon Israel.

This song naturally follows the one in which Jehovah's relation to the home, as building and establishing it, is recognized. It is chiefly interesting as it reveals the singer's conception of the relation between the prosperity of the family and that of the city.

As to the home, the condition of its prosperity is declared to be fear of the Lord, walking in His ways. Then the resulting blessings are promised. This blessedness of home life issues in the good of Jerusalem. The line of development is most important; the God-fearing man, the God-fearing family, the God-fearing city.

This song of the worshippers ascending toward the city and temple is one the application of which is of perpetual importance. The strength of any city lies in its strong family life. The true strength of the family issues from its ordering in the fear of the Lord. It is of real significance that these songs of home and of true civic consciousness are found among those which are sung on the way that leads to worship. It is ever good to carry into the place of our communion with God the interests of home and city. It is only by doing so that we can influence these for their lasting good.

PSALM 129

Jehovah the Confidence of the Pilgrim

MANY a time have they afflicted me from my youth up,
Let Isreal now say,
2 Many a time have they afflicted me from my youth up:
Yet they have not prevailed against me.
3 The plowers plowed upon my back;
They made long their furrows.
4 Jehovah is righteous:
He hath cut asunder the cords of the wicked.
5 Let them be put to shame and turned backward,

All they that hate Zion.
6 Let them be as the grass upon the housetops,
Which withereth before it groweth up;
7 Wherewith the reaper filleth not his hand,
Nor he that bindeth sheaves, his bosom:
8 Neither do they that go by say,
The blessing of Jehovah be upon you;
We bless you in the name of Jehovah.

This song is that of one who ascending toward the much desired place of rest and worship, looks back and sees how in the past Jehovah has delivered from sore perils. The backward look would seem to be inspired by consciousness of present peril, for immediately the song expresses desire for the judgment of Jehovah against those who are described as hating Zion.

On the way to the city and temple those who hate the pilgrims of faith plot and scheme for their overthrow, and it is in the consciousness of this that the song celebrates past deliverances and seeks a continuance of them. While there is evidently a sense of danger in the mind of the singer, there is an utter absence of despair. It is the true attitude of those who have a rich experience of the faithfulness of God. In times of peril it is a good thing for the pilgrim to strengthen the heart by looking back and remembering past deliverances. Such an exercise will invariably create a present confidence.

"His love in time past forbids me to think
He'll leave me at last in trouble to sink;
Each sweet Ebenezer I have in review
Confirms His good pleasure to help me quite through."

PSALM 130

Jehovah the Redeemer of the Pilgrim

OUT of the depths have I cried
    unto thee, O Jehovah.
2 Lord, hear my voice:
  Let thine ears be attentive
  To the voice of my supplications.
3 If thou, Jehovah, shouldest mark
    iniquities,
  O Lord, who could stand?
4 But there is forgiveness with
    thee,
  That thou mayest be feared.
5 I wait for Jehovah, my soul doth
    wait,

And in his word do I hope.
6 My soul *waiteth* for the Lord
  More than watchmen *wait* for
    the morning;
  Yea, more than watchmen for the
    morning.
7 O Israel, hope in Jehovah;
  For with Jehovah there is loving-
    kindness,
  And with him is plenteous re-
    demption.
8 And he will redeem Israel
  From all his iniquities.

After the backward look there would fittingly be an inward look as the worshipper approached the place of worship. This is always a disquieting look. There is no confession here of specific sins, but the cry is "out of the depths," and the figure suggests the singer's sense of deep need.

What the cause is may certainly be gathered from the apprehensive sigh, "If Thou, Lord, shouldest mark iniquities, O Lord, who shall stand?" If the sense is of the nation's distress, it is distinctly conscious of the connection of that distress with sin. All this is background which flings into bright relief the confidence of the soul in Jehovah as a pardoning and redeeming Lord. Some of the most beautiful things in the Psalter, or indeed in the Bible, are here. It was a Welshman in the midst of the wonderful revival of 1905 who rendered verse 4, "There is forgiveness with Thee—enough to frighten us!" which if not accurate translation is fine exposition. The deepest note in all true worship is this sense of "plenteous redemption," and the perfection of Jehovah's love as thus manifested. To mark iniquities would be to fill us with despair. To redeem from all iniquities is to inspire us with hope.

PSALM 131

Jehovah the Satisfaction of the Pilgrim

JEHOVAH, my heart is not haughty, nor mine eyes lofty; Neither do I exercise myself in great matters, Or in things too wonderful for me.
2 Surely I have stilled and quieted my soul;

Like a weaned child with his mother, Like a weaned child is my soul within me.
3 O Israel, hope in Jehovah From this time forth and for evermore.

This is a brief psalm, but it is very full of beauty, as it sets forth the contentment of a restless soul in the will of God. It follows the last as an advance of experience, and as a sequence. Its peculiar note is not that of a natural contentment, but of a satisfaction won in spite of all contrary tendencies.

The thought of weaning is the dominant one. That for which a child craves it at last comes to be content without. So the soul of the singer, which once was ambitious and restlessly attempted to walk in ways for which it was not fitted, is with Him in quietness and contentment. The secret of victory over feverish ambition is divulged in the psalmist's appeal to Israel to hope in the Lord. That, interpreted in the light of the previous psalm, means that in the gracious sense of His forgiving love is the secret of a content which puts an end to all false ambition. Redemption truly apprehended, is more than forgiveness. It is restoration to the quiet peace of being in harmony with all the forces of the universe, because governed by the will of God.

PSALM 132

Jehovah the Assurance of the Pilgrim

JEHOVAH, remember for David
All his affliction;

2 How he sware unto Jehovah,
And vowed unto the Mighty
One of Jacob:

3 Surely I will not come into the
tabernacle of my house,
Nor go up into my bed;

4 I will not give sleep to mine eyes,
Or slumber to mine eye-lids;

5 Until I find out a place for Jehovah,
A tabernacle for the Mighty
One of Jacob.

6 Lo, we heard of it in Ephrathah:
We found it in the field of the
wood.

7 We will go into his tabernacles;
We will worship at his footstool.

8 Arise, O Jehovah, into thy resting-place;

Thou, and the ark of thy
strength.

9 Let thy priests be clothed with
righteousness;
And let thy saints shout for joy.

10 For thy servant David's sake
Turn not away the face of thine
anointed.

11 Jehovah hath sworn unto David
in truth;
He will not turn from it:
Of the fruit of thy body will I
set upon thy throne.

12 If thy children will keep my
covenant
And my testimony that I shall
teach them,
Their children also shall sit
upon thy throne for evermore.

13 For Jehovah hath chosen Zion;

He hath desired it for his habitation.

14 This is my resting-place for ever:
Here will I dwell; for I have desired it.

15 I will abundantly bless her provision:
I will satisfy her poor with bread.

16 Her priests also will I clothe with salvation;

And her saints shall shout aloud for joy.

17 There will I make the born of David to bud:
I have ordained a lamp for mine anointed.

18 His enemies will I clothe with shame;
But upon himself shall his crown flourish.

The pilgrims stand at the very entrance of the Holy City, and their song is one of strong desire, and equally strong confidence.

In the first part the desire is expressed (vers. 1–10). It is for the fulfilment of the God-inspired purpose of David when, through affliction and at cost, he prepared for the building of the sanctuary. The idea of the Theocracy is in mind as they pray, "Arise, O Lord, into Thy resting-place." Jehovah is to be the Centre of gathering, while around Him are priests and saints, and before Him the anointed King.

The desire is answered by the assurance of the fidelity of Jehovah to His word (vers. 11–18). He has sworn to David, and He will not turn from it. The order is then set forth. The faithful Jehovah, the anointed King, the chosen city, the clothed priests, the rejoicing people, the established kingdom. Whatever were the circumstances of the writing of this song, its placing here is significant. The worshipping people are to be conscious of the true order of their life, and the true meaning of their approach. A spacious conception of the purpose of God is ever necessary to a true worship. Lacking this, the exercises of worship may easily degenerate into selfish formalism. Where it is present, every individual is enabled to contribute to the whole, that which makes for the complete realization of the ideal.

NOTES ON THE PSALMS

PSALM 133

Jehovah the Gatherer of the Pilgrim

BEHOLD, how good and how
  pleasant it is
For brethren to dwell together
  in unity!
2 It is like the precious oil upon
  the head,
That ran down upon the beard,
Even Aaron's beard;
That came down upon the skirt
  of his garments;
3 Like the dew of Hermon,
That cometh down upon the
  mountains of Zion:
For there Jehovah commanded
  the blessing,
Even life for evermore.

At last the pilgrims are within the city. After the long and toilsome march their feet actually stand within the city of God. The common impulse of all has been the desire to reach the dwelling-place of Jehovah, and to worship before His face. This desire has brought them together, and in this nearness of souls gathered by a common purpose there is a new blessing, and of that they sing. In finding Jehovah they have found each other, and as a result of common loyalty to Him, a new social order has been created.

Under two figures the singer describes the blessedness of this order. It is like the holy anointing oil. It is like the dew of Hermon. The former suggests joy and richness of experience. The latter describes the freshness of renewal of all life. The source of the new joy is recognized, "Jehovah commanded the blessing." The first matter of importance in individual life is ever that of seeking fellowship with God. When this is sought and found, there always follows the realization of the fellowship of the saints. All lack of union among ourselves is due to failure to realize our union with God.

PSALM 134

Jehovah the Rest of the Pilgrim

BEHOLD, bless ye Jehovah, all ye servants of Jehovah, That by night stand in the house of Jehovah.

2 Lift up your hands to the sanctuary, And bless ye Jehovah. Even he that made heaven and earth.

This is the last of the Songs of Ascents, and breathes the spirit of rest. As in the previous one, the joy of the fellowship of faithful souls was the burden, here it is that of the sense of peace and rest flowing from fellowship with Jehovah. The atmosphere of the song is that of rest. The sun has sunk in the west. The activity of the day is over. Quietness pervades the city. The pilgrims have found the hour of peace. At the centre of the people is the temple. There priests still keep their vigil. They "by night stand in the house of Jehovah." The last thought of the pilgrim is of the goodness of Jehovah, and the song calls to the temple watchers to bless His name.

In the stillness there comes back the answer of the priests. It is one of blessing upon the worshipper. Thus in the silence of night, ere sleep comes, the worshipper blesses Jehovah, and is blessed by Him. It is the fellowship of rest.

By faith the pilgrims of to-day have access to this fellowship every night. There is one Watcher in the Holiest, Who never slumbers, and through Him our worship is perpetual. His voice speaks the word of benediction to us in response to our adoration. This is rest indeed.

PSALM 135

Jehovah the Object of His People's Praise

PRAISE ye Jehovah. Praise ye the name of Jehovah; Praise *him*, O ye servants of Jehovah,

2 Ye that stand in the house of Jehovah, In the courts of the house of our God.

3 Praise ye Jehovah; for Jehovah
is good:
Sing praises unto his name; for
it is pleasant.
4 For Jehovah hath chosen Jacob
unto himself,
And Israel for his own possession.
5 For I know that Jehovah is
great,
And that our Lord is above all
gods.
6 Whatsoever Jehovah pleased,
that hath he done,
In heaven and in earth, in the
seas and in all deeps;
7 Who causeth the vapors to
ascend from the ends of the
earth;
Who maketh lightnings for the
rain;
Who bringeth forth the wind
out of his treasuries;
8 Who smote the first-born of
Egypt,
Both of man and beast;
9 Who sent signs and wonders
into the midst of thee, O
Egypt,
Upon Pharaoh, and upon all his
servants;
10 Who smote many nations,
And slew mighty kings,
11 Sihon king of the Amorites,
And Og king of Bashan,
And all the kingdoms of Canaan,
12 And gave their land for a
heritage,

A heritage unto Israel his people.
13 Thy name, O Jehovah, *endureth*
for ever;
Thy memorial *name*, O Jehovah,
throughout all generations.
14 For Jehovah will judge his people,
And repent himself concerning
his servants.

15 The idols of the nations are
silver and gold,
The work of men's hands.
16 They have mouths, but they
speak not;
Eyes have they, but they see
not;
17 They have ears, but they hear
not;
Neither is there any breath in
their mouths.
18 They that make them shall be
like unto them;
Yea, every one that trusteth in
them.
19 O house of Israel, bless ye Jehovah:
O house of Aaron, bless ye Jehovah:
20 O house of Levi, bless ye Jehovah:
Ye that fear Jehovah, bless ye
Jehovah.
21 Blessed be Jehovah out of Zion,
Who dwelleth at Jerusalem.
Praise ye Jehovah.

After the general movement of this book of the Psalter
which has brought us in thought to the ultimate realization
of worship, and before the final psalms of perfected praise,
we now have a section (cxxxv–cxliv) in which are contained

songs of experience, the inspiration of which is in the conceptions of Jehovah and the way of approach to Him, which the former songs have set forth.

This first of the series is a pure song of praise. It opens with a call to the priests as the representatives of the people to praise (vers. 1, 2). It proceeds to set forth the reasons for this praise (vers. 3–18). The first is that of what He is in Himself, and the fact that He has chosen His people (vers. 3–5). The second is that of His creative might (vers. 6, 7). The third is that of His deliverance of His people from bondage (vers. 8, 9). The fourth is that of His giving them a land (vers. 10–12). The fifth is that of His faithfulness (ver. 13). The sixth is that of His sure judgment and consequent return to His servants (ver. 14). The seventh is that of His superiority as the Living One over all the false and dead idols of the nations (vers. 15–18). Finally the song is an appeal to nation, priests, and Levites to unite in His praise.

PSALM 136

Jehovah the God of Mercy

OH give thanks unto Jehovah;
for he is good;
For his lovingkindness *endureth*
for ever.

2 Oh give thanks unto the God of
gods;
For his lovingkindness *endureth*
for ever.

3 Oh give thanks unto the Lord
of lords;
For his lovingkindness *endureth*
for ever:

4 To him who alone doeth great
wonders;
For his lovingkindness *endureth*
for ever:

5 To him that by understanding
made the heavens;
For his lovingkindness *endureth*
for ever:

6 To him that spread forth the
earth above the waters;
For his lovingkindness *endureth*
for ever:

7 To him that made great lights;
For his lovingkindness *endureth*
for ever:

8 The sun to rule by day;
For his lovingkindness *endureth*
for ever;

9 The moon and stars to rule by
night;

For his lovingkindness *endureth*
for ever:

10 To him that smote Egypt in
their first-born;
For his lovingkindness *endureth*
for ever;

11 And brought out Israel from
among them;
For his lovingkindness *endureth*
for ever;

12 With a strong hand, and with
an outstretched arm;
For his lovingkindness *endureth*
for ever:

13 To him that divided the Red
Sea in sunder;
For his lovingkindness *endureth*
for ever;

14 And made Israel to pass through
the midst of it;
For his lovingkindness *endureth*
for ever;

15 But overthrew Pharaoh and his
host in the Red Sea;
For his lovingkindness *endureth*
for ever:

16 To him that led his people
through the wilderness;
For his lovingkindness *endureth*
for ever:

17 To him that smote great kings;
For his lovingkindness *endureth*
for ever;

18 And slew famous kings;
For his lovingkindness *endureth*
for ever:

19 Sihon king of the Amorites;
For his lovingkindness *endureth*
for ever;

20 And Og king of Bashan;
For his lovingkindness *endureth*
for ever;

21 And gave their land for a
heritage;
For his lovingkindness *endureth*
for ever;

22 Even a heritage unto Israel his
servant;
For his lovingkindness *endureth*
for ever:

23 Who remembered us in our low
estate;
For his lovingkindness *endureth*
for ever;

24 And hath delivered us from our
adversaries;
For his lovingkindness *endureth*
for ever:

25 Who giveth food to all flesh;
For his lovingkindness *endureth*
for ever.

26 Oh give thanks unto the God of
heaven;
For his lovingkindness *endureth*
for ever.

This is a song of the age-abiding mercy of Jehovah. It opens
and closes with a call to praise, and in its main movements
sets forth the reason for such praise. In the opening call the
three great names or titles of God are made use of, viz., Jehovah, Elohim, Adonahy. The first is mentioned in its lonely
splendour, as it always is. There is no attempt at qualifica-
tion or comparison. The second is used in comparison. He is
the God of gods. All other mighty beings, false or true, are

less than He; and subservient to Him. In the same way He is Lord of lords.

The reasons for praise are found in the manifestations of His power and interest in His people. His power as seen in creation is first sung (vers. 1–9). Then His delivering power manifest on behalf of His people (vers. 10–15). This naturally merges into the song of His guidance and government of them, as He brought them into possession (vers. 16–22). And finally His goodness in restoring His people after declension and wandering (vers. 23–25). The dominant note is mercy as manifest in all the activities of God. To see the love and compassion of God in creation, in deliverance, in government, in restoration, is ever to be constrained to praise.

PSALM 137

Jehovah the God of Judgment

BY the rivers of Babylon,
There we sat down, yea, we wept,
When we remembered Zion.
2 Upon the willows in the midst thereof
We hanged up our harps.
3 For there they that led us captive required of us songs,
And they that wasted us *required of us* mirth, *saying*,
Sing us one of the songs of Zion.
4 How shall we sing Jehovah's song
In a foreign land?
5 If I forget thee, O Jerusalem,
Let my right hand forget *her* skill.

6 Let my tongue cleave to the roof of my mouth,
If I remember thee not;
If I prefer not Jerusalem
Above my chief joy.
7 Remember, O Jehovah, against the children of Edom
The day of Jerusalem;
Who said, Rase it, rase it,
Even to the foundation thereof.
8 O daughter of Babylon, that art to be destroyed,
Happy shall he be, that rewardeth thee
As thou hast served us.
9 Happy shall he be, that taketh and dasheth thy little ones
Against the rock

This is a song of memory. From the midst of the circumstances of restoration the singer looks back to days of captivity and sorrow. The picture is graphic. Babylon was far from their own land, and far removed in every way from the city of God and the temple of Jehovah. All its material splendour was nothing to the captive souls who were yet faithful to Jehovah. There they sat, with harps hung, silent, upon the willows, and wept.

Their taunting captors asked them to sing. They sought to be amused by these people of a strange religion, and the request was in itself an insult to their faith. It was impossible, and they refused to sing the song of Jehovah. To have done so would have been to play traitor to their own lost city, and to all that their citizenship stood for. The prayer for vengeance must be interpreted by the first part of the song, with its revelation of the treatment they received. It must of course also be interpreted by the times in which they lived. Our times are different. We have more light. And yet it is well to remember that the deepest sense of justice still makes punishment a necessary thing in the economy of God. That conception of God which denies the equity of retribution is weak and false.

PSALM 138

Jehovah the Perfecter

I WILL give thee thanks with my whole heart:
Before the gods will I sing praises unto thee.
2 I will worship toward thy holy temple,
And give thanks unto thy name for thy lovingkindness and for thy truth:
For thou hast magnified thy word above all thy name.
3 In the day that I called thou answeredst me,
Thou didst encourage me with strength in my soul.
4 All the kings of the earth shall give thee thanks, O Jehovah,
For they have heard the words of thy mouth.
5 Yea, they shall sing of the ways of Jehovah;
For great is the glory of Jehovah.
6 For though Jehovah is high, yet hath he respect unto the lowly:
But the haughty he knoweth from afar.

7 Though I walk in the midst of
trouble, thou wilt revive me;
Thou wilt stretch forth thy hand
against the wrath of mine enemies,
And thy right hand will save me.

8 Jehovah will perfect that which
concerneth me:
Thy lovingkindness, O Jehovah,
endureth for ever;
Forsake not the works of thine
own hands.

The final personal note of this song is reached in the words, "Jehovah will perfect that which concerneth me." It opens with consecration to the sacred duty of praise. This consecration has a threefold aspect. It is personal, and thus is expressed in terms of completeness. "With the whole heart" leaves no room for mixed motives or divided devotion. It has in view the surrounding authorities, "before the gods."

As a testimony to the supreme God the singer will praise. It is directed "towards the holy temple," and so is conscious of the true order of worship as ordained. The reason of praise is next declared to be that of lovingkindness and truth as already proved. The effect of praise is to be that of the revelation of God to others, who if they come to know Him, will also praise Him.

The final movement tells of the singer's confidence as to the future. This is based on His knowledge. He sees the lowly, and the haughty cannot escape Him by distance. Therefore, the deliverance of the trusting soul from all coming trouble is assured, and his final perfecting also. The song closes with the affirmation of the enduring mercy of Jehovah, and a petition which reveals the singer's need of the continual help of God.

PSALM 139

Jehovah the Omniscient

O JEHOVAH, thou hast
searched me, and known *me.*
2 Thou knowest my down-sitting
and mine uprising;

Thou understandest my thoughts
afar off.
3 Thou searchest out my path
and my lying down,

And art acquainted with all my
ways.

4 For there is not a word in my
tongue,

But, lo, O Jehovah, thou knowest it altogether.

5 Thou hast beset me behind and
before,

And laid thy hand upon me.

6 *Such* knowledge is too wonderful for me;

It is high, I cannot attain unto
it.

7 Whither shall I go from thy
Spirit?

Or whither shall I flee from thy
presence?

8 If I ascend up into heaven, thou
art there:

If I make my bed in Sheol, behold, thou art there.

9 If I take the wings of the morning,

And dwell in the uttermost
parts of the sea;

10 Even there shall thy hand lead
me,

And thy right hand shall hold
me.

11 If I say, Surely the darkness
shall overwhelm me,

And the light about me shall be
night;

12 Even the darkness hideth not
from thee,

But the night shineth as the
day:

The darkness and the light are
both alike *to thee.*

13 For thou didst form my inward
parts:

Thou didst cover me in my
mother's womb.

14 I will give thanks unto thee;

for I am fearfully and wonderfully made:

Wonderful are thy works;

And that my soul knoweth right
well.

15 My frame was not hidden from
thee,

When I was made in secret,

And curiously wrought in the
lowest parts of the earth.

16 Thine eyes did see mine unformed substance;

And in thy book they were all
written,

Even the days that were ordained *for me,*

When as yet there was none of
them.

17 How precious also are thy
thoughts unto me, O God!

How great is the sum of them!

18 If I should count them, they
are more in number than the
sand:

When I awake, I am still with
thee.

19 Surely thou wilt slay the wicked,
O God:

Depart from me therefore, ye
bloodthirsty men.

20 For they speak against thee
wickedly,

And thine enemies take *thy
name* in vain.

21 Do not I hate them, O Jehovah,
that hate thee?

And am not I grieved with those
that rise up against thee?

22 I hate them with perfect hatred:

They are become mine enemies.

23 Search me, O God, and know
my heart:

Try me, and know my thoughts;

24 And see if there be any wicked | And lead me in the way ever-
      way in me, | lasting.

The conception of intimate personal relation between God and man is perhaps more remarkably and forcefully dealt with in this song than in any other in the whole collection.

The great facts are first stated. Jehovah's knowledge of personal life is declared. He is familiar with every motion even to the simplest of downsitting and uprising. He knows thought afar off, that is, in the strange and mystic processes of its making. All ways and words are intimately known to the God Who is the nearest environment of human life. And from all this there can be no escape, for the Omniscient is also the Omnipresent. He is in heaven, but Sheol also is full of His presence. Distance is a human term only, and the uttermost parts of the trackless sea are also in the Presence. Darkness is light to Him, and has no hiding place from Him. The deep mysteries of being are not involved to Jehovah, for He presided in wisdom over all the mystic processes of the beginnings of human life. All this does not affright the singer, for he knows the love of Jehovah, and exclaims in glad praise for the preciousness of the unnumbered thoughts of God concerning him.

In view of all this it is hopeless for the wicked to attempt to escape from God, and the singer's desire for separation from all such is the final word of the psalm. The way of separation is that of personal choice. He must and will separate himself. Yet he is also dependent upon God in this matter, and prays for His examination and leading.

PSALM 140

Jehovah the Defender of the Defenceless

DELIVER me, O Jehovah, from
the evil man;
Preserve me from the violent
man:

2 Who devise mischiefs in their
heart;
Continually do they gather
themselves together for war.

3 They have sharpened their
tongue like a serpent;
Adders' poison is under their
lips.

4 Keep me, O Jehovah, from the
hands of the wicked;
Preserve me from the violent
man:
Who have purposed to thrust
aside my steps.

5 The proud have hid a snare for
me, and cords;
They have spread a net by the
wayside;
They have set gins for me.

6 I said unto Jehovah, Thou art
my God:
Give ear unto the voice of my
supplications, O Jehovah.

7 O Jehovah the Lord, the
strength of my salvation,
Thou hast covered my head in
the day of battle.

8 Grant not, O Jehovah, the desires of the wicked;
Further not his evil device, *lest*
they exalt themselves.

9 As for the head of those that
compass me about,
Let the mischief of their own
lips cover them.

10 Let burning coals fall upon
them:
Let them be cast into the fire,
Into deep pits, whence they
shall not rise.

11 An evil speaker shall not be established in the earth:
Evil shall hunt the violent man
to overthrow him.

12 I know that Jehovah will maintain the cause of the afflicted,
And justice for the needy.

13 Surely the righteous shall give
thanks unto thy name:
The upright shall dwell in thy
presence.

The previous five psalms have dealt with the absolute sufficiency of Jehovah. Their titles will indicate this, "Jehovah
the Object of His people's praise, Jehovah the God of mercy,
Jehovah the God of Judgment, Jehovah the Perfecter, Jehovah Omniscient and Omnipresent."

In the four which follow a different note is struck. They
reveal the need of man, and his utter helplessness. Yet they
stand over against the former five. The appeal of all of them
is made out of dire necessity to absolute sufficiency. They
lead up to another which thrills with thanksgiving as it ex-

presses the consciousness of how perfectly the resources of
Jehovah meet the need of man.

The present psalm deals with the subject of foes without.
The singer is conscious that he is surrounded by enemies. The
song begins on a low level, and rises as it proceeds. The first
movement (vers. 1–5) describes the malice of the enemies,
and ends with prayer for preservation. The second (vers.
6–10) commences with earnest prayer, the confidence of which
is based upon past experiences of deliverance; and it ends
with a definite request for the discomfiture of his foes. The
final movement (vers. 11–13) is an affirmation of faith. The
singer is confident that in the government of Jehovah evil
men cannot continue. The afflicted will be delivered, and the
righteous and upright will be perfectly vindicated.

PSALM 141

Jehovah the Keeper of the Trembling

JEHOVAH, I have called upon
thee; make haste unto me:
Give ear unto my voice, when
I call unto thee.
2 Let my prayer be set forth as
incense before thee;
The lifting up of my hands as
the evening sacrifice.
3 Set a watch, O Jehovah, before
my mouth;
Keep the door of my lips.
4 Incline not my heart to any evil
thing,
To practise deeds of wickedness
With men that work iniquity:
And let me not eat of their
dainties.
5 Let the righteous smite me, *it
shall be* a kindness;
And let him reprove me, *it shall
be as* oil upon the head;
Let not my head refuse it:

For even in their wickedness
shall my prayer continue.
6 Their judges are thrown down
by the sides of the rock;
And they shall hear my words;
for they are sweet.
7 As when one ploweth and cleaveth the earth,
Our bones are scattered at the
mouth of Sheol.
8 For mine eyes are unto thee, O
Jehovah the Lord:
In thee do I take refuge; leave
not my soul destitute.
9 Keep me from the snare which
they have laid for me,
And from the gins of the workers of iniquity.
10 Let the wicked fall into their
own nets,
Whilst that I withal escape.

In this song the influence of the external troubles upon the inner life of the singer is revealed. Throughout it breathes the spirit of fear lest the soul should be seduced from the attitude of whole-hearted loyalty to God. The peril most evidently threatening arises from the enticements of the ungodly; and the psalmist earnestly prays that he may be protected by Jehovah in speech and thought and action.

Without in so many words declaring so, the song clearly reveals the fact that the singer has been sorely tempted to turn aside to ways of ungodly men, to share their hospitality, and so escape their hostility. This peril is more subtle than that of the active opposition of these men, and in this distress he turns to God. This is his safety. That he is able to say, "Mine eyes are unto Thee, O God the Lord," is a revelation of the fact that his anchor still holds, not only against the fierce onslaught of enemies, but also against the insidious temptation to turn aside from the path of rectitude in order to escape the vindictive opposition of his enemies. If the former psalm reveals the perils of foes without, this no less clearly deals with the danger of fears within.

PSALM 142

Jehovah the Refuge of the Overwhelmed

I CRY with my voice unto Jehovah;
With my voice unto Jehovah do I make supplication.
2 I pour out my complaint before him;
I show before him my trouble.
3 When my spirit was overwhelmed within me,
Thou knewest my path.
In the way wherein I walk
Have they hidden a snare for me.
4 Look on *my* right hand, and see;

For there is no man that knoweth me:
Refuge hath failed me;
No man careth for my soul.
5 I cried unto thee, O Jehovah;
I said, Thou art my refuge,
My portion in the land of the living.
6 Attend unto my cry;
For I am brought very low:
Deliver me from my persecutors;
For they are stronger than I.

7 Bring my soul out of prison,
That I may give thanks unto thy
name:

The righteous shall compass me
about;
For thou wilt deal bountifully
with me.

In this psalm human need is yet more vividly set forth. Here is seen the consciousness resulting from the difficulties described in the previous psalm. Here there is a combination of fighting and fears within and without.

The onslaught of the foe and the trembling heart constitute an experience which can only be described as that of a spirit overwhelmed. There are two notes running side by side throughout the song. The first is that of this terrible sense of helplessness and hopelessness so far as man is concerned. The other is that of the determined application of the helpless soul to Jehovah. There is the utmost urgency in this method. "I cry with my voice . . . I pour out my complaint . . . I show before Him my trouble." The whole need is gathered up into the tremendous statement, "Refuge hath failed me; no man careth for my soul." This is answered by triumphing faith in the words, "O Jehovah . . . Thou art my refuge." The song ends with an earnest cry for deliverance, and an affirmation of confidence that the cry will be heard and answered.

PSALM 143

Jehovah the Confidence of the Desolate

HEAR my prayer, O Jehovah;
give ear to my supplications:
In thy faithfulness answer me,
and in thy righteousness.
2 And enter not into judgment
with thy servant;
For in thy sight no man living
is righteous.
3 For the enemy hath persecuted
my soul;

He hath smitten my life down
to the ground:
He hath made me to dwell in
dark places, as those that
have been long dead.
4 Therefore is my spirit overwhelmed within me;
My heart within me is desolate.
5 I remember the days of old;
I meditate on all thy doings;

I muse on the work of thy hands.

6 I spread forth my hands unto thee:
My soul *thirsteth* after thee, as a weary land.

7 Make haste to answer me, O Jehovah; my spirit faileth:
Hide not thy face from me,
Lest I become like them that go down into the pit.

8 Cause me to hear thy loving-kindness in the morning;
For in thee do I trust:
Cause me to know the way wherein I should walk;
For I lift up my soul unto thee.

9 Deliver me, O Jehovah, from mine enemies:
I flee unto thee to hide me.

10 Teach me to do thy will;
For thou art my God:
Thy Spirit is good;
Lead me in the land of upright-ness.

11 Quicken me, O Jehovah, for thy name's sake:
In thy righteousness bring my soul out of trouble.

12 And in thy lovingkindness cut off mine enemies,
And destroy all them that afflict my soul;
For I am thy servant.

This is the last of the four psalms, and both in respect of the sense of helplessness and of assurance in God, it is more vivid and striking than either of them. So far as human situation is concerned, it is a cry of despair, and a terrible one indeed. The life is smitten, the spirit is overwhelmed, and the whole complaint ends with a statement, "My heart within me is desolate." That final word "desolate" has in it the sob of an unillumined sea. Yet the psalm opens with an earnest cry to Jehovah, and after the declaration of need, is to the end a determined act of faith.

In the situation of complete helplessness the soul prepares for its prayer, and the words which indicate the method of preparation are interesting. "I remember . . . I meditate . . . I muse." The issue of this is immediately declared, "I spread forth my hands unto Thee." The earnestness of the soul is manifested in the urgent petitions which follow. "Make haste . . . hide not Thy face . . . cause me to hear . . . cause me to know . . . deliver me . . . teach me . . . quicken me." Personal consecration in this endeavour to lay hold upon the infinite resource is manifest in the affirmations. "In Thee do I trust

. . . I lift up my soul unto Thee . . . I flee unto Thee to hide me," and finally, "I am Thy servant." Through all the urgency and the earnestness there is also manifest an unshaken confidence. "Thou art my God" is the central word around which all the others gather.

PSALM 144

Jehovah the Rock of Strength

BLESSED be Jehovah my rock,
    Who teacheth my hands to
    war,
    And my fingers to fight:
2 My lovingkindness, and my
    fortress,
    My high tower, and my de-
    liverer;
    My shield, and he in whom I
    take refuge;
    Who subdueth my people under
    me.
3 Jehovah, what is man, that thou
    takest knowledge of him?
    Or the son of man, that thou
    makest account of him?
4 Man is like to vanity:
    His days are as a shadow that
    passeth away.
5 Bow thy heavens, O Jehovah,
    and come down:
    Touch the mountains, and they
    shall smoke.
6 Cast forth lightning, and scatter
    them;
    Send out thine arrows, and dis-
    comfit them.
7 Stretch forth thy hand from
    above;
    Rescue me, and deliver me out
    of great waters,
    Out of the hand of aliens;
8 Whose mouth speaketh deceit,

And whose right hand is a right
    hand of falsehood.
9 I will sing a new song unto thee,
    O God:
    Upon a psaltery of ten strings
    will I sing praises unto thee.
10 Thou are he that giveth salva-
    tion unto kings;
    Who rescueth David his servant
    from the hurtful sword.
11 Rescue me, and deliver me out
    of the hand of aliens,
    Whose mouth speaketh deceit,
    And whose right hand is a right
    hand of falsehood.
12 When our sons shall be as plants
    grown up in their youth,
    And our daughters as corner-
    stones hewn after the fashion
    of a palace;
13 *When* our garners are full, af-
    fording all manner of store,
    And our sheep bring forth thou-
    sands and ten thousands in
    our fields;
14 *When* our oxen are well laden;
    When there is no breaking in,
    and no going forth,
    And no outcry in our streets:
15 Happy is the people that is in
    such a case;
    Yea, happy is the people whose
    God is Jehovah.

This is a song of triumphant assurance. Its placing at this point in the book suggests the invincible experience of trusting souls. In order to appreciate all its value, the nine psalms immediately preceding must be borne in mind. Five of them celebrate the sufficiency of God. These are followed by four which declare the utter helplessness of man. The present one immediately follows, and in it the two facts are present; but the Divine sufficiency is seen encompassing the human helplessness until it is so lost sight of as hardly to be discoverable.

The opening affirmations thrill with the singer's confidence of ability in the might of Jehovah. There is a conflict, but fear is banished, because Jehovah teaches the hands to war and the fingers to fight; and He is all that the soul in conflict needs. This affirmation is followed by an exclamation of surprise that Jehovah so high, should take any account of man, who by comparison, is vanity. There is no shadow of doubt in the exclamation, for the song immediately becomes a prayer for the operation of Jehovah's might, for the rescue of the trusting soul. It then climbs to the higher level of praise in the new song of confidence which ends in a repetition of the prayer for rescue. Finally the singer describes the peace and prosperity of the people whose God is Jehovah.

PSALM 145

Jehovah the Object of Perfect Praise

I WILL extol thee, my God, O King;
And I will bless thy name for ever and ever.

2 Every day will I bless thee;
And I will praise thy name for ever and ever.

3 Great is Jehovah, and greatly to be praised;
And his greatness is unsearchable.

4 One generation shall laud thy works to another,
And shall declare thy mighty acts.

5 Of the glorious majesty of thine honor,
And of thy wondrous works, will I meditate.

6 And men shall speak of the might of thy terrible acts;
And I will declare thy greatness.

7 They shall utter the memory of
thy great goodness,
And shall sing of thy righteousness.
8 Jehovah is gracious, and merciful;
Slow to anger, and of great lovingkindness.
9 Jehovah is good to all;
And his tender mercies are over
all his works.
10 All thy works shall give thanks
unto thee, O Jehovah;
And thy saints shall bless thee.
11 They shall speak of the glory of
thy kingdom,
And talk of thy power;
12 To make known to the sons of
men his mighty acts,
And the glory of the majesty of
his kingdom.
13 Thy kingdom is an everlasting
kingdom,
And thy dominion *endureth*
throughout all generations.
14 Jehovah upholdeth all that fall,

And raiseth up all those that are
bowed down.
15 The eyes of all wait for thee;
And thou givest them their food
in due season.
16 Thou openest thy hand,
And satisfiest the desire of every
living thing.
17 Jehovah is righteous in all his
ways,
And gracious in all his works.
18 Jehovah is nigh unto all them
that call upon him,
To all that call upon him in
truth.
19 He will fulfil the desire of them
that fear him;
He also will hear their cry, and
will save them.
20 Jehovah preserveth all them
that love him;
But all the wicked will he destroy.
21 My mouth shall speak the praise
of Jehovah;
And let all flesh bless his holy
name for ever and ever.

This is a great psalm of praise standing alone, and serving
as an introduction to the last five, which constitute the final
anthem of thanksgiving, the expression of perfected praise.
It is a solo, but the singer is singing not for himself alone, but
for others. The peoples are in mind.

It has three movements; an introduction (vers. 1–4); a
statement of theme (vers. 5–9); and the full exercise of
thanksgiving (vers. 10–21). The introduction speaks of determination to praise (ver. 1), of continuity in praise (ver. 2),
of reason for praise (ver. 3), and of fellowship in praise (ver.
4). The theme is a threefold one; first, the majesty of the
Divine honour and works (ver. 5). Second, the might of the
acts of God (vers. 6, 7). Third and supremely, the mercy of

God (vers. 8, 9). Then follows the exercise. First, the chorus of the works of Jehovah, and of His saints. This chorus celebrates His glory, His power, His mighty acts, and the majesty of His kingdom.

The rest of the psalm is a song carrying out the thoughts suggested in the statement of theme. The majesty of Jehovah is celebrated (ver. 13). His might as operating in the uplifting of the fallen is declared (ver. 14). Finally, the activity of His mercy is delighted in (vers. 15–20). Everything concludes with the reaffirmation of personal determination to praise, and the expression of desire that all flesh should join in the anthem.

PSALM 146

Jehovah Praised as the Helper of His People

PRAISE ye Jehovah.
Praise Jehovah, O my soul.
2 While I live will I praise Jehovah:
I will sing praises unto my God while I have any being.
3 Put not your trust in princes,
Nor in the son of man, in whom there is no help.
4 His breath goeth forth, he returneth to his earth;
In that very day his thoughts perish.
5 Happy is he that hath the God of Jacob for his help,
Whose hope is in Jehovah his God:
6 Who made heaven and earth,
The sea, and all that in them is;
Who keepeth truth for ever;

7 Who executeth justice for the oppressed;
Who giveth food to the hungry.
Jehovah looseth the prisoners;
8 Jehovah openeth *the eyes of* the blind;
Jehovah raiseth up them that are bowed down;
Jehovah loveth the righteous;
9 Jehovah preserveth the sojourners;
He upholdeth the fatherless and widow;
But the way of the wicked he turneth upside down.
10 Jehovah will reign for ever,
Thy God, O Zion, unto all generations.
Praise ye Jehovah.

We now come to the final psalms of adoration, each one of which opens and closes with the great call to praise. "Hallelujah, praise the Lord."

The theme of this first is that of the sufficiency of God as the Helper of His people. It opens with the personal note of determination to praise (vers. 1, 2). As a background the inability of man to help is declared. He is not to be trusted, for "his breath goeth forth." In contrast with this helplessness the strength of Jehovah is celebrated as manifested in creation, and the maintenance of order (ver. 6), as exercised on behalf of the needy and the oppressed (vers. 7–9). Notice the descriptions of the people whom Jehovah helps. "The oppressed . . . the hungry . . . the prisoners . . . the blind . . . they that are bowed down . . . the righteous . . . the strangers . . . the fatherless and widow."

Then notice how the Divine activity exactly meets the need. "Executeth judgment . . . giveth food . . . looseth . . . openeth the eyes . . . raiseth up . . . loveth . . . preserveth . . . upholdeth." In contrast with the vanishing life of princes and sons of men, Jehovah reigns for ever, and is the God of Zion to all generations.

PSALM 147

Jehovah Praised as the Governor of His People

PRAISE ye Jehovah;
For it is good to sing praises unto our God;
For it is pleasant, *and* praise is comely.
2 Jehovah doth build up Jerusalem;
He gathereth together the outcasts of Israel.
3 He healeth the broken in heart,
And bindeth up their wounds.
4 He counteth the number of the stars;
He calleth them all by *their* names.
5 Great is our Lord, and mighty in power;

His understanding is infinite.
6 Jehovah upholdeth the meek:
He bringeth the wicked down to the ground.
7 Sing unto Jehovah with thanksgiving;
Sing praises upon the harp unto our God,
8 Who covereth the heavens with clouds,
Who prepareth rain for the earth,
Who maketh grass to grow upon the mountains.
9 He giveth to the beast his food,
And to the young ravens which cry.

10 He delighteth not in the strength
of the horse:
He taketh no pleasure in the
legs of a man.
11 Jehovah taketh pleasure in them
that fear him,
In those that hope in his lovingkindness.
12 Praise Jehovah, O Jerusalem;
Praise thy God, O Zion.
13 For he hath strengthened the
bars of thy gates;
He hath blessed thy children
within thee.
14 He maketh peace in thy borders;
He filleth thee with the finest
of the wheat.
15 He sendeth out his commandment upon earth;

His sword runneth very swiftly.
16 He giveth snow like wool;
He scattereth the hoar-frost like
ashes.
17 He casteth forth his ice like
morsels:
Who can stand before his cold?
18 He sendeth out his word, and
melteth them:
He causeth his wind to blow,
and the waters flow.
19 He showeth his word unto Jacob,
His statutes and his ordinances
unto Israel.
20 He hath not dealt so with any
nation;
And as for his ordinances, they
have not known them.
Praise ye Jehovah.

In this psalm, beginning with a call which declares the pleasantness and comeliness of praise (ver. 1), the singer first celebrates the Divine activity in restoring His people (vers. 2–6). He then proceeds to declare how God provides for all human needs (vers. 7–11); and finally rejoices in the perfection of His government (vers. 12–20).

In the first movement dealing with the restoration of Israel, there is a very beautiful suggestion of the inter-relation of the pitying power of God. "He healeth the broken-hearted . . . He telleth the number of the stars." In this activity of restoration there is manifest power and wisdom, and strict discrimination in the upholding of the meek, and the abasing of the wicked. In His providence God provides for all material needs, and yet His purpose in so doing is that of creating the spiritual attitudes towards Himself in which He supremely delights, His delight being finally not in animal strength, but in the fear and hope which constitute spiritual strength.

In the last movement there is a fine recognition of His provision of material supply, which is however, all the way through made parabolic of His sustenance of spiritual strength. Literally He gives His people "the finest of the wheat," and actually gives snow, and hoar frost, and ice; and yet all these things are intended to be revelations of the methods by which He sends His commandment and His word, His statutes and His judgments, for the perfect ordering of life.

PSALM 148

Jehovah Praised by the Whole Creation

PRAISE ye Jehovah.
Praise ye Jehovah from the heavens:
Praise him in the heights.
2 Praise ye him, all his angels:
Praise ye him, all his host.
3 Praise ye him, sun and moon:
Praise him, all ye stars of light.
4 Praise him, ye heavens of heavens,
And ye waters that are above the heavens.
5 Let them praise the name of Jehovah;
For he commanded, and they were created.
6 He hath also established them for ever and ever:
He hath made a decree which shall not pass away.
7 Praise Jehovah from the earth,
Ye sea-monsters, and all deeps;

8 Fire and hail, snow and vapor;
Stormy wind, fulfilling his word;
9 Mountains and all hills;
Fruitful trees and all cedars;
10 Beasts and all cattle;
Creeping things and flying birds;
11 Kings of the earth and all peoples;
Princes and all judges of the earth;
12 Both young men and virgins;
Old men and children:
13 Let them praise the name of Jehovah;
For his name alone is exalted;
His glory is above the earth and the heavens.
14 And he hath lifted up the horn of his people,
The praise of all his saints;
Even of the children of Israel, a people near unto him.
Praise ye Jehovah.

This is the psalm of the whole creation. It has two movements indicated by the words "From the heavens" (ver. 1), and "From the earth" (ver. 7). In the first the scale is a descending one. "In the heights" to "His angels," "Sun and moon." Of all of them it is true that He created and established them. In the second the scale is an ascending one, from the deeps and the dragons, through the elements and Nature, to the sentient life, and onward through kings and princes and all human beings. From the heights and depths and all that lies between, praise is to be offered to Jehovah, for "His glory is above the earth and heaven."

This praise however, in the mind of the singer is to be perfectly expressed through Israel, a people near unto Him. This is an all-encompassing note of adoration, which one of our more recent singers has perfectly expressed in the lines:—

"The whole creation joins in one
To bless the sacred Name
Of Him Who sits upon the Throne,
And to adore the Lamb."

PSALM 149

Jehovah Praised by His Saints

PRAISE ye Jehovah.
Sing unto Jehovah a new song,
And his praise in the assembly of the saints.
2 Let Israel rejoice in him that made him:
Let the children of Zion be joyful in their King.
3 Let them praise his name in the dance:
Let them sing praises unto him with timbrel and harp.
4 For Jehovah taketh pleasure in his people:
He will beautify the meek with salvation.
5 Let the saints exult in glory:
Let them sing for joy upon their beds.
6 *Let* the high praises of God *be* in their mouth,
And a two-edged sword in their hand;
7 To execute vengeance upon the nations,
And punishments upon the peoples;
8 To bind their kings with chains,
And their nobles with fetters of iron;
9 To execute upon them the judgment written:
This honor have all his saints.
Praise ye Jehovah.

As the last song ended by the recognition of the place of the saints in expressing the universal praise of Jehovah, this one enlarges the thought by confining itself wholly to the anthem of the saints. "His praise in the assembly of the saints" (ver. 1); "Let the saints exult in glory" (ver. 5); "This honour have all His saints" (ver. 9). The saints are to praise Him as Creator and King. They are to do this with all the abandon of the dance and of music; because He has taken pleasure in them, and beautified them with salvation.

This praise is to be the perpetual attitude of their lives. They are to "exult in glory," and to "sing for joy upon their beds." Their praise is not merely to be that of the chanting of words. It is also to be in the doing of His will. While the high praises of God are in their mouth, a two-edged sword is to be in their hand, with which they carry out His purposes among the peoples, the kings, and the nobles. The privilege of praise in word and work is an honour, specially conferred upon His saints.

PSALM 150

Jehovah Praised in Perfection

PRAISE ye Jehovah.
Praise God in his sanctuary:
Praise him in the firmament of his power.
2 Praise him for his mighty acts:
Praise him according to his excellent greatness.
3 Praise him with trumpet sound:
Praise him with psaltery and harp.

4 Praise him with timbrel and dance:
Praise him with stringed instruments and pipe.
5 Praise him with loud cymbals:
Praise him with high sounding cymbals.
6 Let everything that hath breath praise Jehovah.
Praise ye Jehovah.

This psalm which concludes the book, and all the Psalter as final doxology, is the most comprehensive, and illuminative illustration of perfect praise in the whole Psalter. In our analysis of it as doxology at the beginning of the book, its essential values are stated. The central place of prayer is the sanctuary, that is, the place of Divine manifestation, whether the earthly temple or the heavenly, matters nothing. The circumference is the firmament of His power which is the outer confine of human consciousness. The reason for praise is that of His mighty acts, whether in creation, redemption, or government. The measure of praise is His excellent greatness, so that it can never end until all the story be exhausted. The method is set forth by a description of the instruments of music constituting a perfect orchestra.

Finally, the one condition of praise is the possession of breath, that is to say, life received from Him must return in praise to Him. The function of life is praise, and the force of praise is life. The note of responsibility and the dignity of choice are alike indicated in the fact that the final psalm is not merely an expression of praise, but a call to its exercise. Thus it is seen that the worship which perfectly glorifies God is not mechanical, but volitional.